Rethinking Market Regulation

Rethinking Market Regulation

Helping Labor by Overcoming Economic Myths

JOHN N. DROBAK

OXFORD
UNIVERSITY PRESS

OXFORD
UNIVERSITY PRESS

Oxford University Press is a department of the University of Oxford. It furthers
the University's objective of excellence in research, scholarship, and education
by publishing worldwide. Oxford is a registered trade mark of Oxford University
Press in the UK and certain other countries.

Published in the United States of America by Oxford University Press
198 Madison Avenue, New York, NY 10016, United States of America.

© Oxford University Press 2021

Library of Congress Cataloging-in-Publication Data
Names: Drobak, John N., author.
Title: Rethinking market regulation : helping labor by overcoming economic myths / John N. Drobak.
Description: New York : Oxford University Press, [2021] | Includes
    bibliographical references and index.
Identifiers: LCCN 2020055607 (print) | LCCN 2020055608 (ebook) |
ISBN 9780197578957 (hardback) | ISBN 9780197578971 (epub) |
    ISBN 9780197578964 (updf) | ISBN 9780197578988 (online)
Subjects: LCSH: Trade regulation—United States. | Antitrust law—United States. |
    Labor policy—United States.
Classification: LCC KF1609 .D76 2021 (print) | LCC KF1609 (ebook) | DDC 331.120973—dc23
LC record available at https://lccn.loc.gov/2020055607
LC ebook record available at https://lccn.loc.gov/2020055608

DOI: 10.1093/oso/9780197578957.001.0001

1 3 5 7 9 8 6 4 2

Printed by Integrated Books International, United States of America

Note to Readers
This publication is designed to provide accurate and authoritative information in regard to the subject
matter covered. It is based upon sources believed to be accurate and reliable and is intended to be
current as of the time it was written. It is sold with the understanding that the publisher is not engaged
in rendering legal, accounting, or other professional services. If legal advice or other expert assistance is
required, the services of a competent professional person should be sought. Also, to confirm that the
information has not been affected or changed by recent developments, traditional legal research
techniques should be used, including checking primary sources where appropriate.

*(Based on the Declaration of Principles jointly adopted by a Committee of the
American Bar Association and a Committee of Publishers and Associations.)*

You may order this or any other Oxford University Press publication
by visiting the Oxford University Press website at www.oup.com.

For Mary

Contents

Preface

This book would not have been possible without the advice and help I received from so many people over the years I was writing the book. My deceased friend and colleague, Doug North, had a tremendous influence on my ideas. In the over twenty-five years we taught and worked together, I grew to understand the core principles that influenced so much of his scholarship. Some of those principles are reflected in this book. Doug always encouraged people to think critically, to question what people say and evaluate the conclusions for yourself. He also emphasized the mismatch between the economic theory taught in universities and written in journals with the way economics is used in the real world. He was part of the new institutional economics movement because he hoped that academic theory could be modified in a way that made it more useful for policy analysis and governance. Those principles led me to ask whether the U.S. economy is a competitive one, the basis for Chapter 3. Doug's emphasis on belief systems, the filters through which people understand the world, is the basis for Chapter 8. Finally, much of Doug's scholarship was devoted to the importance of constraints on human conduct, the "institutional framework" for economic behavior. He emphasized over and over again that there was never a true laissez-faire economy, that the real question was the degree of government involvement in the economy. That question is at the heart of this book.

My work with Doug and my involvement with the International Society for New Institutional Economics (now the Society for Institutional and Organizational Economics) led me to think about where there was a clear mismatch between economic theories and how the theories were used to craft the law. As a longtime teacher of antitrust law, I have focused on the need for competition to make an economy work, while, at the same time, watching the U.S. economy becoming more concentrated and, as I argue in this book, less competitive. I was also aware of the limited scope of merger review, with its disregard of issues that do not directly reflect on the competitive aspects of the merger. I was touched by the loss of jobs that followed many mergers. Even though that causes serious harm to the workers who lose their jobs, that byproduct of a merger is never considered in merger review. Thinking about the loss of jobs through mergers prompted me to examine the massive movement of manufacturing jobs to other countries in the first decades of this century. As with mergers, there was no regulation to limit this kind of corporate action. That brought me back to economic theory and the belief by some economists and law professors that corporations existed solely for the benefit of shareholders.

I grew up in a vibrant region in Upstate New York, the Triple Cities of Binghamton, Johnson City, and Endicott, where abundant manufacturing jobs made it possible for workers to live a good middle-class life. These cities were the home of the Endicott Johnson Shoe Company, one of the largest shoe manufacturers in the country, and the birthplace of IBM, with its large manufacturing facilities. The region had an energy and optimism that came with the ability of so many to achieve upward mobility—until the factories closed and the jobs went away. The same thing happened to many other manufacturing towns throughout the country. Even though these kinds of business decisions changed hundreds of communities for the worse, the government left the business firms unregulated. Part of the justification for this inaction is the acceptance of the shareholder primacy of corporations and the belief that the government need not intervene because the constraints of a competitive market are sufficient. As a result, I tried to tie together my concern for the problems of using economic principles as a justification for the lack of government intervention with the harm that has been caused to workers. A book that started out as a refutation of the utility of some economic principles turned into a book that ties together unworkable economic principles and harm to labor.

In addition to the influence of Doug North and my colleagues in the new institutional economics, there are a few people I want to single out. I am deeply indebted to Claude Menard, who read at least three versions of the text, listened to my ideas, and gave me copious suggestions for improvement. I also appreciate the comments of Tom Ulen and an anonymous referee who carefully reviewed my manuscript. Thráinn Eggertsson's advice not to stray from my main ideas helped me focus on what is important. In addition, his scholarship and ideas are part of the foundation of Chapter 8. Bertrand du Marais gave me helpful comments. I also benefited from the advice of many of my colleagues in the law school and other departments at Washington University. Bob Pollak's comments on an early draft helped me understand the different perspectives among academic economists and realize that many would agree with my conclusions. Ron King introduced me to the concept of residual income, which I use in Chapter 3, while the scholarship of Steve Fazzari and Mark Rank had a strong influence on my ideas. I also benefited from workshops at St. Mary's law school and at the Mercatus Center at George Mason University.

Throughout the years I worked on this book, I received invaluable help from a good number of research assistants at Washington University, as well as from the librarians and administrative staff members at the law school. I want to thank all of them for their assistance. The law students researched many issues, gave me feedback on my ideas, and provided substantial help with citation style. The librarians helped with my research, while members of the administrative staff were invaluable in helping me with word processing, formatting, and organization of the many iterations of the book. I also want to thank my editors at the Oxford University Press, Alex Flach and David Lipp, and their staff who helped bring this book to fruition.

Finally, I want to thank my wife, Mary, for the support she has given me. Not only did she tirelessly listen to my ideas, provide the initial design of the book cover, and tolerate the piles of my research notes (which sure made a mess at times), she was my biggest booster throughout the process, encouraging me to keep working on the book as the topic seemed to expand unceasingly. I cannot thank her enough for all that she did.

1

Introduction

Millions of American workers lost their jobs this century as a result of out-sourcing jobs to other countries and layoffs after mergers. Many were in manufacturing. This did not just result in a loss of income; it caused terrible disruptions in the lives of the workers, with loss of self-esteem, depression, and drug use for many laid-off workers. The massive unemployment also had social effects extending through families and communities. It also played a major role in the election of Donald Trump as president in 2016, with his election turning on victories in the manufacturing states of Pennsylvania, Ohio, Michigan, and Wisconsin, and led to the strong support for Bernie Sanders in the Democratic primary. The problem of displaced workers helped fuel the rise of a new populism that will continue to have political consequences in the United States.

Globalization of the U.S. economy has caused the outsourcing of jobs. With worldwide transportation by sea and air, fast communication between countries by the phone and internet, and English becoming the common language of the world, it has become easy to manufacture products for the U.S. markets in other countries. In addition, the strength of the U.S. dollar when compared to other currencies, especially the Chinese yuan, has exac-erbated the problem. Jobs are lost after mergers through the elimination of redundant jobs and by the trimming of a workforce in order to reduce costs. Merger regulation makes this possible because the regulatory agencies do not consider the effect on labor in their merger review. To the contrary, mergers are more likely to be approved if they result in efficiencies, which often mean the elimination of jobs.

I am far from the first to refer to these initial decades of the twenty-first century as a new Gilded Age, with vastly increasing wealth at the top, a greater disparity between the wealthiest and the rest of society, and huge impediments to the American Dream of achieving prosperity through hard work. In 1890, when the Sherman Antitrust Act was being debated on the Senate floor, Senator John Sherman said:

Rethinking Market Regulation. John N. Drobak, Oxford University Press. © Oxford University Press 2021. DOI: 10.1093/oso/9780197578957.003.0001

The popular mind is agitated with problems that may disturb social order, and among them all none is more threatening than the inequity of condition, of wealth, and opportunity that has grown within a single generation out of the concentration of capital into vast combinations to control production and trade and to break down competition.[1]

Senator Sherman could have been referring to our times. Just as economic conditions in the late nineteenth century led to the passage of the first antitrust laws in the United States, today's economic conditions demand new regulation to soften the impact of market forces on the losers and to undo the inequality of wealth and opportunity.

It is impossible to stop market forces, but government can soften the effects. However, the government has done virtually nothing to slow the elimination of jobs or to help the workers who lost their jobs, in spite of many proposals for action. Unlike our inaction, Canada and countries in the European Union have taken steps to protect the jobs of workers. Although there are many reasons for the lack of concern in our country for displaced labor, I want to focus primarily on the role economic theory has played.

Over the decades I have spent with economists, I have grown skeptical about how descriptive some economic ideas are of the actual economy. There are elegant economic theories based on such unrealistic assumptions that they have little to do with how businesses actually operate. This is not just a lawyer's skepticism; it is something I have learned from economists themselves. Many academic economists openly recognize the limitations of their discipline. However, people use economic ideas to shape public policy without a word about limitations.

I want to examine two economic "principles" that have shaped our world today: (1) the U.S. economy is competitive, making government regulation less necessary, and (2) corporations exist for the financial benefit of their shareholders and not for other stakeholders. Perhaps the word "beliefs" is a better description than "principles" because neither statement is part of the core of economic theory. There is a core theory of economics that explains competitive markets, but whether a particular market is competitive is an empirical question. A lack of competitive markets does not alter the theory of competition itself, although it makes the theory less helpful in understanding the actual economy. Similarly, economists take corporations to be

---

[1] 21 CONG. REC. 2460 (1890) (statement of Sen. Sherman).

actors in a market. They are assumed to act as the theory posits: a corporation, as any business firm, is a producer of goods and services that is assumed to maximize profits. Whether corporations actually take actions solely for shareholders is irrelevant to the theory. Nonetheless, much of the original—and the continued—impetus for the application of these principles as a way to run the U.S. economy comes from economists. Not surprisingly, there is a substantial difference among economists in their belief in these principles. It is the conservative ones, who have an unshakable faith in the market, who espouse these views. Sometimes they are labeled as members of the Chicago School of economics or, pejoratively, free-market zealots. With a patina of academic legitimacy from these economists, these two beliefs have captured government leaders, policymakers, and media commentators. This intellectual capture has had a strong influence on how the U.S. economy is run.

The application of these two economic principles has justified this loss of millions of jobs in the United States in the first two decades of the twenty-first century. Rarely have so many people been harmed in such a short period of time by the workings of an economic system. Although this harm is justified as the normal consequences of a market economy, the economic principles used to support this result are not inviolate laws, like the law of gravity, even though conservative economists state them to be certainties. When the claim that markets are competitive is not true, consumers are hurt by higher prices, poorer quality products, and fewer products to choose. Semi- and unskilled workers are hurt when firms act as monopsonist buyers of labor. Just as troublesome, the lack of competition undermines the common argument that government regulation is unnecessary because the competitive market already provides sufficient constraints. Uncompetitive markets lack the constraints that come from competition, making regulation necessary.

An erroneous belief in the existence of competitive constraints was a major cause of the economic problems stemming from the Great Recession of 2008 and its aftermath. Many argued that the existence of competitive financial markets made it unnecessary to enact regulations that would have prevented or at least softened the effects of the Great Recession. Two examples of this occurred during the Clinton administration. The economists Alan Greenspan, the Chair of the Federal Reserve, Robert Rubin, the Treasury Secretary, and Larry Summers, the Deputy Treasury Secretary, advised President Bill Clinton not to regulate financial derivatives, when the Commodities Futures Trading Commission was considering whether to regulate them. Later, Summers, then Treasury Secretary, also advocated the repeal of the Glass-Steagall Act, which had separated investment and commercial banking in the aftermath of the Great Depression. President Clinton accepted both of those recommendations. The decisions not to regulate derivatives and to deregulate banks turned out to be major causes of the Great Recession of 2008.

There has never been a purely laissez-faire economy. The libertarian longing for a purely laissez-faire economy, free of government intrusion, is fascination with a fantasy.[2] A functioning economy requires, at a bare minimum, laws that protect property rights and exchange. This was just as true in the days of Adam Smith as it is today. A modern market system—with impersonal nonsimultaneous exchange, complex multiparty transactions, and esoteric financing methods, to name just a few attributes—requires significant government involvement. The underlying question is not government versus the market but the extent to which government should regulate—or, we could say, interfere in—the market. There must be some regulation, so the debate is really over the extent of government regulation. That is a debate that depends upon how competitive a market truly is.

Many people have strong beliefs that affect how much government interference in the market they view as appropriate. In making the comparison between government and market, it is important to recognize the truth in what the Spanish economist Benito Arruñada has written: liberal "idealism errs by comparing imperfect markets with perfect politics. Libertarian idealism makes the opposite mistake, by comparing perfect markets with imperfect politics. In so doing, it makes it impossible to understand the role that the state plays in making real markets less imperfect."[3] We all bring biases to our comparison of the market and regulation. The data that we have to show the existence of competition are imprecise, so it is impossible to prove definitively whether some markets are competitive. That makes our preconceived notion of the relative benefits of one over the other even more important. It skews how we see the available facts and creates a presumption of the desirability of one over the other.

Some people consider government regulation to be a four-letter word. With an intuitive sense that any expansion of the government is horrible, they often label it as socialism. These people express a preference for the market over the government as part of an overarching fear of big government. They

[2] DOUGLASS C. NORTH, UNDERSTANDING THE PROCESS OF ECONOMIC CHANGE 122 (2005).

[3] Benito Arruñada, Coase and the Departure from Property, in THE ELGAR COMPANION TO RONALD H. COASE 305, 307 (Claude Menard & Elodie Bertrand eds., 2016).

have a libertarian philosophy that, all things being equal, people are better off being left alone by the government, whether it concerns economic issues or social matters. They fear the "nanny state," in which the government runs every little aspect of our life, from telling us the kind of light bulb or toilet we need to use, to limiting when we can use an outdoor grill. The Affordable Care Act was so controversial because it required people to have health insurance, a mandate that many opposed. Some people dislike regulation because they believe that the government is inefficient and wasteful. There are also people who oppose government action out of a genuine belief that the market itself provides sufficient regulation, making regulation unnecessary. Others are disingenuous in their opposition to regulation because their reasoned arguments mask their desire to become richer free of government interference.[4] Regardless of the source of this opposition to government regulation, this belief makes it much harder to marshal the government to improve economic conditions.

An ideology that arose in the aftermath of World War II, when the Cold War raised the fear of the spread of communism and when countries in Europe were embracing socialism, is still persuasive today. Influential European economists, like Ronald Coase and Fredrick Hayek, lamented Europe's move toward socialism.[5] Their preference for limited regulation of the market, as a counterweight to socialism, influenced economists in the United States, who then in turn had a compelling effect on the public's view of the ideal relationship between government regulation and the market, as well as an influence on the law.[6] It is unrealistic today to fear that the United States will become a socialist country. Nonetheless, an ideology forged during the Cold War persists today and makes it much harder to use the

---

[4] It is impossible to know whether people really act on the beliefs they express as justifications or whether their statements are just a pretext. For example, in discussing whether law and economics really influenced the development of antitrust law, Richard Posner wrote: "To begin with, it is generally believed that law and economics has transformed antitrust law. It can, to be sure, be argued that all law and economics really did, so far as its impact on the practice of antitrust law was concerned, was to provide conservative judges with a vocabulary and conceptual apparatus that enabled then to reach the results to which they were drawn on political grounds. Even if this is all law and economics has done for (or to) antitrust, or for that matter to any other field of law, it would be far from negligible; to enable is to do much." Richard A. Posner, *The Deprofessionalization of Legal Teaching and Scholarship*, 91 MICH. L. REV. 1921, 1925 (1993).

[5] Hayek was among the economists of the Austrian school who had a strong influence on the importance of a free market with minimal government intervention in the United States. MARK BLYTH, AUSTERITY: THE HISTORY OF A DANGEROUS IDEA 143–45 (2013).

[6] For a summary of the history of economic thought and its influence on neoliberalism in the United States, *see id.*

government to correct the market imperfections that have caused tremendous harm throughout society. As John Maynard Keynes wrote:

> [t]he ideas of economists and political philosophers, both when they are right and when they are wrong, are more powerful than is commonly understood. Indeed, the world is ruled by little else. Practical men, who believe themselves to be quite exempt from any intellectual influences, are usually the slaves of some defunct economist.[7]

Over fifty years ago, the conservative economist George Stigler noted that economists had a strong preference for a market free of government regulation because they were drilled in the methods by which a price system solves problems without the aid of the government.[8] Not only do they teach their students and the public about the desirability of relying on the market, they also influence and make government policy.[9] To further compound this issue, some economists may advance theories solely because the theories support the policy outcomes they prefer. Ronald Coase noted this problem when he considered how economists choose which theory to advance:

> In public discussion, in the press, and in politics, theories and findings are adopted not to facilitate the search for truth but because they lead to certain policy conclusions. Theories and findings become weapons in a propaganda battle. In economics, whose subject matter has such a close

---

[7] JOHN MAYNARD KEYNES, THE GENERAL THEORY OF EMPLOYMENT, INTEREST, AND MONEY 383 (1964), *quoted in* BLYTH, *supra* note 5, at 118.

[8] GEORGE J. STIGLER, ESSAYS IN THE HISTORY OF ECONOMICS 52–54, 59 (1965).

[9] There are many economists who are skeptical about the prevalence of competition. However, from my acquaintance with economists in the United States, I believe that the majority of economists are true believers in a competitive market. It is impossible to know what most economists teach in their classes, but university textbooks emphasize the prevalence of markets. In the 1960s and early 1970s, economic textbooks described the U.S. economy as a "mixed economy," meaning a mixture of capitalism and socialism. Sometime in the 1980s, the texts began to describe the U.S. economy as a "market economy." David R. Henderson, *Burying Good Ideas*, REG., Spring. 2011, at 56, 58 (book review). Gregory Mankiw's textbook, which is the most popular, explains at the beginning of the section on markets: "The market for ice cream [an example he just gave], like most markets in the economy, is highly competitive." N. GREGORY MANKIW & MARK P. TAYLOR, ECONOMICS 64 (1st ed. 2006). Mankiw does soften this statement over the next few paragraphs as he introduces monopoly and oligopoly. He ends the section with this:

> Despite the diversity of market types we find in the world, we begin by studying perfect competition. Perfectly competitive markets are the easiest to analyze. Moreover, because some degree of competition is present in most markets, many of the lessons that we learn by studying supply and demand under perfect competition apply in more complicated markets as well.

Id. at 65.

connection with public policy, it would be surprising if some academic economists did not adopt the criteria of public discussion in selecting theories, that is, choose because it lends support to a particular policy.... At the same time, they may belittle the work of other economists because it seems to have the wrong policy conclusions.[10]

The second principle, or belief—that a corporation exists solely for the financial benefit of shareholders—justifies harm to the other corporate stakeholders. Workers can be laid off, labor can be outsourced, plants can be closed, and communities can be destroyed all in the name of improved profits for shareholders. Acceptance of this principle is a relatively recent phenomenon; yet many people accept the principle as a natural result of incorporation. People overlook the fact that the corporate form came about as a way to aggregate capital and to minimize risks, not as a vehicle for maximizing shareholder wealth. They overlook the fact that many corporations served their workers and communities, as well as their investors, for a good part of the twentieth century. Mistreatment of labor is not a prerequisite for a robust economy, as shown by the success of the economies in the E.U. countries that have limited outsourcing and protected labor.

Starting at least from the junk bond crisis in the 1980s, it has become acceptable to many people that getting richer by any means was something to strive for. In effect, greed was legitimatized and applauded. One example of this has been the meteoric rise in the compensation to senior management. The media reinforces the legitimacy of this quest for wealth by constantly publicizing the stock market. It is true that many middle-class people gain wealth in their pension plans when the stock market rises, but more workers have little or no investments. No one reports that the cause of a rise in the value of a stock was the layoff of workers or the closure of plants. The emphasis on increasing the value of capital has been a major cause in the growing disparity in wealth in the United States. Once a society accepts the legitimacy of the all-out quest for wealth, it becomes very hard to change that notion.

Part of the analysis in this book depends on data. However, much of the data is far from certain. Information about corporate profits from the sale of particular goods and services is nearly impossible to obtain because

---

[10] Ronald H. Coase, *How Should Economists Choose?* G. Warren Nutter Lecture in Political Economy at the American Enterprise Institute for Public Policy Research *(Nov. 18, 1981), in* ESSAYS ON ECONOMICS AND ECONOMISTS 15, 30 (1995).

corporate financial reports give aggregate results for a corporation's overall business, not for individual goods and services. Although the degree of the concentration of an industry is relevant to the competitiveness of the industry, the Federal Trade Commission suspended a program that collected data on industry concentration in 1981.[11] As a result, we need to rely on studies by academics who gather their own data from other government and private sources. Data about the number of workers who lost their jobs as a result of mergers or outsourcing is also difficult to obtain. To my surprise, the federal government does not keep this kind of data. In fact, Congress has rejected proposed bills that would have required gathering this kind information. It seems as if some people prefer that the magnitude of job losses remain uncertain as a way to limit public pressure for regulation.[12] As a result, what we know of job losses comes from academics who study these problems, press releases and statements from corporations, and reports from the financial press. This is less precise than systematic data gathered by the government, but it is the best that we have. Another problem stems from the lack of a consensus among economists about how to interpret and explain data. Conservative economists will reject the conclusions of liberal economists out of distrust in their objectivity, and vice versa. The analysis in this book would be more convincing if the data were more certain, but I believe that we have enough information about corporate earnings and job losses to justify my conclusions.

Although I recognize that my conclusions are debatable, I would not have written this book if I did not believe that they are correct. Even if I am completely correct, some readers will still not believe my analysis and conclusions. This stems from their perspective on the world, which makes them blind to contrary views. My late friend and colleague, the economic historian and Nobel laureate Douglass C. North, culminated his sixty years' of economic research by focusing on the importance of belief systems. North believed that we need to understand that people do not perceive the world directly, but through their own mental filters, resulting in different people

---

[11] David Leonhardt, Opinion, *The Monopolization of America*, N.Y. TIMES (Nov. 25, 2018), https://www.nytimes.com/2018/11/25/opinion/monopolies-in-the-us.html   [https://perma.cc/5LJ6-H97G].

[12] Congress did precisely this for gun control in 1996 when it enacted the "Dickey amendment" to a spending bill. The amendment prohibited the Centers for Disease Control and Prevention from using any funds to promote gun control. As a result, the CDC stopped all research on gun violence, including the compiling of statistics for the public. In 2018, Congress allowed the use of funds to study gun violence, but not to advocate gun control. Allen Rostron, *The Dickey Amendment for Federal Funding for Research on Gun Violence*, 108 AM. J. PUB. HEALTH 865 (2018).

seeing the world through different lenses. That people see the world through their own filters is not a novel idea, going back at least to Plato's cave. Once people form their beliefs, confirmation bias reinforces them. This aspect of human decision-making makes it that much harder for people to agree on the ways to resolve social problems.[13]

This book does not explain the benefits of globalization on consumers, shareholders, and business people in the United States. That is a well-known story. I am aware that lower wage rates and regulatory costs have enabled firms in other countries to produce products for the U.S. market at costs significantly lower than the costs of U.S. firms. The strength of the dollar relative to other currencies makes moving jobs overseas even more attractive. In addition, some countries, like China, were known for stealing U.S. intellectual property and erecting import barriers to give their firms an advantage in global competition. This has forced U.S. firms to adapt to foreign competition, with tactics that included layoffs of workers and outsourcing of jobs. There is a real question as to whether the federal government and the firms themselves could have taken other paths this century to minimize the impact of globalization on U.S. workers, as was done in some European countries and Canada. Rather than tackling all the issues of international trade, this book is about only part of a much larger problem, but it is a part that is less known than the benefits of globalization.

This book is organized as follows. Chapter 2 explains the theory of competitive markets, something that will be familiar to readers with just a basic understanding of economics. It also analyzes the assumptions that underlie the theory, emphasizing the problems that stem from the assumption of consumer sovereignty and the ability of producers to manipulate consumer preferences. It also explains how the assumption that markets are competitive became the paradigm of economic education rather than recognizing the prevalence of monopolies and oligopolies.

Chapter 3 analyzes the competitiveness of U.S. markets in four different ways. First, it examines the profitability of business firms to determine if their profits are so high that we can conclude that they operate in markets lacking competition. Second, it looks at the increasing consensus

---

[13] Although North developed his ideas from cognitive science and not from philosophy, what he referred to as a belief system has been a basic tenet of a number of schools of philosophy, including realism, idealism, and pluralism. Even Leo Tolstoy noted this proposition in *War and Peace* in 1869: "For the first time in his life, Pierre was struck by the endless variety of men's minds, which guarantees that no truth is ever seen the same way by any two persons." LEO TOLSTOY, WAR AND PEACE 474 (E. Zaydenshnur trans., Penguin, 2009).

by economists that markets are becoming less competitive, including an issue brief by President Barack Obama's Council of Economic Advisers. Third, it shows how an examination of the conduct of the firms in an industry can help us assess the competitiveness of that industry. Finally, it analyzes the concentration of the firms in a market as a way to determine competitiveness, examining the many studies over the past few years that show greatly increased concentration in many markets. Based on these four perspectives, I argue that there is strong evidence of a lack of competition in many markets, which shifts the burden to those who oppose government regulation to demonstrate that there actually is viable competition that sufficiently constraints the firms.

Chapter 4 shows that part of the decrease in competition has resulted from the recent wave of large mergers. Mergers are thought to be desirable economically because they benefit consumers with lower prices and better products. However, many mergers are justified by a claim of increased efficiencies in the combined firm, which is often the result of layoffs and plant closures. Not only does this change the lives of the workers who lose their jobs, it also hurts their families and communities. When a plant closes, it harms the businesses that had supplied goods and services to the plant. Many studies have shown that the closure or transfer of a corporate headquarters also results in a significant decrease in charitable giving and support for local educational and cultural activities. In economic terms, these spillover effects are externalities. Even though merger regulation does not take these kinds of externalities into account, they are nonetheless harmful consequences of mergers. When I first considered this problem, I wondered about the ways to compare the benefits to consumers with the resulting harms to labor and communities, a comparison I find hard to make. Then I discovered that numerous studies have shown that many mergers do not result in lower prices, while some mergers have even led to price increases. In these mergers, workers suffered not for the sake of consumers but for the financial benefits reaped by the shareholders and managers of the merging firms and by the professionals who put the deals together. It also appears that investment advisors encourage mergers just so that they can profit from the transactions, regardless of the degree of benefit provided to consumers (or even shareholders). With little or no benefit to consumers from some mergers and significant harm to labor, I argue that we need to reassess how the government should review mergers. The current form of merger regulation does not take into account the harm caused by mergers because it solely examines a merger's effect on competition between the firms in the relevant market.

Chapter 5 examines shareholder primacy, the notion that corporations exist to increase shareholder wealth. It traces the origins of this idea and explains how it has come to be accepted as a truism by many scholars, judges, and commentators. When Milton Friedman originally popularized this idea in 1962, he wrote that corporations should serve shareholder interest "within the rules of the game." These days the rules of the game are influenced tremendously by business lobbying. The chapter explains how the political influence of labor waned and was replaced by business influence in the 1970s. Since that time, Congress has done very little to protect labor because business interests have become extremely powerful lobbyists and substantial donors to political campaigns. The chapter ends with a discussion of the growing sentiment that corporations should take into account the interests of their other stakeholders in addition to shareholders.

Chapter 6 analyzes one of the consequences of shareholder primacy: the outsourcing of millions of jobs to other countries. It details the failed attempts in Congress to regulate outsourcing, partly due to lobbying by business but also as a result of the belief that these kinds of activities should be left to the market. The chapter then compares the situation in the United States with the protection of labor and the limits on outsourcing in some countries in the European Union, particularly in Germany. Not only do many European countries have laws protecting labor, they also have a culture respecting the rights of workers. The chapter explains that the prevalent cultural views in the United States toward labor, unions, and government regulation make it impossible to do that. Nonetheless, I argue that we should not only learn from the E.U. experience, but we should also adopt some of the European protections of labor.

Chapter 7 discusses the changes in norms that have made it acceptable to make as much money as possible in any legal way, even at great harm to labor and communities. The chapter also considers the role of the media in glorifying the wealthy, along with its constant reporting of stock prices—which reinforces the belief that corporations exist only for shareholders. The chapter shows how the quest for wealth this century has led to a huge and still-growing disparity in both income and wealth. Then the chapter examines the imprecision of unemployment statistics, showing how the statistics overlook people who are not seeking work and disregard the change in pay and benefits when displaced workers take new jobs. In trying to assess the permanence of the harm caused displaced workers, the chapter examines retaining programs under the Trade Adjustment Assistance program, which was designed to help workers who lost their jobs as a result of outsourcing. In what may be a surprising result, a number of studies have shown that retraining generally does not improve the employment prospects of displaced workers. Finally, the chapter looks at the tragic effects on two communities from the closing of an automobile manufacturing plant in Janesville, Wisconsin, and the shrinkage of a glass manufacturing company in Lancaster, Ohio.

Chapter 8 then examines why so many people are locked into their views about the market and the government. It begins by describing the development of belief systems, the filter through which people see the world. The world is too complex for people to rationally analyze every question that faces them. As a result, we create mental models of the world that simplify decisions for us, and we use heuristics and rules of thumb to help us derive answers to problems. Once we develop our views of how the world works, confirmation bias makes it difficult to change them. We pay attention to the information that reinforces our prior beliefs and disregard information that challenges them. The vast majority of people have much more to think about than the relationship between the market and the government, so they do not pay much attention to details and to what many perceive as boring data. The chapter uses studies about the rigidity of political views as an example to show the difficulty in changing the public's acceptance of the harm done to workers by mergers and outsourcing.

Chapter 9 lays out proposals for change. They range from simple and uncontroversial ones, like requiring the government to collect reliable statistics about the number of jobs lost through mergers and outsourcing, to controversial proposals, like adding labor representation to the corporate boards of directors. Although some antitrust scholars have recently proposed changing merger review to include consideration of the effects on labor, I do not think that changing the current process is feasible. Instead, I propose the creation of a new government panel to review proposed mergers and outsourcing. The board would assess the expected displacement of labor in comparison with a realistic appraisal of the expected gains to consumers. This chapter also deals with political effects, by pointing out that the harm to workers has aggregated over the years, culminating in popular support for both Donald Trump and Bernie Sanders in the 2016 presidential election. There is a dark side to this growing populist movement, however, because disgruntled labor has played a role in nationalistic and fascistic movements during the twentieth century. It would be a tragedy if the problems facing workers worsened so badly that they fueled a violent movement.

The postscript in the last chapter shows the commonality between other economic propositions and the two economic beliefs that are at the heart of this book, that U.S. markets are competitive and that the primary responsibility of a corporation is to make money for its shareholders. Many people believe assertions just because economists make them. Some people take these statements to be absolute truths, even though they are only opinions. Besides the two propositions I discuss, there are other economic narratives that are disputed by many economists. Yet, despite this rejection, policymakers, members of the media, and laypeople still believe that they are true. John Quiggin labels these as "zombie economics" because they "still walk among us."[14] The chapter considers three of these: trickle-down tax policy, austerity, and privatization. No serious economist supports trickle-down tax policy, while the benefits of the other two propositions are disputed by a good number of economists. One of the lessons of this book is the need to question whether economic propositions put forth by policymakers are the absolute truth.

---

[14] JOHN QUIGGIN, ZOMBIE ECONOMICS: HOW DEAD IDEAS STILL WALK AMONG US (2012).

2

The Theory of Competitive Markets

The ideal market postulated by economic theory performs two important so-cial functions. First, it provides a way to allocate goods and services without the need for government direction. Supply and demand respond to each other through the pricing system. Part of this allocative function is to direct investments into activities where they are needed. The result is to maximize resource allocation and to achieve the largest possible breadbasket of goods and services. Second, the ideal market provides constraints on producers through competition. This second function is the one relevant to the ideas in this book.

Perfect competition is the engine that makes the market system work without government intervention. It creates constraints that prevent unde-sirable conduct by business firms. It prevents high prices because the firm that charges above the market price will be underpriced by its competitors and theoretically lose all business because consumers will buy from the firms with lower prices. The constraints of competition force business firms to act in the interests of their customers, rather than in their own interests. Perfect competition also creates incentives for efficient production techniques, better products, and research and development. Although the model assumes per-fect competition, these benefits will arise from vigorous, although less than perfect, competition. But there must be competition for these benefits to arise. If the firms in a market collude or if the firms refuse to compete as in an oligopolistic market, these benefits of competition are lost. To the contrary, if the market does not provide constraints, something else must do that. The only other realistic sources of constraints are self-restraint by firms or gov-ernment regulation.

The discipline of economics provides an elegant model about how a market economy works. It is an intuitive model that can be described with narratives, as Adam Smith did, so it is understandable to most people. It has been mathematized, beginning with Antoine Augustin Cournot in the nineteenth century and popularized by Alfred Marshall in the early twen-tieth century, so it can be manipulated and studied in what seems to be a

Rethinking Market Regulation. John N. Drobak, Oxford University Press. © Oxford University Press 2021.
DOI: 10.1093/oso/9780197578957.003.0002

scientific way. In addition, economists write with a certitude that makes their conclusions seem unshakable.[1] These characteristics make people forget that it is only a model, a theory that only works perfectly on a blackboard. In the messy real world, the model works well at some times and poorly at others. Plus, the rapid pace of technological change and globalization has been altering the real economic world, raising the question of whether a theory that worked in the past works today.

The theory of perfect competition is based on a number of assumptions: (1) a large number of buyers and sellers, each so small relative to the market that no purchase or sale will affect the market price;[2] (2) a homogeneous product, so that products are perfect substitutes for each other; (3) no barriers to entry to or exit from the market; (4) perfect information to buyers and sellers, particularly information about price; (5) producers live by the simple decision rule of maximizing profits; and (6) consumers are sovereign, meaning that each buyer has perfect knowledge of the differences between the various choices in the marketplace and perfect knowledge of what product will bring them the best satisfaction (or utility).[3]

It is obvious that these assumptions are not met in the real world. The mismatches most relevant to my concerns are those that allow firms to take advantage of consumers and workers. In welfare economic terms, consumer surplus is the benefit consumers get above the price they pay for a product. Theoretically, we could measure each consumer's surplus by the difference between the highest price a consumer would pay for a product and the actual price paid. For example, if a consumer would pay $35,000 for a particular car but can buy it for $30,000, that person has a surplus of $5,000. We could view labor surplus to be the difference between the actual wage paid and the lowest wage at which a person would work. In attempting to maximize profits, a producer is trying to decrease consumer surplus by raising price, thus converting consumer surplus into producer surplus, and trying to reduce labor surplus by paying low wages. Competition has the benefit of limiting the amount of producer surplus, while a monopolist can achieve much greater producer surplus than possible in a competitive market. If our economic objective is to increase the breadbasket of goods and services by maximizing resource allocation, we might be agnostic about the transfer

---

[1] Donald N. McCloskey, *The Rhetoric of Economics*, 21 J. ECON. LIT. 481, 493–94 (1983).

[2] Hence the well-known saying that firms in perfect competition are "price takers," unlike monopolists that are "price makers."

[3] *E.g.*, ROBERT COOTER & THOMAS ULEN, LAW AND ECONOMICS 22–41 (1988).

of consumer surplus into producer surplus because we do not know which type of surplus will lead to greater economic productivity. It might be that increased producer surplus will be reinvested in research and development and thus lead to better products, or it might just be passed on to shareholders and managers. Increased consumer surplus may be spent on additional goods and services, thus fueling the economy, or it might be put under a mattress at home for safekeeping. Since the second-order effects of surplus are so uncertain, it is understandable why economists may not take any position of the transfer of surplus.[4]

Supposedly the increase in the breadbasket of goods and services is good for everyone. As the economic pie grows, all of us have a bigger piece, even if our proportional share remains the same. However, the past few decades have shown that not to be true. Inequality in the United States has grown astronomically, with the rich getting an ever-growing share of the country's wealth. Part of the reason for this result is the stagnation of real wages since the late 1970s.[5] That is one of the reasons some economists have recently emphasized that wealth comes from capital accumulation these days, not from labor.[6] The increasing inequality in wealth leads to my concern about the transfer of surplus from consumers to producers.

Economic theory deals with wealth maximization and resource allocation, not with wealth distribution. The discipline assumes that people vote with their dollars to make the system work. The result is that people with less wealth have less power in the market. Many economists care about relative wealth, but they view that as an issue beyond economic theory. They view government programs designed to alleviate adverse wealth effects, like taxation, welfare, and healthcare, as matters of social, not economic, policy, making it acceptable to use a process that depends on people voting with their dollars. However, if progressive social policies are not followed, wealth disparities will increase and decisions based on economic reasoning will lead to the kinds of problems described earlier.[7]

---

[4] This is why the primary economic objection to monopoly is the deadweight loss that results from consumers who are priced out of the market and forced to buy their second-choice product, rather than a transfer of surplus.

[5] Barry Z. Cynamon & Steven M. Fazzari, *Rising Inequality and Stagnation in the US Economy*, 12 EUR. J. ECON. & ECON. POLICIES: INTERVENTION 170 (2015).

[6] *See, e.g.*, THOMAS PIKETTY, CAPITAL IN THE TWENTY-FIRST CENTURY (Arthur Goldhammer trans., 2014).

[7] Joseph Stiglitz has noted that large "behemoths" use their size to avoid taxation, depriving the public of "essential revenues to invest in infrastructure, people, and technology—contributing again to our economy's stagnation and distorting our economy by giving those firms an unfair competitive advantage." Joseph E. Stiglitz, *America Has a Monopoly Problem—And It's Huge*, THE NATION (Oct.

The assumption of consumer sovereignty that underlies the competitive market is an application of rational choice theory. As with most of social science, consumers are assumed to be rational actors. However, everyone knows that most consumers are not all-knowing about the choices available to them, nor are they equipped to foresee the relative benefits (or utility) of choosing one product over another. This mismatch of the assumption of consumer sovereignty and actual consumer behavior makes it easier for producers to increase their surplus at the expense of consumers.

The assumption of consumer sovereignty is unrealistic because information is far from perfect.[8] Consumers often lack enough information about substitute products to be able to make a reasoned choice. That is the reason for the popularity of lists that rank products and services. Consumers believe that the makers of the lists put in the effort to get information and design rankings that are legitimate. In the field of legal education, the ranking of law schools by *U.S. News* has tremendous influence on applicants because they believe that the information on relative quality is accurate, even if that is not correct. Competitive constraints reflect consumer preferences because the theory posits that demand will shift to the firms with lower prices and better quality products. If consumers cannot perceive the price and quality differences, then competitive constraints will not have this positive effect. Of course, they often do not in the real world.

Confusion abounds in consumer choice for many reasons. Not only are people not perfect decision makers, firms create confusion with product differentiation and manipulate demand through advertising.[9] Most products are not homogeneous. Not only is that a natural aspect of some products, other products are not homogeneous as a result of product differentiation. Producers use many different techniques to make their products appear to be different from very similar products of their competitors, in an attempt to make their competitors' products appear not to be substitutes for their

23, 2017), https://www.thenation.com/article/archive/america-has-a-monopoly-problem-and-its-huge/ [https://perma.cc/3ZCN-BQTY].

[8] Another way to describe this problem is to label it as an issue of high transaction costs. *See* Yoram Barzel, Economic Analysis of Property Rights 2–3 (1989).

[9] Advertising by pharmaceutical manufacturers designed to get patients to ask their doctors to prescribe certain drugs has skyrocketed over the past few years into annual advertising expenditures of billions of dollars. Elisabeth Rosenthal, Sunday Review, *Ask Your Doctor If This Ad Is Right for You,* N.Y. Times (Feb. 27, 2016), https://www.nytimes.com/2016/02/28/sunday-review/ask-your-doctor-if-this-ad-is-right-for-you.html [https://perma.cc/C9QU-4DVX]. This type of advertising does not sufficiently inform consumers because there is so much more expertise required to prescribe drugs.

products. Common examples include automobiles, mattresses, and cereal. Advertising is used to convince consumers that products are different and hence more desirable than others.[10] A good example of this use of advertising occurs in the market for American lager beer, which tastes nearly the same no matter the brewer. Steve Jobs, the founder of Apple, put it simply when he said that "[p]eople don't know what they want until you show it to them."[11]

The effect of brands on consumer behavior also undercuts the belief that consumers act rationally. Most people have a desire to fit in, whether at school, at work, or in social circles. For this reason, people sometimes buy brands because they believe the brands will contribute to greater social acceptance. Likewise, some people buy certain brands to support their personal or professional image. For example, a person will buy a Rolex watch not because it tells time better but because it conveys an image to others. Finally, some people rely on brands as indicating quality, regardless of whether that perception is objectively correct.[12] Psychological researchers conclude that some consumers have unconscious perceptions about a brand's authenticity and timelessness—what consumers describe as its "truth." These perceptions evoke emotions, like a sense of trust and security that comes with the purchase of a branded product.[13]

Producers also take advantage of consumers in other ways. Lack of competition in an industry may result in a smaller choice of products than would be available in a competitive market. For example, the four major airlines in the United States comprise an industry that has limited consumer choice, as will be discussed in the next chapter. Planned obsolescence in products is also a way to extract consumer surplus. Apple is a company that constantly introduces new versions of its phones, computers, and watches. Not only does this tap into some consumers' desire to always have the newest versions,

---

[10] Advertising is big business. For example, in 2014, Kellogg spent $32 million advertising Pop-Tarts, Pepsi spent $150 million on Gatorade, and Coca-Cola spent $269 million advertising its premier soda brand Coca-Cola. James Hamblin, *The Money Spent Selling Sugar to Americans Is Staggering*, ATLANTIC (Sept. 27, 2015), https://www.theatlantic.com/health/archive/2015/09/the-money-spent-selling-sugar-to-americans-is-staggering/407350/ [https://perma.cc/Q6PM-PE6S].

[11] WALTER ISAACSON, STEVE JOBS 567 (2011); *see also* Tim Wu, *Blind Spot: The Attention Economy and the Law*, 82 ANTITRUST L.J. 771, 784–86 (2017).

[12] Neil Kokemuller, *Why Do People Buy Brand Names?*, HOUS. CHRONICLE (Jan. 28, 2019), https://smallbusiness.chron.com/people-buy-brand-names-69654.html [https://perma.cc/7PKK-3KCQ]; John Paintcrown, *Why Do People Pay More Just for a Brand Name or Logo?*, QUORA (Mar. 31, 2018), https://www.quora.com/Why-do-people-pay-more-just-for-a-brand-name-or-logo [https://perma.cc/7PFS-YLQB].

[13] Peter Noel Murray, *The Myth of the Rational Consumer*, PSYCHOL. TODAY (Mar. 8, 2016), https://www.psychologytoday.com/us/blog/inside-the-consumer-mind/201603/the-myth-the-rational-consumer [https://perma.cc/8438-5K6D].

Apple uses the upgrades as a way to justify no longer supporting the older products, which limits the functions and workings of the older products.[14] The digital marketplace has made it easier for retailers to manipulate consumers by constant advertising based on a consumer's purchasing and browsing history.[15]

Another problem with the assumption of consumer sovereignty stems from consumer preferences reflecting short-term benefits over long-term ones. Behavioral economics has shown that people routinely give greater importance to short-term consequences than to future effects. Consumers also often overlook social good and focus on only what affects them. For example, to the extent that mileage and safety standards raise the price of cars, many consumers would prefer to have lower-priced cars that guzzle gas and kill people in collisions. As a general proposition, I suspect that many consumers focus primarily on price in making their decisions, leaving out consideration of the other dimensions of the goods and services they are purchasing. That trait is inconsistent with the assumption of consumer sovereignty.[16]

In addition to the unrealistic assumption of consumer sovereignty, the perfect competition model fails to describe many actual markets today that, unlike blackboard markets, lack the large number of buyers and sellers posited by the model. As the next chapter will show, many markets consist of only a few producers, creating oligopolies that are far from the competitive ideal.

All economists understand the mismatch between the assumptions of the theory and the realities of modern markets. For example, Milton Friedman has called competition "an ideal type, like a Euclidean line or point. No one has ever seen a Euclidean line—which has zero width and depth—yet we all find it useful to regard many a Euclidean volume—such as a surveyor's

---

[14] Jeff Sommer, *Apple's Watch Is Smarter, but My Casio Keeps Getting the Job Done*, N.Y. Times (Aug. 23, 2019), https://www.nytimes.com/2019/08/23/business/apple-watch-iphone-casio.html [https://perma.cc/R9RK-D4Y7].

[15] Ryan Calo, *Digital Market Manipulation*, 82 Geo. Wash. L. Rev. 995 (2014).

[16] In discussing the differences between travelers' expectations and reality, one travel writer wrote that "travelers are interested in—even obsessed by—saving money but one reason is that they're barraged by advertising messages that promise they can have it all: a low price, great service, and eventually, if they book enough trips, free flights and hotel stays." In his opinion, travelers need to take into account service as well as price: "It also means giving your business to an airline, hotel, or car rental company that treats you fairly and honestly, instead of the one that quotes you the lowest price." Christopher Elliott, *Got a Complaint About the Travel Industry? It's Got One About You, Too*, Wash. Post (Sept. 27, 2017), https://www.washingtonpost.com/lifestyle/travel/got-a-complaint-about-the-travel-industry-its-got-a-complaint-about-you-too/2017/09/26/707c59ec-97d3-11e7-87fc-c3f7ee4035c9_story.html [https://perma.cc/KSA3-KV5W].

string—as a Euclidean line."[17] Some economists, as a result, are hesitant to claim that the model is appropriate for policymaking.[18] Others, however, popularize the idea that the market works well enough, so we should trust its results over government intervention.

Part of the support for markets is based on the personal beliefs by the economists who take that position. But part simply comes from the way in which economists are educated. Alfred Marshall is generally credited as establishing economics as a discipline separate from philosophy. He is also credited as founding the neoclassical tradition, which mathematized economics and made it more "scientific." In his scholarship, including his highly influential textbook, *Principle of Economics*, Marshall taught that competition was the normal state of most markets. As one commentator explained:

> Although Marshall acknowledged the existence of monopolies and oligopolies, he believed that those market structures were a special case. To Marshall, the microeconomic behavior of firms and individuals was kept in constant check by the competitive nature of markets. The dynamics of free enterprise, of limitless entry to and exit from markets, enforced the norm of perfect competition among buyers and sellers. By his terms, each market is made up of sufficiently large numbers of competing firms buying and selling virtually identical products and services. No single demander or supplier of goods can affect the market price because no single firm has a large enough stake in the market. Given these conditions, the market price for goods will always gravitate to a level equal to the firm's cost of production. As a result, economic profits could not persist. Under the rigors of perfect competition, no firm would be able to rise above its equals.[19]

Clearly, in many modern markets in the United States, one firm has risen above its rivals.

Joan Robinson, who followed Marshall on the University of Cambridge Economics faculty, saw a far different world than Marshall. She believed that

---

[17] MILTON FRIEDMAN, CAPITALISM AND FREEDOM 120 (1962). Friedman also described the the-oretical purpose of the competition model: the concepts of competition and monopoly "are ideal constructs designed to analyze particular problems rather than to describe particular situations." *Id.* at 121.

[18] For example, the existence of transaction costs, frictions in the working of a market system, are important to the new institutional economists.

[19] JAMES D. GWARTNEY ET AL., MICROECONOMICS: PRIVATE AND PUBLIC CHOICE 293 (9th ed. 2000).

monopolies and oligopolies were prevalent in markets, not perfect competition. As she wrote in her book, *The Economics of Imperfect Competition*, "It is customary . . . to open with the analysis of a perfectly competitively world, and to treat monopoly as a special case. . . . [I]t is more proper to set out the analysis of monopoly, treating perfect competition as a special case."[20] She believed that in modern markets, individual firms were large enough to influence market prices on their own. This leads to economic profits, which in turn permits dominant firms to maintain or increase their dominance.

In the battle of intellectual thought, Marshall's insights prevailed over Robinson's. As a result, most people are taught today and come to believe that normal means competitive markets. Marshall and Robinson were trying to describe markets in the early twentieth century, a world very different from our own. Today's world is a global economy in which revolutions in transportation and communication make possible business activities that were inconceivable to Marshall and Robinson. In addition, the antitrust laws developed in a way that makes parallel behavior perfectly legal, resulting in the ability of firms to raise price through tacit coordination rather than through agreement. Oligopolistic markets, with few competitors, are the perfect place in which firms can legally disadvantage consumers by converting consumer surplus into producer surplus. Regardless of whether Marshall or Robinson was correct in describing Britain's prewar economy, I believe that Robinson's insights are an accurate description of many of the markets in our economic world today. It is true that some economists have created models to show that competition can arise in monopolistic and oligopolistic markets.[21] In these models, firms must decide to compete in order for competition to arise. However, modern markets have shown that many oligopolies exhibit no competitive behavior. Firms have learned to share the monopoly profits that are available to oligopolies, rather than competing. In a case involving oligopolistic pricing, Judge Posner has written, "the Sherman Act imposes no duty on firms to compete vigorously, or for that matter at all, in price."[22]

---

[20] Joan Robinson, The Economics of Imperfect Competition 207 (2d ed. 1969).
[21] Antoine Cournot, Researches into the Mathematical Principles of the Theory of Wealth (Macmillan 1897) (1838); Nirvkar Singh & Xavier Vives, *Price and Quantity Competition in a Differentiated Duopoly*, 15 Rand J. 546 (1984).
[22] *In re* Text Messaging Antitrust Litig., 782 F.3d 867, 863 (7th Cir. 2015).

3

Lack of Competition in U.S. Markets

The economy of the United States today is not the agrarian and mercantile economy of Scotland in 1776, when Adam Smith wrote the *Wealth of Nations*, nor is it the post–Industrial Revolution economy of England when Alfred Marshall wrote the *Principles of Economics* in 1890. When Milton Friedman wrote *Capitalism and Freedom* during the Cold War in 1962, a time when many feared that the United States would slide into socialism following the countries in Europe, the U.S. economy was much simpler and more localized than today's economy. Our economy today is much more complex and global than any of those economies. Multinational manufacturing and financial corporations, along with modern transportation and communications, have tied the economies of the world together. In addition, technology and automation have made drastic changes in the workplace. None of these existed when Smith, Marshall, and Friedman developed their ideas about how an economy works. Different economic times may need new theories about how markets work and new regulations for the new markets.

Today's economy is also dominated by huge corporations.[1] Although a few have monopoly power, most operate in oligopolistic markets with few firms. Rather than compete, the firms in many of these markets dance the "minuet of oligopoly" by raising prices just by following the price rise of the other firms. The prevalence of oligopolies is the primary reason that so many markets in the United States are not competitive.

In assessing the ability of firms to take advantage of consumers by converting consumer surplus into producer surplus, we need to determine whether product markets are competitive, such as the market for automobiles, for televisions, for income tax preparation software, and so forth. The question is whether only a few firms control the range of products that are substitutes for each other when we want to purchase a certain product. If they do, they can raise the price for all the substitute products, and

---

[1] TIM WU, THE CURSE OF BIGNESS: ANTITRUST IN THE NEW GILDED AGE 114–26 (2018).

Rethinking Market Regulation. John N. Drobak, Oxford University Press. © Oxford University Press 2021.
DOI: 10.1093/oso/9780197578957.003.0003

we consumers have only the choice of paying the higher price or not buying the good.

My contention is that many product markets in the United States are not competitive, even though we assume them to be. This chapter provides ways to assess my claim and shows the lack of competition in a number of illustrative markets. I recognize that markets are dynamic and subject to exogenous shocks that disrupt the normal workings of the market. The impact of the coronavirus pandemic in 2020 is an example of that. My perspective is on the performance in a market for a long enough time period to give us a sense of the typical characteristics of a market, say over a period of one to three years, depending on the industry. I also recognize that a market that is noncompetitive today may become competitive tomorrow. However, the evidence shows that the trend over a significant number of years has been for many markets to be noncompetitive.

I. Financial Data Relevant to Competitiveness

As Milton Friedman wrote, the ideal of perfect competition is an abstract concept, but it is a standard to which we compare real-world markets. If a market is far from the ideal, we should not label it as being competitive. If we do, we make the term "competitive market" meaningless.[2] One way to determine competitiveness is to examine how firms actually operate. Prices should be kept down to or near a competitive price, with returns to the producers reflecting the cost of capital. If a firm has market power, it has "the power to profitably elevate price above the competitive level, which in the case of perfect competition would be a price equal to firms' marginal cost."[3] The greater the price is above marginal cost, the more market power the firm has and the more consumer surplus can be converted into producer surplus.

---

[2] The term "market" is often used to imply a competitive market that can constrain behavior. A market is any vehicle that permits exchange, many of which do not constrain behavior. I once co-taught about the Microsoft antitrust case with an economist. When I referred to Microsoft's monopoly in operating systems, he replied that the government should have left Microsoft alone because the market was what it was. He claimed that whatever Microsoft did defined the market. That kind of use of the term "market" is misleading because many would assume that it means a functioning market that provides constraints, that is, a competitive market.

[3] Louis Kaplow, *Why (Ever) Define Markets?*, 124 HARV. L. REV. 437, 444 (2010). Market power is often expressed through the Lerner Index. The index indicates the portion of the price that is in excess of marginal cost. It is the price minus the marginal cost divided by the price. The higher the Lerner Index the greater the market power. *Id.* at 445–46.

However, it is very difficult to determine marginal costs.[4] There may be ways to come close, but that cost information is not generally available.[5] Another way to determine market power is to examine profits. Large profit in an industry over a number of years is an indicator of significant market power and a lack of competitiveness. This may be the best indicator that we have, but it is difficult to obtain profit rates for discrete product markets, not only because the data is hard to get but also because large companies generally aggregate the data for all the products they sell. In addition, many firms sell multiple products by allocating overhead in different proportions to their various products, making the determination of profit even harder. Accounting profit does give us some indication of competitiveness, but accounting profit is not what is meant by economic profit. There is really no way to measure the latter. If we want to compare returns, we need to know what would have been the competitive "normal" return in a market. That is extremely difficult to do, since it requires hypothesizing a competitive market as a benchmark. Finally, the ideal of a competitive price usually means a static equilibrium price. Actual markets are dynamic, not static. When we take a snapshot of the behavior of a market, it may be difficult to tell if it is near equilibrium or if it is moving away from or toward equilibrium. Nonetheless, we can get a sense of profit rates for a few products.

In the 1950s, it was popular for academic economists to examine factors that showed the degree of competitiveness of markets. In one of the best-known studies, two economists were able to show that DuPont earned much higher profits from its sales of cellophane than from its sales of rayon. Both products were introduced about the same time, but the profits differed so greatly because cellophane was a monopoly while rayon was sold in a competitive market.[6] These kinds of studies, however, fell out of favor in the academic economics profession, although they would be very helpful to our understanding what actually is going on in U.S. markets.

It is very difficult to get the kind of financial information necessary to determine the profitability of a particular product or all the firm's products in a defined market. The economists who studied DuPont's profitability were fortunate to have had access to DuPont's internal financial information about

[4] Id. at 447; see also Gauti B. Eggertsson et al., Kaldor and Piketty's Facts: The Rise of Monopoly Power in the United States (Nat'l Bureau of Econ. Research, Working Paper No. 24,287, 2018), http://www.nber.org/papers/w24287 [https://perma.cc/D3VT-BZE9].

[5] Kaplow, supra note 3, at 447 n.20.

[6] George W. Stocking & Willard F. Mueller, The Cellophane Case and the New Competition, 45 AM. ECON. REV. 29, 60–63 (1955).

both cellophane and rayon. Publicly available financial information shows the profitability of most companies as a whole, but not the profitability of particular products. However, when a company sells primarily one product or only a few products, public financial information may give us a rough sense of the profitability of its individual products.

Take Apple and the iPhone, as an example. For the iPhone X, released in November 2017 at a retail price of $999, Apple earned a profit of 61 percent based on the cost of the components making up the phone.[7] The actual profit from the sale of an iPhone X was less because the cost used to determine the 61 percent profit rate did not include expenses like marketing, distribution, and research and development of the iPhone X. Those costs are unavailable.[8] Since about 62 percent of Apple's 2017 annual revenue from the sale of all goods and services came from the sale of iPhones, looking at the profitability of the company overall gives us a sense of the profit that Apple makes from iPhone sales.[9] Apple's reported overall profit margin was 38.5, 39.1, and 40.1 percent for the years 2017, 2016, and 2015, respectively.[10] Those are high rates of profit, indicating a company with the ability to charge prices well above costs and to convert sizeable consumer surplus into producer surplus. This demonstrates that the iPhone gives Apple considerable market power and that the iPhone is only subject to limited competitive constraints from Android cell phones.

Another example is the airline industry. Since the December 2013 consummation of the merger between American Airlines and US Airways, only four firms comprise the industry: American, Delta, Southwest, and United. They mostly sell one "product," passenger air transportation, with a small amount of revenue from air cargo.[11] As a result, financial information about

---

[7] Tuan Do, *The Real Production Costs of Smartphones*, TECHWALLS (Nov. 25, 2019), https://www. techwalls.com/production-costs-of-smartphones/ [https://perma.cc/2LRT-3X2D]. The cost of the phone was determined by breaking down the device and determining the cost of the components. What the article referred to as profit margin was akin to the gross margin for the phone in accounting terminology. Another commentator calculated Apple's profit from the sale of an iPhone X at 64 percent. Stephen Nellis, *Apple's iPhone X Has Higher Margin Than iPhone 8: Analysis*, REUTERS (Nov. 6, 2017), https://www.reuters.com/article/us-apple-iphone/apples-iphone-x-has-higher-margin-than-iphone-8-analysis-idUSKBN1D62RZ [https://perma.cc/K8JD-SWCP].

[8] I doubt that the research and development expenses of the iPhone X were great since that phone was only a variation of earlier models. Sales of earlier iPhone models must have recovered most of the research and development costs of the iPhone technology.

[9] Apple Inc., *Annual Report (Form 10-K)* 24 (Sept. 30, 2017). https://www.sec.gov/Archives/edgar/data/320193/000032019317000070/a10-k20179302017.htm#s65EBF38841D3591FA44752C C48FB0D37 [https://perma.cc/YAY4-NQRS].

[10] *Id.* at 26.

[11] Delta Airlines, *Annual Report (Form 10-K)* (Feb. 23, 2018). https://www.sec.gov/Archives/edgar/data/27904/000002790418000006/dal1231201710k.htm [https://perma.cc/C9KY-C6KC].

an airline company gives a rough picture of the returns from the company's product. Since deregulation in 1978, the industry has been volatile financially, with many years of losses. However, consolidation has brought financial stability with large profits.

Appendix A shows the operating margin and residual income for the four airlines over a span of years. The operating margin gives a rough sense of the profitability of a firm's air transportation business. The annual operating margin of the airlines dramatically increased over a five-year period starting in 2012, even though it has not been a constantly steady increase. For example, Delta had an operating margin in the 11.5 to 14 percent range for 2012 to 2014, but then it jumped to 27.8 percent in 2015. For 2017, it was about 23 percent. The other three airlines show similar increases over 2012 to 2017.

Residual income is a managerial accounting concept used to evaluate the profitability of different companies. Unlike gross margin, which measures accounting profit, residual income provides a more realistic measure of the economic profit that is relevant to investors. It is a measure in terms of dollars that attempts to show the relationship between the profit earned by a firm and the cost of the firm's capital.[12] We could roughly equate the cost of capital with normal economic returns and any profit above that as above-normal or excess returns in economic terms. Since the calculation of the cost of capital, especially the cost of equity, is somewhat subjective and there is no publicly available industry benchmark for residual income, it is difficult to reliably compare residual income across companies within the same industry.[13] In comparison, accounting profit is more readily available and comparable because it is calculated according to generally accepted accounting principles. Nonetheless, comparing the residual income for one firm over a span of years gives us a good sense of how the firm has been performing financially.

Appendix A uses the cost of capital for the airlines as determined by two different investment services, *Bloomberg* and *GuruFocus*. The appendix shows that the four airlines had negative residual income until 2013–2015. Since then, annual residual income has been in the billions of dollars for the airlines. For example, the residual income of American Airlines peaked

---

[12] The cost of capital includes interest on debt and earning for shareholders needed to raise new capital.

[13] For the same company, different sources (like *Bloomberg*, *GuruFocus*, and *Yahoo Finance*) may give different betas. Beta, a key figure used to calculate cost of equity, represents the volatility of a stock relative to the market. Therefore, cost of equity is almost always subjective.

in 2015 at $6.2 billion or $2.9 billion, using respectively the data from *GuruFocus* or *Bloomberg*. That year, the residual income for Delta was $3.7 billion, using data from *GuruFocus*, or $3.6 billion, using *Bloomberg* data. As with operating margin, there is some volatility in the residual income from year to year, but the trend has been upward. According to both *GuruFocus* and *Bloomberg*, the residual income of the four major airlines has been in the billions of dollars between 2015 and 2017, except that *Bloomberg* reports American Airlines' at slightly below a billion for 2017 and United Airlines' at $280 million.

Using the residual income of Delta Airlines to determine a percentage return on invested capital, one investment service concludes this about the desirability of investing in Delta:

> Because it costs money to raise capital, a firm that generates a higher [return on invested capital] than it costs to raise the capital needed for that investment is earning excess returns. A firm that expects to continue generating positive excess returns on new investments in the future will see its value increase as growth increases, whereas a firm that earns returns that do not match up to its cost of capital will destroy value as it grows.
>
> As of [December 2017], Delta Airlines Inc.'s weighted cost of capital is 6.85%. Delta Airlines Inc.'s [return on invested capital] is 21%. . . . Delta Airlines Inc. generates higher returns on investment than it costs the company to raise the capital needed for that investment. It is earning excess returns. A firm that expects to continue generating positive excess returns on new investments in the future will see its value increase as growth increase.[14]

The other airlines also generate excess returns like Delta.[15] These kinds of earnings show that the four airlines have considerable market power, which gives them the ability to charge prices well above costs and to convert sizeable consumer surplus into producer surplus. It used to be that airline profits

[14] *Delta Air Lines WACC %*, GuruFocus, https://www.gurufocus.com/term/wacc/NYSE:DAL/WACC-/Delta-Air-Lines-Inc [https://perma.cc/MQJ3-5LQS].

[15] *American Airlines Group WACC %*, GuruFocus, https://www.gurufocus.com/term/wacc/NAS:AAL/WACC-/American-Airlines-Group-Inc [https://perma.cc/2EJJ-8HS7]; *United Airlines Holdings WACC %*, GuruFocus, https://www.gurufocus.com/term/wacc/UAL/WACC-Percentage/United%20Airlines%20Holdings [https://perma.cc/3FUZ-Z4JN]; *Southwest Airlines Co WACC %*, GuruFocus, https://www.gurufocus.com/term/wacc/LUV/WACC-Percentage/Southwest%20Airlines%20Co [https://perma.cc/MK8S-FNZ4].

were heavily dependent on fuel prices, but the major airlines are financially strong enough now to minimize that effect. One Bloomberg report in May 2018 concluded "[t]he largest carriers are still expected to report another year of multibillion dollar profits—gone are the days when the industry would tremble when oil prices rose."[16] This is an industry lacking competition.

The airline industry is very susceptible to exogenous shocks that dramatically decrease demand for air transportation. This was true in the aftermath of the 9/11 terrorist attack in 2001 and during the coronavirus pandemic in 2020. Although the precipitous drop in demand can cause financial losses, it does not demonstrate that the airline industry is competitive. The poor returns are not the result of competition among the four airlines but rather from the abnormally low demand.

It is very difficult, often impossible, to obtain the financial data necessary to analyze a firm's profit on a particular product, as I tried to do for the iPhone and the airline industry. Rather than focusing on the profitability of individual products, some studies have examined the profitability of the firms in a defined industry. For example, a study in 2019 found that a large increase in the concentration of many industries since the late 1990s led to a significant increase in corporate profits.[17] The study's "findings demonstrate that firms in concentrated industries are becoming more profitable predominantly through higher profit margins, rather than via greater efficiency."[18] The study's authors find a robust correlation between market concentration and profits, noting that the increased profitability has been transferred to investors through higher abnormal returns.

In addition to examining profitability, we need to look at other factors to judge competitiveness. Some macro information shows effects that support the conclusion that competition has decreased greatly. Many believe that the road to wealth these days is through capital rather than labor. Investors have done very well this century while real wages have stagnated since the early 1980s. This has led to the largest wealth differential among the American population since World War II. Since 2010, many corporations have done so well financially that they can afford to spend billions to buy other companies. They can also afford massive buy-backs of their own stock. There may

---

[16] Mary Schlangenstein, *Southwest's $49 Fares Signal Summer Bargains Despite Pricier Oil*, BLOOMBERG (May 21, 2018), https://www.bloomberg.com/news/articles/2018-05-21/southwest-s-49-fares-signal-summer-bargains-despite-pricier-oil [https://perma.cc/L53C-VANS].

[17] Gustavo Grullon, Yelena Larkin, & Roni Michaely, *Are US Industries Becoming More Concentrated?*, 23 REV. FIN. 697 (2019).

[18] *Id.* at 699.

be laudable reasons for this great corporate wealth, but it also may be the result of a lack of competition.

There are three other factors that show the decline of competition in the United States. First, many economists have begun to write about this problem. Second, the conduct of the firms in many markets could not occur if there was competition. Finally, numerous studies of specific industries have noted very high concentration of the market shares of the firms.

II. Expert Opinion on Competitiveness

In April 2016, President Obama issued an executive order, entitled "Steps to Increase Competition and Better Inform Consumers and Workers to Support Continued Growth of the American Economy,"[19] which recognizes the problem of decreased competition in many industries. An issue brief, published by the Council of Economic Advisors to support the executive order, concluded that "many industries may be becoming more concentrated, that new firm entry is declining, and that some firms are generating returns that are greatly in excess of historical standards," all indicative of a decline in competition.[20] Prominent liberal economists have warned of the decrease in competition. In *America Has a Monopoly Problem—And It's Huge*, Joseph Stiglitz, wrote:

> Over the past four decades, economic theory and evidence has laid waste to [the] claims and the belief that some variant of the competitive equilibrium model provides a good, or even adequate, description of our economy. But if we begin with the obvious, opposite hypothesis—that what we see in our daily life is true, that our economy is marked in industry after industry by large concentrations of market power—then we can begin to simultaneously understand much of what is going on. There has been an increase in the market power and concentration of a few firms in industry after industry leading to an increase in prices relative to costs (in mark-ups). This lowers the standard of living every bit as much as it lowers workers' wages. . . . This increase in market power helps explain simultaneously the

---

[19] Exec. Order No. 13,725, 3 C.F.R., 2016 Comp., at 452 (2017).
[20] EXEC. OFFICE OF THE PRESIDENT, COUNCIL ECON. ADVISERS, BENEFITS OF COMPETITION AND INDICATORS OF MARKET POWER 14 (2016), https://obamawhitehouse.archives.gov/sites/default/files/page/files/20160414_cea_competition_issue_brief.pdf [https://perma.cc/CS72-XZL3].

slowdown in productivity growth, the sluggishness of the economy, and the growth of inequality—in short, the poor performance of the American economy in so many dimensions.[21]

Similarly, Paul Krugman has written that the twenty-first century is defined by

the growing importance of monopoly rents: profits that don't represent returns on investment, but instead reflect the value of market dominance. [For example,] the price you pay for an iWhatever is disconnected from the cost of producing the gadget. Apple simply charges what the traffic will bear, and given the strength of its market position, the traffic will bear a lot. [This is also true for] Microsoft, which made huge profits for many years, let alone for the financial industry, which is also marked by a lot of what looks like monopoly rents, and these days accounts for roughly 30 percent of total corporate profits. Anyway, whether corporations deserve their privileged status or not, the economy is affected, and not in a good way, when profits increasingly reflect market power than production.[22]

Some economists who have analyzed the causes of the increasing wealth disparity this century have pointed to the great returns to capital, stemming from high profits for business. Probably the best known is Thomas Piketty's emphasis on the accumulation of wealth through capital when returns to capital exceed the rate of economic growth.[23] Three economists from Brown University, Gauti Eggertsson, Jacob Robbins, and Ella Wold, expanded on Piketty's work to model the current economic conditions in the United States based on their hypothesis that an increase in monopoly profits and a reduction in interest rates have been the "key drivers" of the current economy.[24] They note that "there is a growing body of evidence that suggests a marked decrease in competition, an increase in concentration, a decline in business dynamism, and an increase in profits."[25] Their model, which appears

---

[21] Joseph E. Stiglitz, *America Has a Monopoly Problem—And It's Huge*, THE NATION (Oct. 23, 2017), https://www.thenation.com/article/archive/america-has-a-monopoly-problem-and-its-huge/ [https://perma.cc/3ZCN-BQTY].

[22] Paul Krugman, Opinion, *Profits without Production*, N.Y. TIMES (June 20, 2013), https://www.nytimes.com/2013/06/21/opinion/krugman-profits-without-production.html   [https://perma.cc/P5HU-FF3T].

[23] THOMAS PIKETTY, CAPITAL IN THE TWENTY-FIRST CENTURY (Arthur Goldhammer trans., 2014).

[24] Eggertsson et al., *supra* note 4.

[25] *Id.* at 3.

to describe accurately current economic conditions, is strong support for the existence of large corporate profits in a world with greatly diminished competition.

The recent concern for the growth of huge corporations in the United States, particularly in the high-tech industries, such as Facebook, Amazon, Google, and Apple, is not just a concern about political power and privacy; it also recognizes that these companies wield tremendous economic power. Tim Wu's book, *The Curse of Bigness*, lays out proposals for fundamental changes in the antitrust laws to combat the huge size of business. His proposals include the reform of merger review, which I will discuss in Chapter 4, and a reorientation of the underlying goals of the antitrust regulation. His most novel proposal would require the government to intervene and rectify noncompetitive markets in circumstances in which the antitrust laws currently do not apply:

> The United States can and should adopt a market investigations law like that of the UK, and give it to the Federal Trade Commission to enforce. The prerequisite would be persistent dominance of at least 10 years or longer, suggesting that a market remedy is not forthcoming, and proof that the existing industry structure lacked convincing competitiveness or public justifications, and that market forces would be unlikely to remedy the situation by themselves. In practice, the agency would put overly consolidated industries under investigation, recommend remedies through the administrative process, and adopt them, subject to judicial review.[26]

There may be a few markets for which we all agree on whether it is close to the competitive ideal or to a monopoly, but most markets are not so easy to classify. The evidence we have about the degree of competitiveness of those markets is mostly circumstantial, which leads to debatable conclusions. As the next two sections will show, the conduct of firms in many markets and the degree of concentration raise a serious question about the competitiveness of many markets in the United States. This undermines the assumption that most markets are competitive and, I believe, shifts the burden to proponents of the existence of competition to demonstrate that that is an accurate description.

---

[26] Wu, *supra* note 1, at 134.

III. Business Conduct as a Way
to Determine Competitiveness

In addition to profit rates, other conduct by firms in a market can give us a sense of the degree of competitiveness in the market. When there are high profits, we would expect large expenditures on "rent seeking" behavior to preserve or increase these profits by activities like product differentiation, branding, and advertising, which the economic literature often refer to as intangible investment.[27] Besides backing into the determination of high profit rates by observing rent-seeking behavior, we could also observe oligopolistic conduct concerning nonprice aspects of a product or service. The premise of the cellophane study referred to earlier was that the observation of business strategy can help us identify noncompetitive markets.[28] A few examples will illustrate this.

The healthcare market is not competitive for a number of reasons. Information problems confound decisions by patients on their medical treatment. Not only do we not understand the variations of care and the prices available to us, making us far from the sovereign consumers that the competitive model assumes, we fear death and disabilities, making price less important. Price is also less important when an insurance company pays for most of the services. We have a tendency to do what our doctors prescribe because we assume they know best. On top of our information problems, many doctors prescribe treatments and drugs without a regard for their cost.[29] Their goal is to cure us, not to save us or our insurance companies money. Monopoly pricing of pharmaceutical drugs is sometimes outrageous. Valeant increased the price of cardiac care drugs by more than 500 percent. Even a monopolist is constrained by the effects of the marginal revenue when setting monopoly prices. The demand for Valeant's drugs must have been highly inelastic if that kind of price rise was profitable to the company. With about 30 million people in the United States having diabetes, insulin is an important drug with a high demand. Nonetheless, the price of insulin has increased dramatically this century. For example, the price of a 10-milliliter vial of the insulin Lantus has increased from $40 in 2001 to around $275 in 2018. Insulin is overpriced

---

[27] Eggertsson et al., *supra* note 4, at 40.

[28] Stocking & Mueller, *supra* note 6, at 29, 31.

[29] *E.g.*, Doctors testified in a recent Eighth Circuit case that they did not take price into account when choosing between two drugs which used different processes to accomplish the same treatment. F.T.C. v. Lundbeck, Inc., 650 F.3d 1236, 1240 (8th Cir. 2011).

in part because only three pharmaceutical firms manufacture insulin and only three firms dominate the business of pharmacy benefit managers, which negotiate drug prices for health insurance companies.[30] The companies act as an oligopoly to keep prices high. Compounding all of this is the monopoly pricing of some pharmaceutical drugs for "innovations" that legally merit patent protection but do nothing for patients other than raise price. For example, the EpiPen delivers an established drug, epinephrine, in a fancy new delivery system that enables it to reap monopoly profits.[31]

Another noncompetitive market is the market for cellular service. There are four principal cellular companies and a few fringe resellers of cellular service, which is a homogeneous product, creating a market structure that can lead to oligopoly pricing and other noncompetitive actions. That is what has in fact happened. Telecom prices in the United States are higher than in many other countries, while the quality is poorer by some measures.[32] There is some competition in pricing and contract terms as a result of T-Mobile's aggressive marketing, but many consumers view price as significantly less important than other aspects of cell service.[33] When the iPhone was new and only available from AT&T, that phone drew customers to AT&T. For those customers with a strong preference for the iPhone, AT&T was effectively a monopolist of the cellular service market. Now, with the cell companies' networks so similar, many customers choose a cell company for the type of

---

[30] *See, e.g.*, Melody Petersen, *Drug Prices Surge Even When Rivals Join Market*, St. Louis Post-Dispatch (Sept. 3, 2016), https://www.stltoday.com/business/local/drug-prices-surge-even-when-rivals-join-market/article_303648e5-9c27-583f-9bec-37abe05340e1.html [https://perma.cc/8YDQ-4NPV]; Marie Beaugureau, *Here's Why Insulin Is So Expensive—And What You Can Do About It*, GoodRx (Feb. 8, 2018), https://www.goodrx.com/blog/heres-why-insulin-is-so-expensive-and-what-you-can-do-about-it/ [https://perma.cc/H3Y3-7FU8]; *8 Reasons Why Insulin Is So Outrageously Expensive*, T1International (Jan. 20, 2019), https://www.t1international.com/blog/2019/01/20/why-insulin-so-expensive/ [https://perma.cc/W65Z-QLMQ].

[31] *See* Elisabeth Rosenthal, Opinion, *The Lesson of Epipens: Why Drug Prices Spike, Again and Again*, N.Y. Times (Sept. 2, 2016), https://www.nytimes.com/2016/09/04/opinion/sunday/the-lesson-of-epipens-why-drug-prices-spike-again-and-again.html [https://perma.cc/YP2Q-VUC9]; Rachel E. Sachs, *Mylan Announces Generic Epipen; Baffles Health Policy Wonks Everywhere*, Bill of Health (Aug. 30, 2016), https://blog.petrieflom.law.harvard.edu/2016/08/30/mylan-announces-generic-epipen-baffles-health-policy-wonks-everywhere/ [https://perma.cc/9KC4-KHMZ].

[32] Stiglitz, *supra* note 21 ("Is there any reason that US telecom prices should be so much higher than in many countries and service so much poorer? Much of the innovation was done here in the United States. Our publicly supported research and education institutions provided the intellectual foundations. It is now a global technology, requiring little labor—so it cannot be high wages that provide the explanation. The answer is simple: market power.").

[33] Liana B. Baker & Anjali Athavaley, *Sprint, T-Mobile Call Off Merger after Months of Talks*, Reuters (Nov. 4, 2017), https://www.reuters.com/article/us-sprint-corp-m-a-t-mobile-us/sprint-t-mobile-call-off-merger-after-months-of-talks-idUSKBN1D40RY [https://perma.cc/8TFZ-7RXK] (T-Mobile was the first major carrier to eliminate two-year contracts, which the other three cellular companies followed).

phone it provides, not giving much importance to the other aspects of the contract with the cell company.[34] One service provided by cellular companies, text messaging, led to an antitrust lawsuit that provided some evidence of high pricing and an increase in producer surplus. The complaint alleged that the four companies sold 90 percent of U.S. text messaging services, that they raised prices as costs fell, and that they changed heterogeneous and complex pricing structures into a uniform pricing structure while simultaneously raising prices by 30 percent.[35] The litigation was dismissed on summary judgment because there was no evidence of an agreement between the four carriers. In the opinion upholding the dismissal, Judge Posner noted that a market with "few sellers, many buyers, and a homogeneous product, which may preclude nonprice competition, [may] favor convergence by the sellers on a joint profit-maximizing price without their actually agreeing to charge that price."[36] This conduct does not violate the Sherman Act, but it shows an uncompetitive market in which producers can take advantage of consumers.

The deregulations of the airlines in 1979 resulted in significantly lower airfares, as much as 40 percent when adjusted for inflation according to one study.[37] However, a comparison of average airfares between 1979 and the present is far from the only story. The airline industry is an oligopolistic industry in which the air carriers have devised ways to maximize producer surplus at the expense of consumers. At the time of deregulation of the industry in 1978, the industry had eleven national carriers and dozens of regional and commuter carriers. Chaos ensued as some airlines expanded, some went bankrupt, and some merged in the aftermath of deregulation. There were fifty-one mergers in the first nine years after deregulation.[38] For many years, the airlines lost money hand over fist in what appeared to be an industry that exhibited destructive competition, as a result of the short-term marginal cost of an airline seat being near zero. When Alfred Kahn, the economist who

---

[34] Rachel Sandler, *How the iPhone Changed the Telecommunications Industry*, USA TODAY (July 4, 2017), https://www.usatoday.com/story/tech/news/2017/07/04/how-iphone-changed-telecommunications-industry/103154146/ [https://perma.cc/3CE3-8EPE].

[35] The notion that customers do not benefit from declining costs in telecom services is not new. Before telecom deregulation, declining costs of long-distance service did not lead to decreasing rates for long-distance phone service, but instead served as a source of additional revenue for the Bell System. Customers do not know that costs are decreasing from technological advances.

[36] *In re* Text Messaging Antitrust Litig., 782 F.3d 867, 874 (7th Cir. 2015).

[37] Elaine Glusac, *Fly Farther, for Cheaper. For Now.*, N.Y. TIMES (July 13, 2018), https://www.nytimes.com/2018/07/13/travel/summer-airline-fares.html [https://perma.cc/AYQ9-XB29] (citing a study by the Eno Center for Transportation).

[38] SIDNEY A. SHAPIRO & JOSEPH P. TOMAIN, REGULATORY LAW AND POLICY 324 (1993).

led the move to deregulate the airlines, was asked what could be done to end the chaos, he responded that the airlines needed to learn to live as rational oligopolists.[39] With the merger of American Airlines and US Airways in late 2013, the industry shrunk to four major firms, with a few smaller airlines in limited markets. In 2019, the four largest airlines controlled over two-thirds of domestic air travel.[40] In many cities, only one airline dominates service; in many others, only two compete. The industry has become a classic oligopoly, with little competition between the firms and virtually no power in air travelers to negotiate for lower prices or better quality of services. Inflight service has essentially disappeared, while preflight service has been automated and curtailed significantly. Through sophisticated computer programs, the airlines' "yield management" allows the carriers to price discriminate and fill up nearly all the seats on a flight, resulting in very few passengers having the space next to them provided by an empty seat.[41] Seat size and the distance between seats have shrunk. Fees for checked baggage, seats with more space, and reservation changes have exploded to nearly $30 billion in 2016.[42] The plaintiffs in a recent lawsuit alleged that the baggage fees charged by Spirit Airlines, a low-cost regional airline, often exceeded the cost of a ticket.[43] These fees are vehicles for extracting additional revenue from customers far above any cost associated with carrying baggage. The rising number of complaints about uncomfortable seats led to proposals to Congress to regulate this aspect of airline service. The airline industry responded with a

---

[39] Alfred E. Kahn, *Surprises of Airline Deregulation*, 78 AM. ECON. REV. 316, 320 (1988).

[40] *Domestic Market Share of Leading U.S. Airlines from February 2019 to January 2020*, STATISTA, statista.com/statistics/250577/domestic-market-share-of-leading-us-airlines/ [https://perma.cc/5P7X-3VNX].

[41] Julie Weed, *In the Race for Cheap Airfare, It's You vs. the Machine*, N.Y. TIMES (Jan. 27, 2020), https://www.nytimes.com/2020/01/27/business/cheap-airfare.html [https://perma.cc/R7ZT-K3C2].

[42] *See, e.g.*, Christopher Elliott, *Got a Complaint About the Travel Industry? It's Got One About You, Too*, WASH. POST (Sept. 27, 2017), https://www.washingtonpost.com/lifestyle/travel/got-a-complaint-about-the-travel-industry-its-got-a-complaint-about-you-too/2017/09/26/707c59ec-97d3-11e7-87fc-c3f7ee4035c9_story.html [https://perma.cc/KSA3-KV5W] ("The top 10 airlines collected more than $28 billion in revenue from airline fees and services last year, up from about $2 billion a decade ago, according to a recent study by the consulting firm IdeaWorks."). Now hotels are following the lead of airlines by charging fees for various services, like charges for the room safe, restocking fees for the minibar, and storing luggage for a few hours. Stephanie Rosenbloom, *Hotels Rake in Record Fees, and Travelers Foot the Bill*, N.Y. TIMES (Sept. 29, 2017), https://www.nytimes.com/2017/09/29/travel/hotels-rake-in-record-fees-and-travelers-foot-the-bill.html [https://perma.cc/P837-9PNV].

[43] Second Amended Class Action Complaint & Demand for Jury Trial, Cox v. Spirit Airlines, Inc., 340 F. Supp.3d 154 (E.D.N.Y. May 10, 2018). *See* Jonathan Stempel, *Spirit Airlines Must Face Lawsuit over "Gotcha" Carry-on Bag Fees: Court*, REUTERS (Sept. 10, 2019), https://www.reuters.com/article/us-spirit-airlines-lawsuit-bag-fees/spirit-airlines-must-face-lawsuit-over-gotcha-carry-on-bag-fees-court-idUSKCN1VV212 [https://perma.cc/C8LL-QCXH] (discussing Cox v. Spirit Airlines, Inc., 786 F. App'x 283 (2d Cir. 2019)).

claim that this is the kind of issue that should be left to self-regulation by the market.[44] However, there is no competitive market that can constrain this kind of conduct. There have been reports of airplane designs with "seats" in which passengers fly upright, leaning against a back support.[45] Where is the power in consumers to prevent this type of equipment? Some airplanes have decreased the size of lavatories drastically, in order to permit more room for seats. If U.S. airlines decide to start charging a fee for the use of the lavatories (as Ryanair does in Europe), do passengers have the power to prevent this? Of course not. There is little competition among the airlines over product quality, leaving consumers with limited choices.[46]

It would be possible to list many different types of industries that lack competitive behavior. Even the services for weddings in many cities, such as hotels, reception venues, wedding planners, wedding photographers, florists, and so forth, often exhibit noncompetitive behavior, with many charging more for the same service if it is involved with a wedding rather than some other type of event.[47] By examining how the firms in an industry act, we can get a sense of the competitiveness of that industry.

---

[44] The airlines have opposed regulation of seat size based on a claim that the market self-regulates: "The airline industry vehemently opposed the amendment. 'We believe that the government should not regulate, but instead market forces, which reflect consumer decisions, and competition, should determine what is offered,' says Jean Medina, a spokeswoman for Airlines for American, a trade group for airlines." Christopher Elliott, *It's Time for Congress to Stand Up for Air Travelers*, WASH. POST (Feb. 18, 2016), https://www.washingtonpost.com/lifestyle/travel/its-time-for-congress-to-stand-up-for-air-travelers/2016/02/18/2a21b7aa-d4d7-11e5-b195-2e29a4e13425_story.html [https://perma.cc/T3QZ-JNH2].

[45] Sydney Levin, *China's Spring Airlines Lobbies for Vertical Seats*, AOL (Feb. 4, 2015), https://www.aol.com/article/2015/02/04/china-s-spring-airlines-lobbies-for-vertical-seats/21139087/ [https://perma.cc/MH6T-S55N].

[46] The airlines seem to always find new ways to raise revenue, by shifting even more consumer surplus to producer surplus. "Three airlines—American, Delta, and United—quietly changed how they price multicity tickets on-line recently, often displaying dramatically higher fares than they used to." Christopher Elliott, *Three Top Airlines Changed the Pricing of Multi-City Tickets. Here's How to Avoid Paying More.*, WASH. POST (Apr. 14, 2016), https://www.washingtonpost.com/lifestyle/travel/three-top-airlines-changed-the-pricing-of-multi-city-tickets-heres-how-to-avoid-paying-more/2016/04/14/59cf234e-00c8-11e6-b823-707c79ce3504_story.html [https://perma.cc/BK27-E72K]. The airlines have also raised the costs of Wi-Fi on flights, reportedly from what used to be $6–$8 a flight to $30 without any improvement in service. Christopher Elliott, *The Wifi on Planes Makes a Convincing Argument for the In-flight Novel*, WASH. POST (Apr. 21, 2016), https://www.washingtonpost.com/lifestyle/travel/the-wifi-on-planes-makes-a-convincing-argument-for-the-in-flight-novel/2016/04/21/e130c592-df06-11e5-846c-10191d1fc4ec_story.html [https://perma.cc/HS7U-Q8QX].

[47] A recent examination of wedding costs by *Consumer Reports* showed such upcharges as an Atlanta photographer charging double his rates for a wedding when compared to an anniversary party, a $7 per person cake-cutting fee in some caterer's contracts, and an extra 29 percent event fee for wedding receptions held in the St. Louis Westin Hotel. Tobie Stanger, *Get More Wedding for Your Money*, CONSUMER REPS. (Apr. 26, 2016), https://www.consumerreports.org/weddings/get-more-wedding-for-your-money/ [https://perma.cc/9BLD-LK54].

IV. Market Concentration as a Way to Determine Competitiveness

The most common way to examine the likelihood of competition in a market is to examine the concentration of market power, which is an indication of "the extent to which a small number of firms control most of the sales."[48] Market concentration is usually determined by various types of ratios. Among the more common methods, courts have looked at the market shares of the two or four largest firms in an industry, referred to respectively as the two- or four-firm concentration ratio. The Justice Department and the Federal Trade Commission rely on a ratio using the squares of the firms' market shares, called the Herfindahl-Hirschman Index (HHI), in merger analysis.[49] An HHI over 2,500 indicates a highly concentrated market. (Appendix B contains technical information about market definition and about the various methods used to determine market concentration.)

Market concentration can help provide insight into whether markets are competitive. Among industrial organization scholars, the convention is "to use concentration ratios as a measure of monopoly power, both within particular industries and across industries generally."[50] Monopoly power is the power to control prices or exclude competition.[51] Furthermore, as the Department of Justice has explained, "[m]arket concentration is often one useful indicator of likely competitive effect of a merger."[52] Therefore, the more concentrated industries and markets present concerns about a lack of competition.[53] Additionally, the U.S. Supreme Court has stated, "a merger which produces a firm controlling an undue percentage share of the relevant market, and results in a significant increase in the concentration of firms in that market is so inherently likely to lessen competition substantially that it must be enjoined in the absence of evidence clearly showing that the merger is not likely to have such anticompetitive effects."[54]

---

[48] Dennis A. Shields, Cong. Research Serv., Consolidation and Concentration in the U.S. Dairy Industry, RL41224 1 (2010).

[49] U.S. Dep't of Justice & Fed. Trade Comm'n, Horizontal Merger Guidelines 18–19 (2010), https://www.justice.gov/atr/file/810276/download [https://perma.cc/672Q-5RSB].

[50] Thomas R. Saving, Concentration Ratios and the Degree of Monopoly, 11 Int'l Econ. Rev. 139, 139 (1970).

[51] U.S. Dep't of Justice, Competition and Monopoly: Single-Firm Conduct under Section 2 of the Sherman Act 19 (2008), https://www.justice.gov/sites/default/files/atr/legacy/2009/05/11/236681.pdf [https://perma.cc/Z8RK-AVDU].

[52] U.S. Dep't of Justice & Fed. Trade Comm'n, supra note 49, at 18.

[53] Id.

[54] United States v. Phila. Nat'l Bank, 374 U.S. 321, 363 (1963).

Although market concentration studies can provide insight into whether markets are competitive, they may also understate or overstate the competitiveness of a market.[55] Concentration indexes can be imprecise, and the methodology of many studies is debatable.[56] However, virtually all the studies point to increasing concentration across the U.S. economy. As Tim Wu has noted, "since the year 2000, the [HHI] has increased in over 75 percent of industries."[57] This result is a strong indication that many markets do not operate as competitively as most believe.

Relying on recent economic scholarship, the *Wall Street Journal* recently noted that "[i]n nearly a third of industries, most U.S. companies compete in markets that would be considered highly concentrated under current federal antitrust standards, up from about a quarter in 1996."[58] The *Journal* noted that "the four biggest firms controlled at least half of the market in 40% of individual manufacturing sectors, up from 30% in 1992"[59] and that "among more than 1,700 public companies operating in 1996 and 2013, 62% had a bigger share of the markets in which they competed at the end of the period than at the beginning."[60] The article cited the example of the "consumer staples sector," which "in 2013 had an HHI for their products above 2,893, up from 2,661 in 1996,"[61] both of which indicate a concentrated market over an HHI of 2,500.

A number of studies have examined the concentration level in various industries. To return to the cellular industry, the Federal Communications Commission analyzed HHI in the mobile wireless services industry. It found that at the end of 2013, the HHI "for the mobile wireless services industry was 3,027, a small increase from 2,966 at the end of 2012, which in turn was an increase from 2,874 at the end of 2011."[62] This is an HHI considerably above the 2,500 threshold for a concentrated market.[63] The "special access"

---

[55] U.S. DEP'T OF JUSTICE & FED. TRADE COMM'N, *supra* note 49.

[56] Hal R. Varian, *Recent Trends in Concentration, Competition, and Entry*, 82 ANTITRUST L.J. 807, 808–10 (2019); Seth B. Sacher & John M. Yun, *Twelve Fallacies of the "Neo-Antitrust" Movement*, 26 GEO. MASON L. REV. 1491, 1495–96 (2019), https://papers.ssrn.com/sol3/papers.cfm?abstract_id=3369013 [https://perma.cc/R9GZ-TFU7].

[57] WU, *supra* note 1, at 21.

[58] Theo Francis & Ryan Knutson, *Wave of Megadeals Tests Antitrust Limits in U.S.*, WALL ST. J. (Oct. 18, 2015), https://www.wsj.com/articles/wave-of-megadeals-tests-antitrust-limits-in-u-s-1445213306 [https://perma.cc/XH9A-2MMX].

[59] *Id.*

[60] *Id.*

[61] *Id.*

[62] Seventeenth Mobile Wireless Competition Report, 29 FCC Rcd. 15311 (19), 17 (2014), https://www.fcc.gov/document/17th-annual-competition-report [https://perma.cc/9YCD-CM5B].

[63] *Id.*

industry involves the transportation of voice and data over a transmission line. Wireless providers use high-capacity special access lines to send voice and data from cell towers to their mobile switching center, where the call is switched to the intended recipient. A study by the Consumer Federation of America found that the HHI for that industry was between 7,000 and 8,300, an extremely highly concentrated market.[64]

Many other industries are concentrated. For example, studies showed that in 2010, the six largest bank holding companies had assets equal to 64 percent of U.S. GDP, up from 17 percent in 1995, and that the four largest banks had 38 percent of all loans and 37 percent of all deposits in 2010 compared to 11 and 10 percent, respectively, in 1976.[65] Healthcare is concentrated in various geographic regions. One study found the median four-firm concentration ratio for health insurance companies is about 90 percent.[66] Another found the HHI index to range from 4,000 to 8,000 in some states, while a third study examined concentration in counties and concluded that 24 percent of counties had an HHI over 3,600 and 55 percent had an HHI between 1,800 and 3,600.[67] The last study also reported that hospital markets are highly concentrated, with concentration increasing over time.[68] Specifically, "[i]n 1987, the mean HHI was 2,340 and by 2006 the HHI was 3,161."[69] The authors also determined that "[t]he market for physician services is generally unconcentrated, but there is meaningful variation across geography . . . 10% of cardiology and orthopedic patients are treated in markets where the HHI is greater than 2,200."[70]

Some studies have looked at the trend toward concentration by examining the decreasing number of firms traded on public markets in the

---

[64] MARK COOPER, CONSUMER FED'N OF AM., THE SPECIAL PROBLEM OF SPECIAL ACCESS: CONSUMER OVERCHARGES AND TELEPHONE COMPANY EXCESS PROFITS 2 (2016), https://consumerfed.org/wp-content/uploads/2016/04/4-16-The-Special-Problem-of-Special-Access.pdf [https://perma.cc/8HLN-BVYX].

[65] John Bellamy Foster et al., *Monopoly and Competition in Twenty-First Century Capitalism*, MONTHLY REV., Apr. 2011, at 1, 5; Dean Corbae & Pablo D'Erasmo, *A Quantitative Model of Banking Industry Dynamics* (Mar. 21, 2013), at 12, https://02e278dc-a-62cb3a1a-s-sites.googlegroups.com/site/deancorbae/research/bank032113.pdf [https://perma.cc/L8L8-4RUC].

[66] Martin Gaynor et al., *The Industrial Organization of Health Care Markets* (Nat'l Bureau of Econ. Research, Working Paper No. 19800, 2014), at 7 https://www.nber.org/papers/w19800.pdf [https://perma.cc/8NUG-Q98G].

[67] Sam Batkins et al., *Market Concentration Grew During Obama Administration*, AM. ACTION F. (Apr. 7, 2016), at 3, https://www.americanactionforum.org/print/?url=https://www.americanactionforum.org/research/market-concentration-grew-obama-administration/ [https://perma.cc/5FKW-CUU9].

[68] Gaynor et al., *supra* note 66, at 5.

[69] *Id.*

[70] *Id.*

United States. About half of the publicly traded firms disappeared between 1996 and 2012, resulting in a level that is lower than the number of publicly traded firms in the 1970s.[71] One study found "that the number of publicly traded firms has significantly declined in most industries. Out of seventy-one industries, sixty-six have experienced a negative change between 1997 and 2014. Moreover, the largest portion of the distribution is concentrated in the extreme range, indicating that 73% of the industries have lost over 40% of their publicly traded peers."[72] These studies have concluded that mergers have played a key role in the disappearance of so many publicly traded firms.

Another study tried to get a handle on the consolidation of business by looking at the percentage of workers employed in small firms versus the number employed in big firms. The study found that in the late 1980s, small companies were still a lot bigger, when combined, than big companies. In 1989, firms with fewer than fifty workers employed about one-third of American workers—accounting for millions more jobs than companies with at least 10,000 employees. However, in 2014, the last year for which data was available, the share of workers in small companies fell to 27.4 percent, and companies with more than 10,000 workers employed more people than firms that employed fewer than fifty workers.[73] (Appendix C contains additional information about concentration levels in various markets.)

I am well aware that some readers will remain skeptical of my claim of a lack of competition. They will focus on different activities in the market. They will observe firms appearing to be competitors by selling slightly different products at different prices. They will see some firms becoming more successful than others. They will conclude that competition is the norm in U.S. markets. To those readers, I want to emphasize that there is conduct in many markets that is uncharacteristic of competitive markets and consumers acting as sovereign. There are also many studies showing increasing concentration rates in many markets. For some markets discussed earlier, the evidence is pretty conclusive that those markets lack competition. For other markets, however, the data only raises the likelihood that those markets

[71] Grullon, Larkin, & Michaely, *supra* note 17, at 697, 701, 702 Fig. 1B (the number decreased from more than 7,500 in 1997 to under 4,000 in 2013); Craig Doidge, G. Andrew Karolyi, & René M. Stulz, *The U.S. Listing Gap* (Nat'l Bureau of Econ. Research, Working Paper No. 21181, May 2015) (from 8,025 in 1996 to 4,101 in 2012), https://www.nber.org/papers/w21181 [https://perma.cc/748L-LWTR].

[72] Grullon, Larkin, & Michaely, *supra* note 17, at 697, 706–07.

[73] David Leonhardt, Opinion, *The Charts That Show How Big Business Is Winning*, N.Y. TIMES (June 17, 2018), https://www.nytimes.com/2018/06/17/opinion/big-business-mergers.html [https://perma.cc/JPG7-S4ZA].

are not competitive. Nonetheless, uncertainty over the competitiveness of markets means that we should not just assume that a particular market is competitive. The burden has shifted to those who claim that a market is competitive. Likewise, if people oppose government regulation by claiming that competition in a market provides all the constraints necessary to make an economic system work, they bear the burden of showing that the market is actually competitive.

4

The Effects of Mega-Mergers

Mergers are one of the causes of increasing concentration in U.S. markets. The economy periodically experiences waves of merger activity.[1] Since the Great Recession of 2008, many firms have been reluctant to invest in their own business out of a concern for stagnant demand, even though they have been making large profits.[2] As a result, many firms have used their accumulated cash to buy other firms. Not only are the number of mergers on the rise, the size of the firms involved in mergers is huge.[3] It seems as if every few months another large merger occurs. In 2008, InBev acquired Anheuser-Busch for $52 billion;[4] then the merged company acquired SABMiller for $107 billion in 2016.[5] Bayer purchased Monsanto for $66 billion.[6] Aetna tried to consolidate the health insurance market with acquisitions of Humana for $37 billion[7] and Cigna for $54 billion,[8] although both mergers were blocked by

[1] Between 1890 and the 1990s, the United States has experienced five periods of large merger activity, W. Kip Viscusi et al., Economics of Regulation and Antitrust 204–07 (2005). The United States is in the midst of its sixth wave of merger activity.

[2] See, e.g., Paul Krugman, Opinion, *Profits without Production*, N.Y. Times (June 20, 2013), https://www.nytimes.com/2013/06/21/opinion/krugman-profits-without-production.html [https://perma.cc/P5HU-FF3T] ("Apple is a case in point: It is hugely profitable, yet it's sitting on a giant pile of cash, which it evidently sees no need to reinvest in its business.").

[3] For example, there were 716 mergers subject to approval by the government under the Hart-Scott-Rodino Act in 2009; in 2018, there were 2,111 mergers. U.S. Fed. Trade Comm'n & Dep't of Justice, Hart-Scott-Rodino Annual Report: Fiscal Year 2018, at 1, https://www.ftc.gov/system/files/documents/reports/federal-trade-commission-bureau-competition-department-justice-antitrust-division-hart-scott-rodino/fy18hsrreport.pdf [https://perma.cc/MF2C-TBF5].

[4] Michael J. de la Merced, *InBev to Buy Anheuser-Busch for $52 Billion*, N.Y. Times (July 14, 2008), https://www.nytimes.com/2008/07/14/business/worldbusiness/14iht-14beer.14460585.html [https://perma.cc/2Y7W-SQRM].

[5] Lauren Hirsch & Chris Prentice, *AB InBev, SABMiller Deal Wins U.S. Approval, Adds Craft Beer Protections*, Reuters (July 20, 2016), https://www.reuters.com/article/us-sabmiller-m-a-abinbev-idUSKCN1002HJ [https://perma.cc/PB4K-GYP6].

[6] Greg Roumeliotis & Ludwig Burger, *Bayer Clinches Monsanto with Improved $66 Billion Bid*, Reuters (Sept. 14, 2016), https://www.reuters.com/article/us-monsanto-m-a-bayer-deal-idUSKCN11K128 [https://perma.cc/XK2A-S8EJ].

[7] Chad Bray & Reed Abelson, *Aetna Agrees to Acquire Humana for $37 Billion in Cash and Stock*, N.Y. Times: Dealbook (July 3, 2015), https://www.nytimes.com/2015/07/04/business/dealbook/aetna-agrees-to-acquire-humana-for-37-billion-in-cash-and-stock.html [https://perma.cc/FJH3-SFZY].

[8] Chad Terhune, *Health Insurer Cigna Rejects Anthem's $54-Billion Takeover Bid*, L.A. Times (June 21, 2015), https://www.latimes.com/business/la-fi-anthem-cigna-talks-20150621-story.html [https://perma.cc/6ECA-W4RK].

Rethinking Market Regulation. John N. Drobak, Oxford University Press. © Oxford University Press 2021.
DOI: 10.1093/oso/9780197578957.003.0004

the courts.[9] Kraft Heinz (the result of a $45 billion merger in 2015)[10] offered to buy Unilever for $143 billion, a bid that was rejected.[11] AT&T bought Time Warner for $65 billion in a merger approved by the court in 2018.[12] Late 2018 saw significant consolidation in the healthcare industry. The insurance company Cigna acquired the last stand-alone major pharmacy benefit manager Express Scripts for $67 billion, while CVS Health, a pharmacy benefit manager and retail pharmacy, took over the insurance company Aetna for $69 billion.[13] In 2019, T-Mobile took over Sprint, its rival in the cell phone industry, for $26.5 billion.[14] Raytheon and United Technologies announced a stock merger in June 2019 that would result in the second largest company in the defense industry with an expected stock market value of $100 billion.[15] According to *The Economist*, the United States and Europe have seen "15 transactions each worth more than $10 billion [for the first five months of 2014], the most since the M&A [mergers and acquisitions] rush of 2007. Taking in smaller deals, mergers are up nearly 50% on last year."[16] While mergers and acquisitions for 2015 in the United States exceeded $1.6

[9] United States v. Aetna, Inc., 240 F. Supp. 3d 1 (D.D.C. 2017). *See* Aaron Smith & Jackie Wattles, *Aetna-Humana & Anthem-Cigna: Two Mergers Die in One Day*, CNN MONEY (Feb. 14, 2017), https://money.cnn.com/2017/02/14/investing/aetna-humana/index.html   [https://perma.cc/6VCR-NCXB].

[10] Drew Harwell, *Heinz to Acquire Kraft Foods in Mega-Merger*, WASH. POST (Mar. 25, 2015), https://www.washingtonpost.com/business/economy/heinz-will-buy-kraft-foods-in-megamerger-for-american-food/2015/03/25/9ed45bd4-d316-11e4-8fce-3941fc548f1c_story.html   [https://perma.cc/T82K-RWA3].

[11] Michael J. de la Merced & Chad Bray, *Kraft Heinz Withdraws $143 Billion Offer to Merge with Unilever*, N.Y. TIMES: DEALBOOK (Feb. 19, 2017), https://www.nytimes.com/2017/02/19/business/dealbook/kraft-heinz-unilever-merger.html [https://perma.cc/C4XC-YPZF].

[12] United States v. AT&T Inc., 310 F. Supp. 3d 161 (D.D.C. 2018), *aff'd*, 916 F.3d 1029 (D.C. Cir. 2019); Edmund Lee & Cecilia Kang, *U.S. Loses Appeal Seeking to Block AT&T-Time Warner Merger*, N.Y. TIMES (Feb. 26, 2019), https://www.nytimes.com/2019/02/26/business/media/att-time-warner-appeal.html [https://perma.cc/2U7H-S89D].

[13] Reed Abelson, *Merger of Cigna and Express Scripts Gets Approval from Justice Dept.*, N.Y. TIMES (Sept. 17, 2018), https://www.nytimes.com/2018/09/17/health/cigna-express-scripts-merger.html [https://perma.cc/EJ6R-6V64]; Reed Abelson, *CVS Health and Aetna $69 Billion Merger Is Approved with Conditions*, N.Y. TIMES (Oct. 10, 2018), https://www.nytimes.com/2018/10/10/health/cvs-aetna-merger.html [https://perma.cc/3FKY-JMXT].

[14] Tali Arbel & Marcy Gordon, *T-Mobile's $26.5b Sprint Deal Ok'd Despite Competition Fears*, ASSOCIATED PRESS (July 26, 2019), https://apnews.com/7cd71d5aae224188a93d679ac74d24d7 [https://perma.cc/8TY3-GB9C].

[15] Aaron Gregg, *Raytheon to Merge with United Technologies, Creating a Military-Industrial Behemoth*, WASH. POST (June 9, 2019), https://www.washingtonpost.com/business/2019/06/09/raytheon-merge-with-united-technologies-creating-military-industrial-behemoth/ [https://perma.cc/CF9G-VMZL].

[16] *Return of the Big Deal*, ECONOMIST (May 1, 2014), https://www.economist.com/business/2014/05/01/return-of-the-big-deal [https://perma.cc/X79S-BQDM].

trillion,[17] companies announced a record $2.5 trillion in mergers for the first half of 2018.[18]

The regulation of mergers is limited. The Clayton Act bans mergers that "may be substantially to lessen competition, or to tend to create a monopoly,"[19] while the Hart-Scott-Rodino Act requires pre-merger notification of large mergers to be reported to the federal government.[20] Of the large mergers reported to the government, fewer than 2 percent have been challenged since the Reagan administration.[21] In the early twentieth century, the Supreme Court viewed bigness as bad, recognizing that the Sherman Act was enacted to control large firms.[22] This understanding continued through the decades, with the Warren Court embracing a goal of preserving small business in merger cases.[23] Until the 1980s, government enforcement of the Clayton Act mirrored the Supreme Court by trying to maintain low levels of market concentration.[24] By then, however, economists began to win the intellectual battle and establish that antitrust law should be based solely on economic principles, rather than on an ad hoc consideration of social factors or good business practices.[25] Their perspective influenced the application of merger law at the Justice Department and the FTC, the agencies that do most of the merger regulation, and the courts. As a result, merger regulation today focuses only on the competitive aspects of the merger, that is, whether the merger tends to create a monopoly or facilitate oligopolistic coordination.[26]

---

[17] By September 2015, global mergers were over $3.5 trillion, close to setting an all-time record. David Nicklaus, *Merger Boom Is a Sign of Confidence, or Maybe Overconfidence*, St. Louis Post-Dispatch (Sept. 22, 2015), https://www.stltoday.com/business/columns/david-nicklaus/nicklaus-merger-boom-is-a-sign-of-confidence-or-maybe/article_f41e7d73-e47d-521f-802b-3202cc3a2c76.html [https://perma.cc/8WYY-UZ47].

[18] Stephen Grocer, *A Record $2.5 Trillion in Mergers Were Announced in the First Half of 2018*, N.Y Times (July 3, 2018), https://www.nytimes.com/2018/07/03/business/dealbook/mergers-record-levels.html [https://perma.cc/G5KF-HX7Y].

[19] Clayton Act § 7, 15 U.S.C. § 18 (2018).

[20] Hart-Scott-Rodino Act, 15 U.S.C. § 18a (2018).

[21] Herbert J. Hovenkamp, *Appraising Merger Efficiencies*, 24 Geo. Mason L. Rev. 703, 709, 709 n.43 (2017).

[22] N. Sec. Co. v. United States, 193 U.S. 197 (1904).

[23] Brown Shoe Co. v. United States, 370 U.S.C. 294 (1962).

[24] Orley Ashenfelter et al., *Did Robert Bork Understate the Competitive Impact of Mergers? Evidence from Consummated Mergers*, 57 J.L. & Econ. S67, S67–68 (2014).

[25] Robert Bork and Oliver Williamson are best known for the change in merger law to focus on economic issues. *See* Robert H. Bork, The Antitrust Paradox: A Policy at War with Itself 107–15 (1978); Oliver E. Williamson, *Economies as an Antitrust Defense: The Welfare Tradeoffs*, Am. Econ. Rev., Mar. 1968, at 18.

[26] When the Sherman Act was passed in 1895, as part of the Progressives' reform, antitrust regulation was not just based upon economic theory. Antitrust law originally accommodated recognition

This is an economic analysis that primarily focuses on mergers between competitors. Under the merger review process, the efficiency gains from a merger are an important justification supporting the legality of a merger.[27]

The ironic aspect of this approach is that it applauds the loss of jobs. Efficiency often comes from the consolidation of the operations of the two companies that merged. Two accounting departments become one; two production lines become one. If the merging firms do not operate in the same markets, say one firm produces autos and the other motorcycles, they will not even get a glance from the government, even if they lay off thousands of workers.

While there is no comprehensive database on merger-related mass layoffs, the media does report on the expected layoffs that will result from a proposed merger and on the number of actual layoffs that occurred following a merger.[28] For example, *CNN Money* reported in 2005 that Proctor & Gamble's acquisition of Gillette would result in 6,000 job losses—4 percent of their combined workforce.[29] According to the *Cincinnati Business Courier*, 2,700 employees were laid off when Procter & Gamble transferred its Duracell battery division to Berkshire Hathaway, Inc. in 2016.[30] *The New York Times* reported in 2015 that Microsoft's acquisition of Nokia would result in 7,800 more layoffs in addition to the 18,000 job cuts that occurred the year before.[31]

---

of the non-economic effects of mergers, but that is impossible today with the embrace of economics as the only standard for merger approval.

[27] Hovenkamp, *supra* note 21.

[28] There is currently no publicly available repository collecting the data on layoffs resulting specifically from changes in ownership. The closest thing available is the Mass Layoffs Statistics program from the Department of Labor that collected data on mass layoffs by looking at employers who filed at least fifty unemployment insurance claims within a five-week period. *See Mass Layoff Statistics*, U.S. BUREAU OF LABOR STATISTICS, https://www.bls.gov/mls/home.htm [https://perma.cc/JF74-NLGK]. This database allows users to look at the number of insurance claims filed due to "organizational changes," which would encompass changes in ownership from a merger or an acquisition. *See MLS Databases*, U.S. BUREAU OF LABOR STATISTICS, https://www.bls.gov/mls/data.htm [https://perma.cc/PC6U-CU29]. However, "organizational changes" would also include strategic reorganization and restructuring, making the dataset overinclusive if users only want data on layoffs resulting from mergers. The program only collected data from 1995 through 2013 (the program was discontinued due to budget cuts); this database is incomplete at best. *BLS 2013 Sequestration Information*, U.S. BUREAU OF LABOR STATISTICS (Mar. 4, 2013), https://www.bls.gov/bls/sequester_info.htm [https://perma.cc/89FN-JT7E].

[29] Chris Isidore, *P&G to Buy Gillette for $57b*, CNN MONEY (Jan. 28, 2005), https://money.cnn.com/2005/01/28/news/fortune500/pg_gillette/ [https://perma.cc/8X6C-E9RU].

[30] Barrett J. Brunsman, *P&G Sheds 2,700 Jobs as Buffett Deal Closes*, CINCINNATI BUS. J. (Mar. 1, 2016), https://www.bizjournals.com/cincinnati/news/2016/03/01/p-g-sheds-2-700-jobs-as-buffett-deal-closes.html [https://perma.cc/5TNV-36EN].

[31] Nick Wingfield, *Cutting Jobs, Microsoft Turns Page on Nokia Deal*, N.Y. TIMES (July 8, 2015), https://www.nytimes.com/2015/07/09/technology/microsoft-layoffs.html [https://perma.cc/VR7J-GR7E].

In 2015, *Forbes* reported that Kraft's merger with Heinz would result in 2,600 layoffs in addition to the 2,500 jobs that were cut a few months prior to the merger.[32] Seven plants were scheduled to close over the next year or so as well, which would result in a 10 percent reduction of Kraft's legacy workforce.[33] *Forbes* also reported in 2016 that Dow Chemical's takeover of Dow Corning was expected to result in 2,500 layoffs.[34] According to Anheuser-Busch's 10-Q filed a few months after InBev took over Anheuser-Busch in July 2008, it instituted an enhanced retirement program in order to "reduce costs and improve efficiency."[35] This program, which seems to be in response

It is difficult to tell how many of the job losses occurred in the United States rather than in other countries. Nokia is based in Finland. According to the 10-K filed by Microsoft shortly after the merger, Microsoft expected to eliminate up to 18,000 employees in 2015, with 12,500 professional and factory positions related to the acquisition of Nokia. Microsoft Corp., *Annual Report (Form 10-K)* 15 (July 31, 2014), https://www.sec.gov/Archives/edgar/data/789019/000119312514289961/0001193125-14-289961-index.htm [https://perma.cc/7QT7-PCZ4]. In its next 10-K, Microsoft reported only 10,000 fewer employees, but it also reported that it planned to eliminate 7,800 positions in 2016 due to restructuring. Microsoft Corp., *Annual Report (Form 10-K)* 17 (July 31, 2015), https://www.sec.gov/Archives/edgar/data/789019/000119312515272806/d918813d10k.htm [https://perma.cc/FLC8-6MFC]. In its next 10-K, Microsoft reported that it did eliminate the 7,800 positions, primarily in its phone hardware division, which it had acquired from Nokia. Microsoft Corp., *Annual Report (Form 10-K)* 16 (July 28, 2016), https://www.sec.gov/Archives/edgar/data/789019/000119312516662209/d187868d10k.htm [https://perma.cc/2QVD-ZU65].

[32] Antoine Gara, *More Job Cuts at Kraft Heinz under 3G Capital and Warren Buffett*, FORBES (Nov. 4, 2015), https://www.forbes.com/sites/antoinegara/2015/11/04/more-job-cuts-at-kraft-heinz-under-3g-capital-and-warren-buffett/ [https://perma.cc/J6SM-TAZ4].

[33] *Id.* Kraft and Heinz merged in July 2015. According to Kraft Heinz's 10-K for the fiscal year that ended on December 31, 2016, they implemented a multiyear "Integration Program" to reduce costs and optimize production following the merger. Kraft Heinz Co., *Annual Report (Form 10-K)* (Feb. 23, 2017), https://www.sec.gov/Archives/edgar/data/1637459/000163745917000007/0001637459-17-000007-index.htm [https://perma.cc/MQH6-R5TK]. As stated in the 10-K, Kraft Heinz expected to eliminate 5,150 positions and close six factories as part of the Integration Program. *Id.* Kraft Heinz had already cut 3,350 general salaried and factory positions in the United States and Canada as of December 31, 2016. *Id.* As of December 31, 2016, Kraft Heinz had 41,000 employees, so eliminating 5,150 positions would be a 12.6 percent reduction in its total workforce. *Id.* According to its 10-Q, Kraft Heinz cut 4,100 employees as of July 1, 2017 as part of the Integration Program. Kraft Heinz Co., *Quarterly Report (Form 10-Q)* 8 (Aug. 4, 2017), https://www.sec.gov/Archives/edgar/data/1637459/000163745917000101/form10-qq22017.htm [https://perma.cc/7FK6-PWH7].

[34] Laura Debter, *Dow Chemical to Cut 2,500 Jobs Ahead of Dupont Merger*, FORBES (June 28, 2016), https://www.forbes.com/sites/laurengensler/2016/06/28/dow-chemical-to-cut-2500-jobs-ahead-of-dupont-merger/ [https://perma.cc/8T5Y-ZPSH]. According to Dow Chemical's most recent 10-K (for the fiscal year that ended on December 31, 2016), Dow Chemical expects to reduce 2,500 of its global workforce by June 30, 2018, because of the ownership restructuring with Dow Corning. Dow Chemical Co., *Annual Report (Form 10-K)* (Feb. 9, 2017), https://www.sec.gov/Archives/edgar/data/29915/000002991517000011/dow201610k.htm [https://perma.cc/NM68-P3BR]. Looking at the severance costs of the restructuring plan in the most recent 10-Q, Dow Chemical gave out severance packages to 800 employees as of December 31, 2016, and another 880 employees as of June 30, 2017 (with 820 more to go). Dow Chemical Co., *Quarterly Report (Form 10-Q)* (July 27, 2017), https://www.sec.gov/Archives/edgar/data/29915/000002991517000035/dow-q2x6302017.htm [https://perma.cc/7AP9-8JRH].

[35] Anheuser-Busch Cos., *Quarterly Report (Form 10-Q)* 12 (Nov. 6, 2008), https://www.sec.gov/Archives/edgar/data/310569/000095013708013472/c47434e10vq.htm [https://perma.cc/44Z2-2WRV].

to the merger, resulted in significant loss of jobs at Anheuser-Busch in the St. Louis region. Ten years after the merger, 2,000 jobs were lost in the St. Louis facilities of Anheuser-Busch.[36] In fall 2017, when TD Ameritrade took over another online brokerage service, Scottrade, it laid off more than 1,000 workers.[37] From media reports and government filings, it is fair to estimate that at least 100,000 workers lost their jobs this century as a result of mergers.

Despite the lack of comprehensive data, business and economics scholars have analyzed and hypothesized the causes and effects of such mass layoffs.[38] While some scholars lament the negative effect mass layoffs can have on displaced workers and "survivors,"[39] others hypothesize that mass layoffs resulting from mergers and acquisitions can be a "mechanism for improving the matching of workers and managers to firms and industries that best suit their skills."[40] In other words, mass layoffs can improve productivity by reallocating the best employees for the job. Scholars also argue that mass layoffs due to "joint economies in management, production, distribution, and purchasing" can result in "significant cost savings" and efficiency improvements.[41] Many economists and business school scholars emphasize the efficiency gains from layoffs that follow mergers. They applaud the current system without giving much consideration to the harm to people who lose their jobs.

Although laid-off workers suffer dearly from these mergers, one could view that consequence as justified by the benefits consumers get from the mergers. Consumers should benefit because merger law is based on a consumer welfare standard in which mergers are to be approved only if the analysis shows an overall benefit to consumers, regardless of the benefit to

---

[36] Brian Feldt, *A Decade after Anheuser-Busch's Sale, Beer Still Pours from St. Louis Brewery but Much Has Changed*, St. Louis Post-Dispatch (July 13, 2018), https://www.stltoday.com/business/local/a-decade-after-anheuser-busch-s-sale-beer-still-pours/article_5a9faf1c-d7c9-5d46-99de-b11b1e22f703.html [https://perma.cc/HW7K-FPLV].

[37] Brian Feldt, *Scottrade Layoffs Climb to over 1,000*, St. Louis Post-Dispatch (Mar. 22, 2018), https://www.stltoday.com/business/local/scottrade-layoffs-climb-to-over/article_6dc4f951-b4ae-53b1-8066-63e4b9436222.html [https://perma.cc/4C64-7CB9].

[38] Economic scholars also studied the effects of mergers on top management and executives. *See* Donald C. Hambrick & Albert A. Cannella Jr., *Relative Standing: A Framework for Understanding Departures of Acquired Executives*, 36 Acad. Mgmt. J. 733 (1993); James P. Walsh, *Top Management Turnover Following Mergers and Acquisitions*, 9 Strategic Mgmt. J. 173 (1988).

[39] Joel Brockner et al., *Survivors' Reactions to Layoffs: We Get By with a Little Help for Our Friends*, 32 Admin. Sci. Q. 526 (1987).

[40] Donald S. Siegel & Kenneth L. Simons, *Assessing the Effects of Mergers and Acquisitions on Firm Performance, Plant Productivity, and Workers: New Evidence from Matched Employer-Employee Data*, 31 Strategic Mgmt. J. 903, 904 (2010).

[41] Sanjai Bhagat et al., *Hostile Takeovers in the 1980s: The Return to Corporate Specialization*, 1990 Brookings Papers on Econ. Activity 1, 50 (1990).

the merging firms.[42] When I first started to examine this issue, I was concerned about how to weigh the benefits to consumers against the harm to labor. I had assumed that firms would not decide to merge together and that the government would not approve the mergers unless consumers benefited. I recognized that laid-off workers were consumers who lost their buying power, thereby decreasing consumer benefit somewhat, but nonetheless believed that there was still considerable benefit to consumers. Perhaps my belief came from teaching merger law for decades or from my naiveté. Ironically, a number of recent studies have made it easier for me to weigh consumer benefits against labor harm from mergers. These studies show that many mergers achieve no benefit in price reductions; in fact, some mergers result in higher prices.[43] These retrospective studies look back at mergers to determine the impact on consumers of the mergers. Even if a firm reduces costs from a merger, no legal rule requires the firm to pass the savings on to customers in reduced prices. The only economic "law" that compels that result is competition, which, I have argued, is lacking in many markets. One article that examined the numerous retrospective merger studies concluded that the "empirical evidence that mergers can cause economically significant increases in price is overwhelming."[44] As a result, for many mergers we are not comparing the harm to workers against the benefit to consumers. Rather we are comparing the harm to workers with the benefits to shareholders, managers, and the professionals who structure the deals. That is a very different comparison than if benefits of mergers flow to consumers. Even if there are reductions in price for consumers, the question is the magnitude of those benefits. It may be that each consumer benefits by only pennies. The

[42] The original economic analysis by Bork and Williamson used a general welfare standard that argued that mergers should be approved as long as the efficiency gains from the merger outweighed any losses to the consumers. As a result, a $5 million gain in efficiency justified a merger even if the merger raised prices by $4 million. Hovenkamp, *supra* note 21, at 713. Today, consumer welfare, not general welfare, is the accepted standard. *See* F.T.C. v. Actavis, Inc., 570 U.S. 136, 154, 159–60 (2013); *see also* Hovenkamp, *supra* note 21, at 714.

[43] For a summary of many of these studies, *see* Ashenfelter et al., *supra* note 24; John E. Kwoka Jr., *Does Merger Control Work: A Retrospective on US Enforcement Actions and Merger Outcomes*, 78 ANTITRUST L.J. 619 (2013).

[44] Ashenfelter et al., *supra* note 24, at S78. One could respond to this criticism of merger approval by pointing out that price effects might be felt for a few years or that consumers benefit in other ways, such as by better research and development. This may be true, but there is no way to know if those claims are correct. At least in the pharmaceutical industry, some scholars conclude that mergers have hindered research and development of new drugs because the mergers "have significantly decreased the number of large, traditional pharmaceutical firms that possess the capacity to develop a drug in-house from its inception to approval." Rachel E. Sachs, *The Uneasy Case for Patent Law*, 117 MICH. L. REV. 499, 508 (2018).

question then becomes a comparison of that benefit to consumers against the jobs lost by workers.

Mergers were thought to occur when firms believed that they could help their business. For example, Boeing took over McDonnell Douglas because it could add an aerospace firm to a commercial airplane firm.[45] With the two types of businesses closely related, the merged companies would have synergies not possible to the stand-alone companies. I'm sure there are still mergers taken to improve the business of the merged companies, but I think that today there are mergers consummated to enrich the people who participate in the mergers. Investment advisors, who play a key role in mergers and acquisitions, convince firms to merge with other firms so that the advisors can make money from putting the deal together (and sometimes make money when they undo the deal). They assess the proper value of the target company, issue a fairness opinion judging the terms of the deal from the company stockholders' perspective, represent and assist corporate clients during negotiation and bidding process, act as brokers by identifying potential buyers or sellers, and act as financing agents by lining up the necessary financing for the transactions.[46] The fee structure for merger work provides investment banks with a strong economic interest in closing deals, because their fees are tied to the consummation of the deal and to the ultimate acquisition price.[47] Therefore, investment banks are compensated for the successful closure of a deal, instead of the deal's long-term success. In addition to the advisors, lawyers, and other experts who benefit from putting together mergers, the senior management of both firms often benefit financially. Buyouts of the management team who leave are often at a very high price, while mangers who stay often receive new positions, pay raises, and bonuses.

Moreover, the degree of the benefits to shareholders from mergers is far from clear. Stock prices provide a treasure trove of data for scholars who want to assess the benefits from corporate actions. Studies have identified numerous mergers where post-merger stock performance has been disappointing in the long run, often with the shareholders of the acquiring company incurring losses greater than the acquired company's shareholders' gain.[48] Of course it is hard to predict the future, but the poor

---

[45] *Building a New Boeing*, ECONOMIST, Aug. 12, 2000, at 83 (reviewing the 1997 merger).

[46] Rita D. Kosnik & Debra L. Shapiro, *Agency Conflicts between Investment Banks and Corporate Clients in Merger and Acquisition Transactions: Causes and Remedies*, ACAD. MGMT. PERSP., Feb. 1997, at 7, 9.

[47] *Id.* at 11; Michael Schuldt, Comment, *A Statutory Proposal for the Regulation of Fairness Opinions in Corporate Control Transactions*, 56 MO. L. REV. 103, 110 (1991).

[48] *See, e.g.,* Thomas Lee Hazen, *The Short-Term/Long-Term Dichotomy and Investment Theory: Implications for Securities Market Regulation and for Corporate Law*, 70 N.C. L. REV. 137, 190 (1991);

stock performances result from the self-interest of the dealmakers pushing mergers. Even if there are uncertain benefits to the resulting business and the shareholders from mergers, the harm to workers is certain.

To put the harm to workers in economic terms, we could label this as an externality. Economists recognize the legitimacy of other types of externalities, like pollution, but they disregard these types of economic externalities.[49] Nonetheless, job losses are negative consequences of mergers. There are also other negative consequences of a merger. Numerous studies have shown that charitable contributions decrease considerably when a corporate headquarters moves away from a city.[50] To give one example, Anheuser-Busch donated $13 million to St. Louis charities in 2007, while InBev donated $50 million over ten years after it took over Anheuser-Busch.[51] In addition, there are other negative consequences to communities from mergers. Leo Strine, when he was Vice Chancellor of the Delaware Court of Chancery, which oversees corporate matters, noted that mergers have hollowed out "the civic leadership in many communities by converting business leaders from the CEOs of independent, locally run corporations into branch managers for national organizations with no particular interest in the cities where they made acquisitions."[52] There is also a geographic dimension to recent mergers. They have tended to move corporate headquarters from Midwestern cities to cities on the coast. This has not only resulted in job losses, it has made those cities less important, with a decrease in prestige and a likely loss of other business with the loss of a corporate headquarters.[53]

Frederic M. Scherer, *Some Principles for Post-Chicago Antitrust Analysis*, 52 CASE W. RES. L. REV. 5 (2001).

[49] *See, e.g.*, Ronald H. Coase, *The Problem of Social Cost*, 3 J.L. & ECON. 1 (1960).
[50] *See, e.g.*, David Card et al., *The Geography of Giving: The Effect of Corporate Headquarters on Local Charities*, 94 J. PUB. ECON. 222 (2010); Mike Faulk, *Nonprofits Fishing for Dollars in a More Crowded Pond*, ST. LOUIS POST-DISPATCH (Sept. 19, 2016), https://www.stltoday.com/business/local/nonprofits-fishing-for-dollars-in-a-more-crowded-pond/article_70cff4cd-429f-5329-b65e-b1fd5d5d4dab.html [https://perma.cc/3JJY-25NC] ("Over the last two decades, individual donors have become even more important as more corporations based in St. Louis have closed or moved elsewhere. 'Corporate giving in St. Louis years ago accounted for about 20 percent of all giving, and that's just no longer the case.' ").
[51] Feldt, *supra* note 36.
[52] Leo E. Strine Jr., *Human Freedom and Two Friedmen: Musings on the Implications of Globalization for the Effective Regulation of Corporate Behaviour*, 58 U. TORONTO L.J. 241, 261 (2008).
[53] *See* Brian S. Feldman, *How America's Coastal Cities Left the Heartland Behind*, ATLANTIC (Apr. 18, 2016), https://www.theatlantic.com/business/archive/2016/04/how-americas-coastal-cities-left-the-heartland-behind/478296/ [https://perma.cc/JWE9-D9J8].

Regardless of who benefits from a merger, we need to remember that one postulate of economic theory holds that it is improper to make interpersonal comparisons of utility, the notion that underlies Pareto optimality.[54] A change is not Pareto optimal if one person loses from the change even if someone else gains more. Who are we to willingly impose harm on someone, even if it is to benefit someone else? Lionel Robbins argued in 1932 that "[i]ntrospection does not enable A to discover what is going on in B's mind, nor B to discover what is going on in A's. There is no way of comparing the satisfaction of two different people."[55] Similarly, Arrow's Impossibility Theorem is premised on the notion "that interpersonal comparison of utilities has no meaning and, in fact, that there is no meaning relevant to welfare comparisons in the measurability of individual utility."[56] Nonetheless, economic decisions have to be made by firms and by the government, always resulting in winners and losers.[57] That we cannot really make interpersonal comparisons of utility should caution us that we need to care for the losers. Workers are human beings, many of whom suffer tragically when they lose their jobs. In the context of mergers, it means that we need to reform merger regulation to account for the adverse effects on labor and communities.

Some economists believe that mergers have led to lower wages. With increased concentration, there are fewer options for jobs, which causes a downward pressure on wages. One estimate concluded that all the mergers have depressed wages by 13 to 31 percent.[58] Beginning in 2017, a few scholars began to explore the use of the antitrust laws to help workers and to stem the rising inequality of wealth in the United States.[59] A few expressed concerns over the use of noncompete clauses and antipoaching agreements in labor contracts, while others dealt directly with the effect of mergers on wages.

---

[54] Christopher T. Wonnell, *Efficiency and Conservatism*, 80 NEB. L. REV. 643, 646 (2001); *see* Gerrit De Geest, *Any Normative Policy Analysis Not Based on Kaldor-Hicks Efficiency Violates Scholarly Transparency Norms, in* LAW AND ECONOMICS: PHILOSOPHICAL ISSUES AND FUNDAMENTAL QUESTIONS 183, 184 (Aristides N. Hatzis & Nicholas Mercuro eds., 2015).

[55] LIONEL ROBBINS, AN ESSAY ON THE NATURE AND SIGNIFICANCE OF ECONOMIC SCIENCE 124 (1932).

[56] KENNETH J. ARROW, SOCIAL CHOICE AND INDIVIDUAL VALUES 9 (1963).

[57] Matthew D. Adler & Eric A. Posner, *Rethinking Cost-Benefit Analysis*, 109 YALE L.J. 165, 204–09 (1999); Guido Calabresi, *The Pointlessness of Pareto: Carrying Coase Further*, 100 YALE L.J. 1211 (1990).

[58] Bryce Covert, Opinion, *When Companies Supersize, Paychecks Shrink*, N.Y. TIMES (May 13, 2018), https://www.nytimes.com/2018/05/13/opinion/mergers-companies-supersize-workers-wages.html [https://perma.cc/R3VU-U5MN].

[59] RANDY M. STUTZ, AM. ANTITRUST INST., THE EVOLVING ANTITRUST TREATMENT OF LABOR-MARKET RESTRAINTS: FROM THEORY TO PRACTICE (2018) (summary of the literature).

Novel proposals included turning around the tools used to judge concentration in product markets to judge concentration in labor markets. The authors were concerned that mergers in concentrated labor markets could lead to monopsony power in employers, thereby leading to lower wages. To remedy this, they advocate changing the merger review process to include an examination of the concentration of labor markets in addition to the examination of the concentration in product markets.[60] However, it is difficult to use the available data to determine the concentration of local labor markets; plus, the techniques used to define product markets, such as substitution analysis, seem not to work as well in examining labor. Nonetheless, these proposals are the first to try to modify merger regulation for the benefit of workers. The current process of merger review is so well-entrenched and dominated by the concern for product market concentration and consumer welfare that I think it will be difficult to convince the Justice Department and the FTC to add consideration of a merger's predictive effects on labor. At least the proposals mimic the current process by using similar economic techniques to determine labor market concentration.

The concern for wages is terribly important, but I want to focus on the loss of jobs from mergers. It makes no sense to propose that the Justice Department or the FTC modify their current merger review process to take lost employment into account. It would cause cognitive dissonance to regulators who are used to finding layoffs to be a positive efficiency factor favoring merger approval. Plus, a concern for lost jobs is not part of an economic analysis that focuses on concentration in the product market and on consumer welfare. As I will explain in Chapter 9, a better solution would be the creation of a new board, independent of the Justice Department and the FTC, to review the unemployment aspects of mergers.

---

[60] *E.g.*, Ioana Elena Marinescu & Eric A. Posner, *Why Has Antitrust Law Failed Workers?* (Mar. 7, 2019) (manuscript at 38–39), https://papers.ssrn.com/sol3/papers.cfm?abstract_id=3335174 [https://perma.cc/32N7-5P8G].

5

Corporate Stakeholders

There is one market in which it is hard to dispute a lack of competition, the market for unskilled and semiskilled factory workers. When labor is abundant, or when poor economic times make workers willing to work for lower wages, workers have little bargaining power. As a result, workers are not protected by competition between firms for their labor. This is the reason for unions. They aggregate the bargaining power of individual workers to try to make the market for labor more competitive. With so much opposition to unions these days, workers are losing bargaining power, making them even more susceptible to whatever employers desire. This is exacerbated by a belief held by many people that the sole role of the management of corporations is to advance the interest of shareholders, which they equate to increasing shareholder value both through the payment of dividends and the rising of stock prices. This is a very narrow view of the role of management, since corporations affect many different constituencies, including workers, customers, suppliers, and the communities where their facilities are located. If there were competition, the constraints imposed by a competitive market could act to protect those other constituencies. In addition, even if there is robust competition between producers, which would act to protect customers and suppliers, there is generally no competitive pressure protecting labor or communities.

The popular conception of the limited role of management follows from a battle of ideas among intellectuals in the 1950s and 1960s. Today the work of Adolph Berle and Gardiner Means is known for its description of the separation and control in a modern large corporation, with managers in effect acting as trustees for the shareholders.[1] However, in their famous book, they recognized the importance of the various stakeholders of a corporation. As they wrote, a corporation "involves the interrelation of a wide diversity

---

[1] *E.g.*, Henry G. Manne, *The "Higher Criticism" of the Modern Corporation*, 62 COLUM. L. REV. 399, 407–13 (1962); Dalia Tsuk, *From Pluralism to Individualism: Berle and Means and 20th-Century American Legal Thought*, 30 L. & SOC. INQUIRY 179, 210–11 (2005).

Rethinking Market Regulation. John N. Drobak, Oxford University Press. © Oxford University Press 2021.
DOI: 10.1093/oso/9780197578957.003.0005

of economic interests—those of 'owners' who supply capital, those of the workers who 'create,' those of the customers who give value to the products of the enterprise, and above all those of the control who wield power."[2] Berle's vision of shareholders was not the wealthy but "the middle and working classes" who would entrust their wealth to corporations. They were representatives of the community.[3] Berle and Means wrote their book to call attention to the extent of the power of corporations and the abuses that stemmed from that power. They viewed large corporations as being so powerful that they were like a state. As a result, they considered ways to curb that power. As one commentator wrote:

> The book's position anticipates that of today's constituency rights advocates: since shareholders had given up responsibility for corporate property, other constituents should join them as corporate beneficiaries. Corporations could be asked to serve the public with fair wages, job security, and good service to their customers.[4]

Although Berle originally argued that corporations were organized and carried on primarily for the profit of stockholders, which he argued in his famous debate with E. Merrick Dodd, he grew to accept Dodd's position that modern directors were not just limited to running a corporation for the benefit of shareholders but also were administrators of the community good.[5]

Competing with Berle and Means' vision of a corporation, conservative economists argued that management's only duty was to increase shareholder wealth. Milton Friedman was one of the more prominent and forceful economists to advance that proposition. The issue of a corporation's social responsibility arose during the 1960s, when many problems brought that to the forefront of the social agenda. For example, President John Kennedy called for the steel companies to roll back a price increase for the good of the economy, President Richard Nixon wanted private groups to help

---

[2] ADOLF A. BERLE & GARDINER C. MEANS, THE MODERN CORPORATION AND PRIVATE PROPERTY 309–10 (Transaction Publishers 1991) (1932).

[3] Tsuk, *supra* note 1, at 207.

[4] William W. Bratton, *Berle and Means Reconsidered at the Century's Turn*, 26 J. CORP. L. 737, 761 (2000).

[5] ADOLF A. BERLE, THE TWENTIETH-CENTURY CAPITALIST REVOLUTION 169 (1954); *see* LYNN A. STOUT, THE SHAREHOLDER VALUE MYTH: HOW PUTTING SHAREHOLDERS FIRST HARMS INVESTORS, CORPORATIONS, AND THE PUBLIC 16 (2012).

remedy social problems,[6] and Ralph Nader mobilized against irresponsible corporations. Conservative economists and business leaders pushed back by arguing that corporate management's only responsibility was to the shareholders. Friedman explained the position as follows:

> The view has been gaining widespread acceptance that corporate officials and labor leaders have a "social responsibility" that goes beyond serving the interests of their stockholders or their members. This view shows a fundamental misconception of the character and nature of a free economy. In such an economy, there is one and only one social responsibility of business—to use its resources and engage in activities designed to increase its profits so long as it stays within the rules of the game, which is to say, engage in open and free competition, without deception or fraud. . . . It is the responsibility of the rest of us to establish a framework of law such that an individual pursuing his own interest is, to quote Adam Smith, again, "led by an invisible hand to promote an end which was no part of his intention. Nor is it always the worse for society that it was no part of it. By pursuing his own interest, he frequently promotes that of the society more effectively than when he really intends to promote it. I have never known much good done by those who affected to trade for the public good."
>
> Few trends could so thoroughly undermine the very foundations of our free society as the acceptance by corporate officials of a social responsibility other than to make as much money for their stockholders as possible. This is a fundamentally subversive doctrine. If businessmen do have a social responsibility other than making maximum profit for stockholders, how are they to know what it is? Can self-selected private individuals decide what the social interest is? Can they decide how great a burden they are justified in placing on themselves or their stockholders to serve the public interest?[7]

It is important to recognize that Friedman's ideas are normative and not based on economic expertise. Although people credit Friedman as speaking from his expertise as an economist, his remarks are really social commentary about the role of a corporation in a society. He tells the reader that those who support corporate social responsibility "have a fundamental misconception

---

[6] Alan L. Otten, *Call for Volunteers: Nixon Plans to Foster Private-Group Attacks on Big Social Problems*, WALL ST. J., Jan. 21 1969, at 1.

[7] MILTON FRIEDMAN, CAPITALISM AND FREEDOM 133–34 (1962).

of the character and nature of a free economy," implying that he, as an econ-omist, would know better than lay readers. Plus, he invokes Adam Smith to show that he and Smith share the same views.[8] Typical of some economists, he writes with a certitude that tries to make his conclusions appear to be the only possible ones. He tries to make the assertion of corporate social respon-sibility go to the bedrock of our society, by noting that we should not "un-dermine the very foundation of our free society" and that corporate social responsibility is a "*fundamentally* subversive doctrine."[9] Much worse than his rhetorical techniques, the substance of his statement supports a cruel regime in our society, which is now dominated by a Congress that is more responsive to business lobbying than to creating the framework of laws that Friedman states that society needs.

With profit as its only motive, corporations, according to the Friedman view, should be able to use slave and child labor; they should be able to force workers to work twelve-hour days, seven days a week; they need not pay a fair wage; they should be able to do anything that reduces cost and raises profit. It is up to "the rest of us" to pass laws that prevent these types of cor-porate conduct. Like Pontius Pilate, Friedman absolves corporations of any responsibility for moral conduct. It is this kind of belief in unbounded profit-seeking that led to the acceptance of greed as a creed to live by. This justifies cost-cutting even if it devastates labor. It supports outsourcing jobs to other countries at the expense of American labor. It means that we should not be concerned about corporate managers setting their income as high as they do these days. Greed is okay unless government passes laws to limit it.[10]

Actually, Friedman does say that corporations have an obligation to "en-gage in open and free competition, without deception or fraud."[11] That is correct, but why is corporate duty so limited? Once he concludes that corporations should not act fraudulently, he acknowledges that corporations have some social obligations. He just chooses to identify a very limited set of obligations. His answer is that corporate managers should not be expected to know what social responsibility means.[12] But that is refuted by the history of good acts by many businesses throughout the twentieth century.

---

[8] Adam Smith applauded the greed of the butcher and the baker, but in a competitive world, it was the constraints of competition that made self-interest of individuals work for the good of society. 2 ADAM SMITH, THE WEALTH OF NATIONS 15 (Edwin Cannan ed., Modern Library 1994) (1776).

[9] FRIEDMAN, *supra* note 7, at 134 (emphasis added).

[10] *See* Lynn A. Stout, *The Toxic Side Effects of Shareholder Primacy*, 161 U. PA. L. REV. 2003 (2013).

[11] FRIEDMAN, *supra* note 7, at 133.

[12] *See also* Ben Lewis, *The Social Responsibility of Big Business*, in MONOPOLY POWER AND ECONOMIC PERFORMANCE; THE PROBLEM OF INDUSTRIAL CONCENTRATION 95, 102 (Edwin

Perhaps when Friedman wrote in 1962, we would have expected that Congress would legislate with the social good in mind, without interference from business. Things changed, however, in the 1970s. In response to the political successes of the public interest movement in the 1960s and early 1970s with the passage of new laws like the Environmental Protection Act and the Occupational Safety and Health Act, business firms banded together to become much more influential with Congress. They expanded lobbying efforts greatly:

> In 1971, only 175 business firms had registered lobbyists; by 1979, 650 had them. . . . All told, as of 1980 there were in Washington 12,000 lawyers representing business before federal regulatory agencies and federal courts, 9,000 business lobbyists, 50,000 trade association personnel, 8,000 public-relations specialists, 1,300 public-affairs consultants, and 12,000 specialized journalists reporting to particular industries on government developments affecting them. The number of individuals employed by the "private service industry" exceeded the number of federal employees in the Washington metropolitan area for the first time since before the New Deal.[13]

Business firms also began to mobilize their constituencies to help with their political efforts. For example, in 1975 Atlantic Richfield began organizing 53,000 shareholders, 6,000 employees, 2,000 retirees into forty-five regional committees to take public stands on the regulatory issues affecting the company and to become politically active on the company's behalf in their communities.[14] Nearly two hundred of the country's leading corporations formed the Business Round Table in 1972 to organize and coordinate business lobbying efforts. That decade also saw a dramatic increase in political action committees funded by business and an emphasis on advocacy advertising aimed at persuading the public of the merits of particular pro-business government actions. Also, in an attempt to build public support, some business leaders funded university education and research that was favorable to business interests. Corporate and foundation grants were also funneled

---

Mansfield ed., 1964) ("Only society is suited and fitted to" identify the ways corporations should act in a socially responsible manner; managers are not).

[13] DAVID VOGEL, FLUCTUATING FORTUNES: THE POLITICAL POWER OF BUSINESS IN AMERICA 197–98 (2003).

[14] DAVID VOGEL, KINDRED STRANGERS: THE UNEASY RELATIONSHIP BETWEEN POLITICS AND BUSINESS IN AMERICA 280 (2016).

to pro-business research groups like the Hoover Institute at Stanford. This support of academia has been effective in legitimizing and popularizing the kinds of economic beliefs criticized in this book.[15]

Lobbying tends to skew public policy toward those narrow groups that can overcome collective action problems and pursue their policy goals at the expense of the general public.[16] In the late 1970s, unified business interests were able to defeat labor on two proposals before Congress, marking a turning point in the ability of business to defeat legislation benefiting labor. In 1976, Congress had enacted a common situs picketing law that allowed the picketing of a construction site even though a union had a dispute with only one of the subcontractors on the job site.[17] However, President Gerald Ford vetoed the law.[18] With the election of Jimmy Carter as president in 1977 and the Democrats in control of both houses of Congress, organized labor saw an excellent opportunity to have the common situs picketing law enacted. However, in a stunning defeat for labor, the bill was rejected in the House by a slight margin of twelve votes.[19] The business community was emboldened by the success of its lobbying efforts and grass-roots campaign against that law. When President Carter proposed a number of changes in the federal labor laws to benefit unions, business mounted another campaign against those changes.[20] Large corporations financed a lobbying campaign and small business owners mobilized grass-roots opposition. Senators received more than eight million pieces of mail in opposition, as well as thousands of visits from their constituents.[21] The bill was eventually sent back to committee, where it died. "Conservative politicians were elated. Senator Hatch characterized the battle over labor-law reform as the beginning of a new era of business assertiveness in Washington."[22] These two defeats marked the end of labor's influence in Congress. Since then, business has prevented all attempts to increase protections for workers, including all proposals to limit outsourcing by business firms. It is ironic that the beginning of government programs

---

[15] *Id.* at 278–90.

[16] Richard L. Hasen, *Lobbying, Rent-Seeking, and the Constitution*, 64 STAN. L. REV. 191, 226–27 (2012).

[17] JAMES A. REICHLEY, CONSERVATIVES IN AN AGE OF CHANGE: THE NIXON AND FORD ADMINISTRATIONS 395–96 (1981).

[18] *Id.*

[19] Gary M. Fink, *F. Ray Marshall: Secretary of Labor and Jimmy Carter's Ambassador to Organized Labor*, 37 LAB. HIST. 463, 473–74 (1996).

[20] VOGEL, *supra* note 13, at 156.

[21] *Id.*

[22] *Id.*

that benefit business and the wealthy started under a Democratic president and a Democratic Congress in the 1970s and then continued under all administrations, whether Democrat or Republican, since then (with the rare exception like the Affordable Care Act).

Lobbying by business is a huge activity today, very different than when Friedman wrote. Businesses know this is an effective way to influence policy. Even Adam Smith, who viewed business leaders as smarter and more effective than government officials, warned of the danger of business leaders influencing government. He believed that businesspeople would use government to promote their own interests rather than the interests of the public.[23] Data on lobbying the federal government began to be collected in 1947. From then through the 1960s, business spent about $5 million annually on lobbying. It is big business today. Annual spending on lobbying has exceeded $1 billion at least since the 1990s. In 2015, companies spent $3.3 billion on lobbying, with 11,554 people registered as lobbyists.[24] To give one industry as an example, "the energy industry spends about $300 million a year lobbying Congress, deploying an army of three lobbyists for each member. It also contributed more than $160 million during the most recent election cycle to federal candidates, with 80 percent of that going to Republicans."[25] Studies have shown that investment in lobbying the federal government has proved very profitable in many industries.[26] One commentator noted that "[a]s a corporation's only goal is to make a profit, and close to $3.32 billion was spent by corporations to lobby the government in 2011 alone, the only logical conclusion is that corporations receive billions in benefits from their lobbying

[23] Samuel Fleischacker, *Adam Smith's Moral and Political Philosophy*, STAN. ENCYCLOPEDIA OF PHIL. (Jan. 27, 2017), https://plato.stanford.edu/entries/smith-moral-political/ [https://perma.cc/T9US-LPE6].

[24] *Trends in Spending*, CTR. FOR RESPONSIVE POL., https://www.opensecrets.org/federal-lobbying/trends-in-spending [https://perma.cc/G9CY-K5XL].

[25] Eric Lipton, *G.O.P. Hurries to Slash Oil and Gas Rules, Ending Industries' 8-Year Wait*, N.Y. TIMES (Feb. 4, 2017), https://www.nytimes.com/2017/02/04/us/politics/republicans-oil-gas-regulations.html [https://perma.cc/7MVP-2HHG] (citing the Center for Responsive Politics).

[26] A 2011 study of the fifty firms that spent the most on lobbying relative to their assets compared their financial performance against that of the S&P 500 in the stock market concluded that spending on lobbying was a "spectacular investment" yielding "blistering" returns comparable to a high-flying hedge fund, even despite the financial downturn of the past few years. Brad Plumer, *The Outsized Returns from Lobbying*, WASH. POST (Oct. 10, 2011), https://www.washingtonpost.com/blogs/ezra-klein/post/the-outsized-returns-from-lobbying/2011/10/10/gIQADSNEaL_blog.html [https://perma.cc/8W7W-RB2R]. *See also* Raquel Alexander et al., *Measuring Rates of Return on Lobbying Expenditures: An Empirical Case Study of Tax Breaks for Multinational Corporations*, 25 J.L. & POL. 401 (2009).

campaigns."[27] Although business firms are not unified in their lobbying activities on some issues, they have been consistent in their opposition to laws that would benefit labor—and they have been very successful.

In addition to increased lobbying, business firms have redoubled their efforts to influence Congress through their campaign contributions. Unions contribute to campaigns too, but their efforts are meager when compared to business. "The amount of money contributed to the Democratic National, Congressional, and Senatorial Committees by organized labor is pocket change—$5.4 million in 2013–14—compared with the $42.7 million from the pro-trade computer and electronics industry; $62.8 million from finance and securities; and over $11 million from other pro-trade interests, according to the Center for Responsive Politics."[28] The scale of lobbying and political contributions today by business means that we cannot rely on Congress to provide those rules of the game for corporate behavior that Friedman used to justify shareholder primacy. As one commentator said:

> The foremost obstacle to sustainable reform is the enormous imbalance in organizational resources between the chief economic beneficiaries of the status quo and those who seek to strengthen middle-class democracy. Powerful groups defending the winner-take-all economy—business coalitions, Wall Street lobbyists, medical industry players—are fully cognizant of the massive stakes involved, and they are battle-ready after years of training.[29]

It is ironic that corporations are supposed to work within this framework of laws, as Friedman says, while they use their influence in Congress to be sure that the framework is very limited. For example, every attempt in Congress to regulate outsourcing of jobs by U.S. business failed, in part as a result of lobbying by the businesses that wished to outsource. There have been at least

[27] Josh Sager, *The Effects of Corporate Lobbying, Pt. 1*, Sarcastic Liberal (May 29, 2012), http://sarcasticliberal.blogspot.com/2012/05/wolf-pac-effects-of-corporate-lobbying.html [https://perma.cc/N54R-Z2BW].

[28] Thomas B. Edsall, Opinion, *Whose Party Is It Anyway?*, N.Y. Times (July 8, 2015), https://www.nytimes.com/2015/07/08/opinion/thomas-b-edsall-whose-party-is-it-anyway.html [https://perma.cc/4GNZ-25AX]. The nonpartisan Center for Responsive Politics provides thorough information about lobbying and campaign finance. *Lobbying*, Ctr. for Responsive Pol., https://www.opensecrets.org/federal-lobbying [https://perma.cc/WM9A-JQFC].

[29] Jacob S. Hacker & Paul Pierson, Winner-Take-All Politics: How Washington Made the Rich Richer—And Turned Its Back on the Middle Class 291 (2011).

eight bills to limit outsourcing by businesses in various ways since 2004. None made it out of committee.[30]

Friedman's view is typical of many people these days. One of the most prominent modern scholars to emphasize shareholder well-being as the goal of corporations is Harvard Business School Professor Michael Jensen. He has argued that long-term value maximization of the firm should be the corporation's sole objective, while stakeholder theory is actually detrimental to society because of the lack of a concrete, singular corporate objective.[31] As he explained, "[w]hereas value maximization provides corporate managers with a single objective, stakeholder theory directs corporate managers to serve 'many masters . . . Without the clarity of mission provided by single-valued objective function, companies embracing stakeholder theory will experience managerial confusion, conflict, inefficiency, and perhaps even competitive failure.'"[32] Jensen has espoused an agency theory of the corporation under which management is the agent of the shareholders. Other stakeholders of a corporation, however, lack an agent. Naively, he believes that the goal of value maximization assures fair treatment of all the stakeholders: "Indeed, it is a basic principle of enlightened value maximization that *we cannot maximize the long-term market value of an organization if we ignore or mistreat any important constituency.*"[33] That is a naive commentary because enhancing shareholder value often comes at a loss to labor and communities. In addition, Jensen was a strong proponent of tying executive compensation to stock market performance, which overly emphasizes short-term performance.[34] Even Donald Trump has contributed to the idea that it is permissible to hurt people in the pursuit of profit. When asked about the difference between being president and being a business person, Trump responded: "Well, in business, you don't necessarily need heart . . . whereas [in government], almost everything affects people. . . . [P]retty much everything

---

[30] *See* Appendix D.

[31] Michael C. Jensen, *Value Maximization, Stakeholder Theory, and the Corporate Objective Function*, J. APPLIED CORP. FIN., Fall 2001, at 8.

[32] *Id.* at 9. He implies that his position is correct because value maximization is based on economics and finance, while stakeholder theory is based in sociology, organizational behavior, and special/ managerial self-interests.

[33] *Id.* at 16.

[34] Michael C. Jensen & Kevin J. Murphy, *CEO Incentives—It's Not How Much You Pay, but How*, J. APPLIED CORP. FIN., Winter 2010, at 64; *see* DUFF MCDONALD, THE GOLDEN PASSPORT: HARVARD BUSINESS SCHOOL, THE LIMITS OF CAPITALISM, AND THE MORAL FAILURE OF THE MBA ELITE 365–82 (2017).

you do in government, involves heart, whereas in business, most things don't involve heart."[35]

Over the years, the notion of shareholder primacy became entrenched in parts of academia and grew in acceptance by others. Lynn Stout has explained why this happened:

To tenure-seeking law professors, the Chicago School's application of economic theory to corporate law lent an attractive patina of scientific rigor to the shareholder side of the longstanding "shareholders versus society" and "shareholders versus stakeholders" disputes. Thus shareholder value thinking quickly became central to the so-called Law and Economics School of legal jurisprudence. . . . Meanwhile, the idea that corporate performance could be simply and easily measured through the single metric of share price invited a generation of economists and business school professors to produce countless statistical studies of the relationship of stock price and variables like board size, capital structure, merger activity, state of incorporation, and so forth, in a grail-like quest to discover the secret of "optimal corporate governance."

Shareholder primacy rhetoric also appealed to the popular press and business media. First, it gave their readers a simple, easy-to-understand, sound-bite description of what corporations are and what they are supposed to do. Second and perhaps more important, it offered up an obvious suspect for every headline-grabbing corporate failure and scandal: misbehaving corporate "agents." If a firm ran into trouble, it was because directors and executives were selfishly indulging themselves at the expense of the firm's shareholders. . . .

Lawmakers, consultants, and would be reformers also were attracted to the gospel of shareholder value, because it allowed them to suggest obvious solutions to just about every business problem imaginable. The prescription for good governance had three simple ingredients: (1) give boards of directors less power, (2) give shareholders more power, and (3) "incentivize" executives and shareholders by tying their pay to share price. . . .

Finally, shareholder value thinking came to appeal, though the direct result of self-interest, to the growing ranks of CEOs and other top executives

[35] Interview by Julie Pace with President Donald Trump, in Washington, D.C. (Apr. 23, 2017), https://apnews.com/c810d7de280a47e88848b0ac74690c83/Transcript-of-AP-interview-with-Trump [https://perma.cc/M2FY-9Z3Q].

who were being showered, in the name of the shareholders with options, shares, and bonuses tied to stock performance.[36]

Leo Strine, when he was Vice Chancellor of the Delaware Court of Chancery, emphasized the market pressures on directors and executives to continually increase stock prices. This has prompted CEOs to cut costs through activities like plant closings, downsizing, outsourcing, and wage and benefit cuts in order to avoid "unwanted attention from hungry bidders or dissatisfied institutional investors. CEOs realized that independent directors would cashier them if push came to shove and stockholder unrest became commonplace. Therefore, rhetoric about focusing sharply on stockholder value became standard for CEOs who obsessed over ensuring that the financial markets were happy with their performance."[37] Strine points at the investors who now have made the academic claim of shareholder primacy a reality. Their constant push for higher returns has resulted in many actions that harm workers. This returns us to the trade-off discussed in the preceding chapter. Why should we favor the investor class over labor? Why should we accept the higher returns to investors at the expense to labor? Just because we have done that up to now, that does not make it right.

Even though proponents of the shareholder primacy theory claim that managers will not know how to balance the interests of all the stakeholders if they have to take them into account, that kind of management was not a problem for much of the twentieth century, when companies adhered to a philosophy of "managerial capitalism." The directors of large public corporations "viewed themselves not as shareholders' servants but as trustees for great institutions that should serve not only shareholders but other corporate stakeholders as well, including customers, creditors, employees, and the community. Equity investors were treated as an important corporate constituency, but not the only constituency that mattered. Nor was share price assumed to be the best proxy for corporate performance."[38]

There are many examples of this type of managerial capitalism. For example, the Endicott-Johnson Shoe Company, which was the largest shoe

---

[36] Lynn A. Stout, The Shareholder Value Myth: How Putting Shareholders First Harms Investors, Corporations, and the Public 19–20 (2012).

[37] Leo E. Strine Jr., *Human Freedom and Two Friedmen: Musings on the Implications of Globalization for the Effective Regulation of Corporate Behaviour*, 58 U. Toronto L.J. 241, 261 (2008).

[38] Lynn A. Stout, *The Dumbest Business Idea Ever. The Myth of Maximizing Shareholder Value: The Dominant Business Philosophy Debunked*, Evonomics, https://evonomics.com/maximizing-shareholder-value-dumbest-idea/ [https://perma.cc/RT2X-PVBB].

company in the United States in the 1940s and 1950s, cared for its workers and communities during the first half of the twentieth century.[39] George F. Johnson, the president of the company, was the first to give shoe company workers a six-day workweek. Prior to that, shoe factory workers (as well as steel and other types of factory workers) worked seven days a week, with Christmas as their only holiday. Johnson also provided the workers with financing for company-built homes, provided healthcare and medical clinics, and recreational facilities. In addition, the company did many good works for the town in which the plants were located, such as building parks (with carousels that are now famous), public libraries, theaters, a golf course, and swimming pools, all open to the public for free. This led the town of Leistershire, New York, to change its name to Johnson City to honor George F. Johnson.[40] These types of good works for workers and towns were not atypical for many factory owners in New England and the Mid-Atlantic states in the pre–World War II era.

There are other progressive commentators on corporations, in addition to Lynn Stout and Leo Strine, who have tried to get business firms to take into account other stakeholders in addition to investors. For example, Kent Greenfield has forcefully argued that the rationales used to support shareholder primacy also support making management the fiduciaries of workers.[41] In response to the argument that it is counterproductive for corporate law to mandate that managers do anything but look after shareholder interests, he writes:

> A rejoinder to this counterargument starts by pointing out how truly awkward it is to assert that corporate managers best advance societal well-being by ignoring it. Not even Adam Smith's invisible hand was assumed to be so powerful that people should be *prohibited* from taking into account the interests of others or of society in general. Yet that is exactly what corporate law claims to do and what most corporate law scholars assert it *should* do.[42]

---

[39] GERALD ZAHAVI, WORKERS, MANAGERS, AND WELFARE CAPITALISM: THE SHOEWORKERS AND TANNERS OF ENDICOTT JOHNSON, 1890–1950 (1988); Gerald Zahavi, *Negotiated Loyalty: Welfare Capitalism and the Shoeworkers of Endicott Johnson, 1920–1940*, 70 J. AM. HIST. 602 (1983).

[40] *The History of Johnson City, NY*, VILL. JOHNSON CITY, N.Y., http://www.villageofjc.com/history.html [https://perma.cc/8GWU-LJE9].

[41] KENT GREENFIELD, THE FAILURE OF CORPORATE LAW: FUNDAMENTAL FLAWS AND PROGRESSIVE POSSIBILITIES 43–71 (2006). Greenfield develops this fiduciary obligation to workers by using property rights theory, principle/agent theory, contractarian theory, and the relevance of being a residual claimant, all ideas that have been used to support shareholder primacy.

[42] *Id.* at 136.

These progressive commentators have had little success so far in changing the dominant view of corporations. However, it does not have to be that way. Unlike the United States, other countries have been successful in giving employees a voice in corporate decision-making. For example, as explained in the next chapter, countries in the European Union provide significant protection of workers. Germany even has a law requiring that the corporate board include representatives of labor. Recently, the U.K. government has expressed a concern about the overemphasis of shareholder interests. With the approval of the government, a corporate governance institute issued a paper in September 2017 setting forth core principles inherent in U.K. corporate law, which includes the board's duty to take into account the interests of employees and the community.[43]

One glimmer of change in the United States is the Business Roundtable's new Statement of Corporate Purpose issued in August 2019. Since 1978, the Roundtable has issued Principles of Corporate Governance that included a statement that corporations exist primarily to serve their shareholders. For the first time, the 2019 statement said that corporations had a fundamental commitment to all their stakeholders, not to just shareholders, but to customers, employees, suppliers, and communities.[44] However, given the history of business's disregard of its employees and communities at least since the 1970s, it is difficult to believe that changes will result from a new change of corporate purpose from the Business Roundtable. In fact, within a month of signing on to that new purpose, Amazon's Whole Foods subsidiary announced that it was eliminating medical benefits for nearly 2,000 part-time employees.[45] The members of the Business Roundtable can prove that their new commitment to all stakeholders is real by taking concrete actions, like putting representatives of labor on their boards; curtailing outsourcing, layoffs, and plant closings; and proposing new laws to protect their workers and communities. Only those kinds of actions will demonstrate a real commitment to stakeholders other than shareholders.

---

[43] INST. CHARTERED SEC'Y & ADM'RS & INV. ASS'N, THE STAKEHOLDER VOICE IN BOARD DECISION MAKING: STRENGTHENING THE BUSINESS, PROMOTING LONG-TERM SUCCESS (Sept. 2017), https://www.icsa.org.uk/assets/files/free-guidance-notes/the-stakeholder-voice-in-Board-Decision-Making-09-2017.pdf [https://perma.cc/LWD5-7BY8].

[44] *Statement on the Purpose of a Corporation*, BUS. ROUNDTABLE (Aug. 19, 2019), https://opportunity.businessroundtable.org/ourcommitment/ [https://perma.cc/NZM5-FFCA].

[45] Hayley Peterson, *Whole Foods Is Cutting Medical Benefits for Hundreds of Part-Time Workers*, BUS. INSIDER (Sept. 12, 2019), https://www.businessinsider.com/whole-foods-cuts-medical-benefits-for-part-time-workers-2019-9 [https://perma.cc/PY2D-WQZD].

As things stand today, the United States is an outlier when compared to Europe and Canada in its complete disregard of labor and communities. The only way change can come about is through legislation. I will explain the kinds of regulations that can help in Chapter 9. However, with business's success in influencing Congress, I fear that new legislation is impossible unless the culture in the United States changes to respect the interests of labor and communities.

6

Outsourcing in the United States and Europe

Over the last three decades the treatment of manufacturing workers has been diametrically different from owners like George Johnson. Manufacturing began to move from New England and the Mid-Atlantic states to the south beginning after World War II because wages were lower and unions weaker there. When workers in a shoe factory in Massachusetts or in a textile mill in Pennsylvania lost their jobs, they suffered; in exchange workers in the south got a better life. Painful as this may have been to some, this was an ordinary consequence of the open markets among the states, constitutionalized in the interstate commerce clause. With global transportation by sea and air, fast communication between countries by the phone and internet, and English becoming the worldwide common language, it has become easy to manufacture products for the U.S. markets in other countries. These days, manufacturing workers in Ohio can lose their jobs to workers in Mexico or China, rather than to workers in Georgia.[1] This is a different kind of problem because American workers are not benefiting when other American workers are harmed.[2]

No doubt, global trade has benefited consumers with quality products at lower prices. In addition, countries can specialize in different kinds of products, achieving specialization and division of labor on a global scale.

---

[1] In addition to moving jobs overseas, firms have used the H-1B visa system to bring in workers from other countries to replace U.S. workers at lower wages. *See* Kenneth M. Geisler II, Note, *Fissures in the Valley: Searching for a Remedy for US Tech Workers Indirectly Displaced by H-1b Visa Outsourcing Firms*, 95 WASH. U.L. REV. 465 (2017). For an example of one businessman's repeated use of outsourcing to become rich, *see* Azam Ahmed & Elisabeth Malkin, *For Commerce Pick Wilbur Ross, "Inherently Bad" Deals Paid Off*, N.Y. TIMES (Feb. 25, 2017), https://www.nytimes.com/2017/02/25/world/americas/wilbur-ross-trump-commerce-secretary.html [https://perma.cc/BP65-FZ3F].

[2] Those who view themselves as citizens of the world will not object to the movement of jobs from the United States to other countries. I think that the recent public concern for jobs for U.S. workers shows that most people reject that view. If business firms continue to move labor from country to minimize production costs, there will come a time when jobs will move from Asian countries to African countries. Only when labor costs (and returns to investment) are equal around the world will the movement of production facilities stop. My guess is that kind of equalization will never occur.

Rethinking Market Regulation. John N. Drobak, Oxford University Press. © Oxford University Press 2021.
DOI: 10.1093/oso/9780197578957.003.0006

Everyone emphasizes these gains, but they do come at a cost to U.S. workers. Just as data is lacking about the number of workers laid off as a result of mergers, it is difficult to know with any degree of certainty how many people have lost their job through outsourcing to other countries. The Mass Layoffs Statistics Program of the Bureau of Labor Statistics in the Department of Labor gathered some of this information until it was canceled in 2013 as a result of federal spending cuts.[3] Using state unemployment filings and self-reporting by firms, that program reported about 87,000 jobs outsourced overseas between 2004 and May 2013. That method of gathering data about job losses significantly understated the actual number of outsourced jobs. Some estimates of the actual number of jobs lost overseas show immense losses. The biggest cause is not NAFTA, as President Trump had claimed, but China, which began when China joined the World Trade Organization in 2001. One economic study estimated the job loss to China between 1999 and 2011 to be 2 million jobs, with almost half in manufacturing.[4] Another estimate puts the job loss at 3.2 million jobs, with 2.4 million in manufacturing.[5] According to the St. Louis Federal Reserve, 5.5 million manufacturing jobs were lost between 2000 and 2010.[6] Job losses to Mexico as a result of NAFTA, while less than the losses to China, are still large. One estimate puts the number of job losses in the United States by 2011 at 773,900, with three-fifths of those in manufacturing, while 91,000 jobs were gained.[7] Another study estimated that by 2013, more than 845,000 U.S. workers lost their jobs as a result of imports from Canada and Mexico or relocated factories.[8]

[3] *See* Mass Layoff Statistics, U.S. BUREAU OF LABOR STATISTICS, https://www.bls.gov/mls/home. htm [https://perma.cc/JF74-NLGK].

[4] David H. Autor et al., *The China Shock: Learning from Labor-Market Adjustment to Large Changes in Trade*, 8 ANN. REV. ECON. 205, 227 (2016). In another study, the authors estimate the total job loss to be 2.37 million. Daron Acemoglu et al., *Import Competition and the Great US Employment Sag of the 2000s*, 34 J. LAB. ECON. S141, S181 (2016).

[5] ROBERT E. SCOTT & WILL KIMBALL, ECON. POL'Y INST., CHINA TRADE, OUTSOURCING AND JOBS (Dec. 11, 2014), https://www.epi.org/files/2014/bp385-china-trade-deficit.pdf [https://perma. cc/3ASC-KURD]. The methodology of this study is criticized in Tim Worstall, Opinion, *The Epi's Terribly Strange Calculation About Trade and the Effect on Jobs*, FORBES (Mar. 13, 2016), https://www. forbes.com/sites/timworstall/2016/03/13/the-epis-terribly-strange-calculation-about-trade-and-the-effect-on-jobs/ [https://perma.cc/A5ZW-NNU9].

[6] Thomas B. Edsall, Opinion, *Whose Party Is It Anyway?*, N.Y. TIMES (July 8, 2015), https://www. nytimes.com/2015/07/08/opinion/thomas-b-edsall-whose-party-is-it-anyway.html [https://perma. cc/4GNZ-25AX].

[7] ROBERT E. SCOTT, ECON. POL'Y INST., HEADING SOUTH: U.S.-MEXICO TRADE AND JOB DISPLACEMENT AFTER NAFTA 11–12, 19 (May 3, 2011), https://www.epi.org/files/page/-/ BriefingPaper308.pdf [https://perma.cc/VSW9-U7ER].

[8] BEN BEACHY, NAFTA's 20-YEAR LEGACY AND THE FATE OF THE TRANS-PACIFIC PARTNERSHIP, PUB. CITIZEN (Feb. 2014), https://www.citizen.org/wp-content/uploads/migration/nafta-at-20-embargoed.pdf [https://perma.cc/VV98-N5KA]. This study based job losses on the number of employees who received Trade Adjustment Assistance.

Regardless of the precise number, outsourcing has caused a tremendous loss of U.S. manufacturing jobs.[9]

The loss of jobs is compounded by the lack of growth in real wages since the 1970s. In fact, wages have gone down slightly for male full-time workers. In 1973, the inflation-adjusted median income for those workers was $54,030, compared with $51,640 in 2016.[10] Many labor economists consider lower wages to be a byproduct of the outsourcing of jobs.[11] Paul Samuelson, a Nobel laureate in economics, wrote that outsourcing had similar economic effects to mass immigration of workers who are willing to work for service jobs at extremely low wages.[12] They can drive down income for a good part of the middle class.[13] In addition, the shrinkage of starting salaries results in lower lifetime earnings. For example, someone who worked for thirty years beginning in 1967 would earn as much as $250,000 more, after adjustment for inflation, than someone who had the same type of career but started work fifteen years later.[14] This factor contributes to the increasing disparity of wealth in the United States today.

Congress has done nothing to regulate the outsourcing of jobs by business. There have been at least eight bills proposed in Congress since 2003 that deal with outsourcing.[15] None would have limited it in any significant way. Most would have required the government to compile data on and study outsourcing or to limit tax deductions for those activities. Even these mild bills never made it out of committee, while some were not even referred to a committee.[16] For example, despite the Republicans being in the minority in the Senate in 2012, they were still able to block the "Bring Jobs Home Act,"

---

[9] Outsourcing is not just limited to manufacturing. For example, IBM now has a larger workforce in India than in the United States, many workers performing consulting services, writing software, monitoring cloud-based computer systems, and engaging in research and development. Vindu Goel, *IBM Now Has More Employees in India Than in the U.S.*, N.Y. Times (Sept. 28, 2017), https://www.nytimes.com/2017/09/28/technology/ibm-india.html [https://perma.cc/2UZV-N8TJ].

[10] Patricia Cohen, *Bump in U.S. Incomes Doesn't Erase 50 Years of Pain*, N.Y. Times (Sept. 16, 2017), https://www.nytimes.com/2017/09/16/business/economy/bump-in-us-incomes-doesnt-erase-50-years-of-pain.html [https://perma.cc/FQL4-UC5X].

[11] Autor et al., *supra* note 4, at 229–34.

[12] Paul A. Samuelson, *Where Ricardo and Mill Rebut and Confirm Arguments of Mainstream Economists Supporting Globalization*, 18 J. Econ. Persp. 135, 144 (2004).

[13] *Outsourcing: Where's Uncle Sam?*, BusinessWeek: The Debate Room (2007), https://web.archive.org/web/20070305113458/http://www.businessweek.com/debateroom/archives/2007/02/outsourcing_whe.html [https://perma.cc/2BEX-J3S6].

[14] *Id.*

[15] The bills are described in Appendix D.

[16] In 2004, Congress did enact one law to limit the outsourcing of government work. American Jobs Creation Act of 2004, Pub. L. No. 108-357, 118 Stat. 1418 (Codified in Scattered Sections of 26 U.S.C.), https://www.congress.gov/bill/108th-congress/house-bill/4520/ [https://perma.cc/HK4E-FCNS].

which would have eliminated the existing tax deductions for the costs associated with moving jobs overseas.[17] The Senate Majority Leader, Harry Reid, claimed that that the Republicans were not just representing the interests of business, they were also defending the Republican nominee for president, Mitt Romney, "who of course made a fortune by shipping jobs overseas."[18] Romney worked for the private investment firm Bain Capital, which was known for buying companies and then outsourcing the jobs. This inaction of Congress is contrary to the general sense of the public. A Zogby International poll in 2015 found that 71 percent of Americans believed that outsourcing jobs hurts the U.S. economy, while 62 percent said that the government should tax or legislate to stop the sending of jobs overseas.[19]

The United States stands alone in the world with this degree of loss of manufacturing jobs, even in per capita numbers. Many readers will justify the loss of jobs and harm to communities by pointing out that this is just the normal result of a capitalist system, that Joseph Schumpeter reminded us of the benefits of destructive competition. However, other countries with successful market economics have not outsourced jobs as we did. Again, data is sparse for other countries. One outsourcing survey of companies in fifteen European countries between 2009 and 2011 disclosed job losses of 83,000, with about 50,000 in manufacturing.[20] There is no doubt that the amount of outsourcing of manufacturing jobs in Europe pales in comparison to what happened in the United States. This raises the question about why some European countries have been able to maintain successful economies with so little outsourcing.

One cause is the type of manufacturing economy we had, with many unskilled and low-skilled workers doing the kind of jobs that can be taught to workers in emerging economies. Another reason stems from the relative influence of shareholders. In the United States, there is a constant push for increased returns to shareholders, with large institutional investors and shareholder activists pushing for short-term profits. Germany is a counterexample. While Germany has many large, global companies, like BMW,

---

[17] Bring Jobs Home Act, S. 3364, 112th Cong. (2012).

[18] Ned Potter, *Senate Kills Anti-Outsourcing Bill; Democrats Point to Romney*, ABC News (July 19, 2012), https://abcnews.go.com/blogs/politics/2012/07/senate-kills-anti-outsourcing-bill-democrats-point-to-romney [https://perma.cc/BT6T-46FZ].

[19] *Outsourcing: Where's Uncle Sam, supra* note 13.

[20] Samuli Rikama et al., *International Sourcing of Business Functions*, Eurostat (June 2013), https://ec.europa.eu/eurostat/statistics-explained/index.php/Archive:International_sourcing_of_business_functions [https://perma.cc/TT7H-V5A5], Fig. 14. The survey does not include Germany, which has a large manufacturing sector.

Volkswagen, and Siemens, the backbone of German manufacturing is small and midsize firms, many family-owned. These firms do not face constant pressure from shareholders for higher and higher returns. In addition, they are often managed with a focus on the longer term when compared with U.S. businesses.[21] German industrial exports are known for their high quality; they have the lowest price elasticities in the world.[22] As a result, many manufacturing jobs in Germany are higher skilled, which are harder to outsource.[23] Finally, there is a greater respect for manufacturing workers in Germany than in the United States. One of the reasons for that is the influence of the country's "ordoliberal" economic philosophy, which emphasizes the importance of the state providing the conditions within which markets can operate, including helping labor to develop skills that meet market needs.[24] Taking the vocation track in high school in Germany does not have the stigma that it does to many people in the United States.[25] As one commentator said about how many Americans think about the working class: "If you worked for $10, $12, $15 an hour, you were a loser, and you know people thought of you as a loser. They didn't want to see you, didn't want to know you, didn't want their children to play with your children."[26] In addition to these differences, the countries in the European Union give many more legal protections to their workers.

[21] Michael Schuman, *Does Germany Know the Secret to Creating Jobs?*, TIME (Feb. 25, 2011), https://business.time.com/2011/02/25/does-germany-know-the-secret-to-creating-jobs/ [https://perma.cc/N2AA-AGLR]; Charles W. Wessner, *How Does Germany Do It?*, MECHANICAL ENGINEERING (Nov. 13, 2013), https://www.asme.org/topics-resources/content/how-does-germany-do-it [https://perma.cc/4VEH-8R79].

[22] MARK BLYTH, AUSTERITY: THE HISTORY OF A DANGEROUS IDEA 76 (2013).

[23] Average pay for German manufacturing workers is significantly higher than in the United States. Nicholas Kristof, Opinion, *Trump Finds a Brawler for His War on Workers*, N.Y. TIMES (Aug. 10, 2019), https://www.nytimes.com/2019/08/10/opinion/sunday/labor-unions.html [https://perma.cc/CSE6-TQ9U].

[24] MARK BLYTH, AUSTERITY: THE HISTORY OF A DANGEROUS IDEA 57 (2013).

[25] In Germany's educational system, students choose between three types of high schools: blue collar, white collar, and university. Students in the blue-collar schools apprentice as part of their high school education. This has led to the highly skilled work force in Germany. A student must pick one type of high school at the end of primary school, effectively choosing a career at a young age. The German educational system is often criticized for requiring such an important choice at such a young age. However, the system of educational tracking may be an important factor contributing to Germany's successful employment policies. OREN CASS, MANHATTAN INSTITUTE, THE WORKFORCE-TRAINING GRANT: A NEW BRIDGE FROM HIGH SCHOOL TO CAREER (July 2019), https://media4.manhattan-institute.org/sites/default/files/R-0719-OCass.pdf [https://perma.cc/U5TB-QBSN].

[26] BRIAN ALEXANDER, GLASS HOUSE: THE 1% ECONOMY AND THE SHATTERING OF THE ALL-AMERICAN TOWN 291 (2017). *See* OREN CASS, THE ONCE AND FUTURE WORKER: A VISION FOR THE RENEWAL OF WORK IN AMERICA, 195–208 (2018); Oren Cass, *The Culture War on Work* (Dec. 12, 2018), https://medium.com/@orencass/the-culture-war-on-work-d1c6cae9db08 [https://perma.cc/MJT4-69P7].

The Charter of Fundamental Rights of the European Union is the equivalent of a constitution and binding on all countries in the European Union. Many of its provisions protect workers.[27] Article 15 gives everyone the right to work and to pursue a freely chosen occupation.[28] It makes the right to work one of the fundamental human rights, linking work to human dignity and self-realization. Article 30 gives workers a right against unjustified dismissal.[29] This right has been interpreted to require both procedural and substantive standards in connection with a workplace dismissal, as well as compensation for a dismissal in some circumstances. The Charter gives workers the right to assert its protections in litigation in national courts. Although workers' rights are not absolute but limited by other rights and the interests of government in many circumstances, the Charter is a powerful acknowledgment of the importance of work and workers' rights.

Every country in the European Union also has its own provisions protecting workers. To use Germany as an example again, the German constitution (called the "Basic Law") includes freedom of association for workers as a constitutionally protected fundamental right by giving them the "right to form associations to safeguard and improve working and economic conditions."[30] In addition, the specialized Federal Labor Court has used values in the Basic Law to support workers' rights through the judicial process.[31] The German Parliament has gone even further than the courts to help workers. For example, the German Works Constitution Act requires that employees participate in the day-to-day management of plant operations through "works councils."[32] The Codetermination Act gives workers considerable input in the management of the firm. German corporations have a supervisory board (similar to a board of directors of a U.S. corporation) that supervises and appoints the members of a firm's board of management.

---

[27] Charter of Fundamental Rights of the European Union, 2012 O.J. (C 326) 391. *See id.* at 398, 401 (Art. 12 (freedom of association), art. 15 (right to engage in work and freedom to choose an occupation), art. 27 (workers' rights to information and consultation), art. 28 (right of collective bargaining), art. 30 (protection from unjustified dismissal), and art. 31 (right to fair and just working conditions).

[28] *Id.* at 398.

[29] *Id.* at 401.

[30] GRUNDEGESETZ [GG] [Basic Law], art. 9(3) (Ger.), *translation at* https://www.gesetze-im-internet.de/englisch_gg/englisch_gg.html#p0054 [https://perma.cc/E6CR-6729], *quoted in* Ian Holloway, *The Constitutionalization of Employment Rights: A Comparative View*, 14 BERKELEY J. EMP. & LAB. L. 113, 126 n.86 (1993).

[31] Holloway, *supra* note 30, at 127–29.

[32] Betriebsverfassungsgesetz [Betrvg] [Works Constitution Act], Sept. 25, 2001, BGBL I at 2518, § 1 (Ger.), https://www.gesetze-im-internet.de/englisch_betrvg/englisch_betrvg.pdf; *see also* Holloway, *supra* note 30, at 125.

Under the Codetermination Act, up to one-half of the members of the supervisory boards are elected by the firm's employees.[33] Through the works council and labor's participation in the supervisory board, the workers of a firm have considerable input about decisions to outsource. Perhaps even more important, German law gives the works council the ability to influence severance pay in connection with layoffs and outsourcing.[34] This combination of formal legal rights to workers and their ability to influence business decisions has acted like a brake on outsourcing by German firms. Other countries in the European Union provide similar protections to labor as Germany. This is not just the result of the Charter of Fundamental Rights but also as a result of domestic laws and practices.[35]

France's response to a proposed merger between Renault and Fiat Chrysler in 2019 is an example of a country attempting to preserve manufacturing jobs. The $35 billion merger would have created the third largest automobile manufacturing firm in the world. Once the merger proposal went public, France, which owns 15 percent of Renault's stock, announced that it would support the merger as long as industrial jobs would be preserved and factories would not be closed in France. Reports said that the companies had agreed to the French ultimatum, while leaving room for the elimination of some white-collar and engineering jobs.[36] Ultimately, the merger did not go through.[37]

Although the countries in the European Union are more protective of workers, they have their own labor problems. One common problem is the unemployment of youths between fifteen and twenty-four years old. The

---

[33] Mitbestimmungsgesetz [Mitbestg] [Codetermination Act], May 4, 1976, BGBl I at 1153, § 9 (Ger.), https://www.gesetze-im-internet.de/mitbestg/BJNR011530976.html; *see also Fundamentals of German Corporate Governance*, SGL Group, https://web.archive.org/web/20190201194846/ http://www.sglgroup.com/cms/international/investor-relations/corporate-governance/principles-of-german-corporate-governance/index.html?__locale=en [https://perma.cc/4J9B-K66C].

[34] *Termination of an Employment Contract in Germany*, How to Germany, https://www.howtogermany.com/pages/termination-employment-contract.html [https://perma.cc/77DZ-PNGQ].

[35] For example, the Italian constitution provides that every citizen has the right to work, art. 4 Constitutzione [Cost.] (It.), that workers have a right to "fair pay," *id.* art. 36, that they have the ability to create unions through the freedom of association, and that they have a right to strike, *id.* art. 40. Italian statutes give workers strong protections from "unfair dismissal," including the payment of compensation and reinstatement, and severance pay. Legge 23 Luglio 1991, N. 223, G.U. July 27, 1991, N.175 (It.).

[36] Sudip Kar-Gupta, *France Wants FCA-Renault Job Guarantees and Nissan on Board*, Reuters (May 28, 2019), https://www.reuters.com/article/us-renault-m-a-fiat-chrysler/france-wants-fca-renault-job-guarantees-and-nissan-on-board-idUSKCN1SY0FR [https://perma.cc/547N-Y8KJ].

[37] Julia Kollewe, *Renault-Fiat Chrysler Merger Collapses*, Guardian (June 6, 2019), https://www.theguardian.com/business/2019/jun/06/renault-fiat-chrysler-merger-collapses [https://perma.cc/43A3-4R2A].

Great Recession of 2008 had a devastating effect on some E.U. countries. For example, Greece and Spain had youth unemployment rates, respectively, of 23 and 18 percent before the financial crisis, but both were above 50 percent in 2013.[38] The sovereign debt crisis also influenced the high unemployment rate for some countries because the financial obligations of the countries in the red lacked the funds to help with unemployment. Six years later, by August 2019, the youth unemployment rate in Greece and Spain had fallen to about 33 percent. France had a youth unemployment rate of 19 percent. At the lower end, the United Kingdom had a youth employment rate of 11 percent and Germany of about 6 percent.[39] Not only does the high youth unemployment rate cause serious economic problems, it can lead to social and political problems.

There are a number of causes of the youth unemployment problem. I suspect that there are just not enough jobs that would pay a middle-class wage with some permanence. So the youth suffer from a lack of opportunity. A lack of education also appears to be a major factor in youth unemployment. Some scholars believe that Germany has been an outlier because of its educational, vocational, and apprentice system.[40] For the educated but unemployed youths, there is often a mismatch of their skills and the skills needed by employers.[41] There may also be a relationship between the protection some countries afford workers and the difficulty the young have in getting jobs. The high minimum wage and the strong protection of permanent workers in France have led many companies to hire temporary workers who lack those protections. As a result, young job seekers are less likely to be hired into permanent positions. As one commentator explained,

> In France, a short-term contract may not extend beyond 24 months. The employed work force has thus acquired a dual structure: on one side, the "insiders"—regular workers protected against dismissal; on the other side, the "outsiders," who survive on short-term contracts and hop from job

[38] Mario Draghi, President, Eur. Cent. Bank, Keynote Speech at Henry Grattan Lecture Series at Trinity College, Dublin: Youth Unemployment in the Euro Area (Sept. 22, 2017), https://www.ecb.europa.eu/press/key/date/2017/html/ecb.sp170922_1.en.html [https://perma.cc/VJB8-G4CM].

[39] H. Plecher, *Youth Unemployment Rate in Europe August 2019*, STATISTA (Oct. 15, 2019), https://www.statista.com/statistics/266228/youth-unemployment-rate-in-eu-countries/ [https://perma.cc/Y7LD-K4B7].

[40] Pierre Cahuc et al., *Youth Unemployment in Old Europe: The Polar Cases of France and Germany*, 2:18 IZA J. EUR. LAB. STUD. 1 (2013).

[41] Draghi, *supra* note 38.

to job. Outsiders make up about 15% of the employed, a proportion that climbs over 50% in the 15–24 age category.[42]

The lack of employment opportunities for young workers is a serious problem in the European Union, but it is different than the elimination of jobs from a merger or from outsourcing in the United States. Just because some European countries have problems with youth unemployment does not mean that we cannot learn from them. All countries have social problems of some sort; there is no nirvana. We can learn from the positive steps these countries take to help labor. I am not proposing that we do what Germany or France does. With the differences between the United States and the European countries, it would be impossible to duplicate the European experience. However, we can move closer to what those countries do to help their workers.

The underlying, fundamental question is why the countries of the European Union are so protective of workers' rights while the United States is not. There is a cultural difference across the Atlantic concerning both the importance of workers' rights and the role of regulation. The notion of path dependence can help us understand the difference between countries. Path dependence reminds us that where we are today depends on where we were in the past and affects where we will be in the future. Yesterday's decisions open new avenues and close others. Over time, these incremental actions shape a country. As John Godard, a Canadian labor economist, explained, the "formative economic, social, and political conditions in a nation's history come to be reflected in deeply held institutional norms, or beliefs, values, and principles."[43]

Relying on a long list of scholars who have tried to identify the social norms that make the United States different from the rest of the world in our treatment of workers, Godard identified the relevant founding conditions as our "history of individualistic frontier development, with limited state involvement; its Calvinistic religious settlement and hence traditions; its history of large markets and large, economically powerful employers; its revolutionary birth; and it tradition of democratic governance."[44] Godard sees these founding conditions as playing an important role in the development of three key characteristics of U.S. society:

---

[42] Pierre Lemieux, *France: The End of the Road, Again*, Reg., Fall 2016, at 34, 38.
[43] John Godard, *The Exceptional Decline of the American Labor Movement*, 63 Indus. & Lab. Rel. Rev. 82, 83 (2009).
[44] *Id.* at 84.

First, these conditions meant that the United States, even more than other liberal democracies, came to be known for its "possessive individualism," under which individual wealth and consumption came to be the primary signifiers of self-wealth, and for its unique "spirit," characterized by optimism, entrepreneurialism, and risk-taking. . . .

Second, these meant that the United States came to be characterized by strong Lockean norms as to the sanctity of property and of ownership rights deriving from property, more than in Europe and even Britain, where these norms originated. . . .

Finally, they meant that the United States came to be characterized by strong norms of formal democracy in the political sphere and by a distrust of centralized state power, both of which have been seen to reflect the circumstances associated with the American Revolution. Coupled with the perception of unlimited opportunity, these circumstances formed the basis for norms under which the state is not expected to play a significant role in addressing economic and social problems. Instead, there is a strong "self-help" tradition in the United States, under which individuals and communities are expected to overcome adversity on their own.[45]

I believe that Godard is correct in his conclusion that these norms have influenced the United States to have "a variant of capitalism more hostile to independent workplace representation than perhaps any other."[46] This is compounded by a number of other factors. Unlike the political activities of workers in Europe, unions in the United States have tended to focus primarily on economic issues, not political ones. Their efforts have emphasized bread-and-butter issues, like wages, benefits, and working conditions. In Europe, corporations came back to life after World War II, just as European countries were formalizing protection of workers. Workers in Europe were active politically, governments were philosophically concerned about workers' rights, and business did not stop the impetus to protect workers.[47]

---

[45] *Id.* at 84–85 (citations omitted).

[46] *Id.* at 85.

[47] To take Germany as an example again, the prevalent economic theory that drove the birth of a new West Germany after World War II was ordoliberalism, a philosophy of using the government to bring order to markets. Although it was a fiscally conservative doctrine, "ordoliberals keenly appreciated that the 'stability and security [of] the working class was a prerequisite to securing the market economy.'" MARK BLYTH, AUSTERITY: THE HISTORY OF A DANGEROUS IDEA 138 (2013) (quoting Ralf Ptak, *Neoliberalism in Germany: Revisiting the Ordoliberal Foundations of the Social Market Economy*, *in* THE ROAD FROM MONT PELERIN: THE MAKING OF THE NEOLIBERAL THOUGHT COLLECTIVE 98, 102 (Philip Mirowski & Dieter Plehwe eds., 2009)).

Rather than resist the rights of labor, management in the European Union has come to recognize the legitimacy of unions and hence worked to accommodate their interests. In the United States, businesses were powerful and well-established when the union movement among industrial workers began at the late nineteenth century. Business has a long history of antagonism to unions, fighting workers tooth and nail to limit their power, using violence and political influence with state and local governments, as well as using the courts. A famous commentary on labor relations concluded that the United States has the "bloodiest and most violent labor history of any industrial nation in the world."[48] The New Deal finally gave workers and unions formal legal protections, but much of the antagonism between business and labor remained. As a result, business has kept up its political and marketing campaign against labor and unions, influencing the public perception of workers' rights. Today the unions representing industrial workers are less powerful and influential than they have been since World War II.[49]

The lack of power of unions also stems from the relative conservativism of the working class in the United States. You would expect opposition to workers' interests to come from investors and management, but, strangely, many workers oppose unions and government intervention to protect workers' rights. This stems from a belief in the ethic of self-reliance, the distrust of government, and the norms that affirm the primacy of property rights.

All of these factors are part of our culture, making a barrier to government regulation of layoffs from mergers and outsourcing. Once norms and beliefs become embedded in culture, they are hard to change. Usually cultural change is generational, so there may be hope that the political power of the millennials will be an effective start to a greater concern for labor in the United States. However, that is far from certain. Another aspect of our culture that stymies change is the legitimization of greed as a socially acceptable—and often laudable—goal.

---

[48] Philip Taft & Philip Ross, *American Labor Violence: Its Causes, Character, and Outcome,* in VIOLENCE IN AMERICA: HISTORICAL AND COMPARATIVE PERSPECTIVES: A REPORT TO THE NATIONAL COMMISSION ON THE CAUSES AND PREVENTION OF VIOLENCE 221, 221 (Hugh Davis Graham & Ted Robert Gurr eds., 1969).

[49] Public sector unions have remained powerful.

7

Legitimization of Greed—Heartbreak to Workers

I. The Quest for Profits

The Wealth of Nations is known for its claim that the market channels self-interested conduct to make it useful for society:

> It is not from the benevolence of the butcher, the brewer, or the baker, that we expect our dinner, but from their regard to their own interest. We address ourselves, not to their humanity but to their self-love, and never talk to them of our necessities but of their advantages. . . .[1]

> Every individual . . . neither intends to promote the public interest, nor knows how much he is promoting it. . . . [H]e intends only his own security; and by directing that industry in such a manner as its produce may be of the greatest value, he intends only his own gain, and he is in this, as in many other cases, led by an invisible hand to promote an end which was no part of his intention.[2]

Competition turns self-interest into something that benefits all. However, if there is no serious competition, self-interested actions are not constrained by market forces. In that case, where do the limitations on self-serving conduct come from?

In his writings, Adam Smith sometimes expressed an optimistic view of humanity in which people act in the self-interest of others. Our empathy for others, or "sympathy" as he puts it, results in other-regarding conduct. Smith wrote that we take actions that benefit others even when it is against our own self-interest. I wish this were true as a general proposition. However,

---

[1] 1 ADAM SMITH, THE WEALTH OF NATIONS 15 (Edwin Cannan ed., Modern Library 1994) (1776); 1 ADAM SMITH, THE WEALTH OF NATIONS 26–27 (Collier 1902).

[2] *Id.* bk. 4, at 483–84.

Rethinking Market Regulation. John N. Drobak, Oxford University Press. © Oxford University Press 2021.
DOI: 10.1093/oso/9780197578957.003.0007

the history of humankind is a history of people trying to enrich themselves or to gain power at the expense of others. After all, greed is one of the seven deadly sins. For some people, greed has the unusual characteristic of being insatiable.

Becoming wealthy makes some people want to become even wealthier, rather than satisfying their financial goals. The more money they have, the more money they want. Many wealthy people measure their personal worth by their financial worth. "Among the rarefied group of the extreme rich, social status depends on net worth."[3] They associate and compete with other wealthy people, measuring their worth relative to their wealthy friends. To some of these people, money becomes addictive. This is a self-centered and selfish view of the world. All the major religions emphasize the need to help others, to adhere to the Golden Rule as doing unto others as you would have them do unto you. Sadly, the affirmation against greed seems to be a thing of the past for too many today. A good number of people view anything that makes shareholders and managers richer and richer, even at the expense of others, as desirable.

Investors are bold in their quest for higher returns these days. Corporate raiders and private equity firms are famous for buying companies and doing all they can to squeeze wealth out of them, including dismantling them, selling off divisions, and laying off workers, actions that seem not to trouble many people. There are also investors with large amounts of stock, like hedge funds and pension funds, who wield considerable clout with management. Many of them push for high returns with no consideration of how that may harm workers. This is also true for activist investors who constantly argue for higher returns.[4]

The rich have been popularized in the media for what seems forever. I think that today's acceptance of increasing shareholder returns at the expense of harm to others has its roots in the era of the junk bond euphoria of the 1980s, an era of "greed is good . . . of yellow ties, nigiri rolls and designer expresso machines that has come to symbolize gilded excess in popular

---

[3] Alex Williams, *Why Don't Rich People Just Stop Working?*, N.Y. TIMES (Oct. 17, 2019), https://www.nytimes.com/2019/10/17/style/rich-people-things.html [https://perma.cc/VPQ8-KFUZ] (quoting Edward Wolff, an economist who studies wealth).

[4] Julie Creswell & Michael J. de la Merced, *Struggles at Procter & Gamble Draw Scrutiny of Nelson Peltz*, N.Y. TIMES (July 17, 2017), https://www.nytimes.com/2017/07/17/business/dealbook/procter-gamble-nelson-peltz-trian.html [https://perma.cc/J8HP-5JLT]; Stephanie Strom, *Shareholders Demand More Drastic Shifts at Nestlé*, N.Y. TIMES (June 26, 2017), https://www.nytimes.com/2017/06/26/business/nestle-activist-investor.html [https://perma.cc/LE8X-VUDN].

imagination."[5] That was a time when the media heavily publicized the wealth of the traders. It became apparent that investment bankers could become enormously wealthy. Business school graduates wanted jobs on Wall Street rather than in other sectors of business. This was not only for the money but also because those jobs were viewed as more prestigious than running a factory. When mathematics became a tool to devise new investment vehicles, "quants" became famous in books and movies.

Another example of glorified wealth is the enormous growth of CEO and other upper-management salaries. In the 1960s, the ratio of the salary of the CEO to the average worker was about twenty to one. In 2017, it was seventy to one; by 2019, the salaries of some CEOs were more than 1,000 times the median employee pay. For example, the compensation of Disney's CEO in 2019 was $65 million, which was 1,424 times the wages of the median Disney worker.[6] Abigail Disney, the granddaughter of Walt Disney, the company's founder, called that compensation "insane."[7] Relying on the pay ratio filings required by the 2010 Dodd-Frank banking law, one commentator pointed out:

A Walmart employee earning the company's median salary of $19,177 would have to work for more than a thousand years to earn the $22.2 million that Doug McMillion, the company's chief executive, was awarded in 2017.

At Nation Entertainment, the concert and ticketing company, an employee earning the median pay of $24,406 would need to work for 2,893 years to earn the $70.6 million that its chief executive, Michael Rapino, made last year.

And at Time Warner, where the median compensation is a relatively handsome $75,217, an employee earning that much would still need to work for 651 years to earn the $49 million that Jeffrey Bewkes, the chief executive, earned in the past 12 months.[8]

---

[5] Williams, *supra* note 3.

[6] Bill Saporito, Opinion, *C.E.O. Pay, America's Economic "Miracle,"* N.Y. TIMES (May 17, 2019), https://www.nytimes.com/2019/05/17/opinion/ceo-pay-raises.html   [https://perma.cc/TBJ7-NUYN].

[7] Brooks Barnes, *Disney Heiress Escalates Attack on Company's Pay Practices*, N.Y. TIMES (Apr. 23, 2019), https://www.nytimes.com/2019/04/23/business/media/disney-heiress-attacks-pay-practices.html [https://perma.cc/B6XT-Q4CV].

[8] David Gelles, *Want to Make Money Like a C.E.O.? Work for 275 Years*, N.Y. TIMES (May 25, 2018), https://www.nytimes.com/2018/05/25/business/highest-paid-ceos-2017.html   [https://perma.cc/2CM8-VAZE].

In addition, the financial compensation of senior management does not reflect the perks they often receive, like the use of corporate jets for personal purposes.[9]

There are other factors that reinforce the desire to maximize corporate profits. CEOs, other corporate officers, and financiers are competitive people, who often validate their actions by the profits they achieve for their firms. They are taught in business schools that their job is to maximize returns. One commentator, an MIT professor who researches the relationship between neuroscience and economics, speculates that the corporate culture of the early twenty-first century created an environment that might have persistently compelled CEOs to earn more and more money for themselves and their companies.[10] Another business commentator wrote:

> "Socialist" is the label you get branded with if you suggest that the senior managers and owners of America's corporations should share more of their vast wealth with the employees who create it. This view of capitalism is that it is a sort of Lord-Of-The-Flies economic system in which the only consideration should be "every man for himself." In this style of capitalism, leaders do not manage teams and organizations in a way that creates value for everyone—customers, shareholders, and employees. Rather, in this view of capitalism, a handful of winners extract as much value as they can from hapless losers who don't have the skills, knowledge, or time necessary to "demand a raise" or "go get a better job."[11]

The media reinforces the importance of shareholder returns with its constant reporting of movements of the stock market. If the Dow goes down today, things are bad, but if it goes up a bit, the world is better off. No one asks whether a firm's stock has gained because it has become more "efficient" through layoffs. It is easy for the media to constantly report stock prices because they change every day. That provides enough information

---

[9] Tim McLaughlin, *Off the Radar: U.S. CEOs' Jet Perks Add Millions to Corporate Tax Bills*, REUTERS (Dec. 2, 2019), https://www.reuters.com/article/us-usa-taxes-jets-insight/off-the-radar-u-s-ceos-jet-perks-add-millions-to-corporate-tax-bills-idUSKBN1Y6131 [https://perma.cc/ZV4C-A9NK].

[10] Stuart Fox, *What Causes Corporate Greed?*, LIVESCIENCE (Apr. 30, 2010), https://www.livescience.com/6394-corporate-greed.html [https://perma.cc/G2TA-CUUT] (quoting Andrew Lo).

[11] Henry Blodget, *This One Tweet Reveals What's Wrong with American Business Culture and the Economy*, BUS. INSIDER (July 31, 2013), https://www.businessinsider.com/business-and-the-economy-2013-7 [https://perma.cc/5M48-ATYK].

to sustain television programs devoted to the stock market. Some television stations even celebrate the opening of the stock market by showing the excitement when different groups ring the opening bell each day. No one rings a bell when a union negotiates higher wages. Perhaps if wage rate or layoff statistics changed every minute, they might be tracked as much as stock prices. As a result, the media constantly publicizes what happens to stock prices, giving importance to that, but not to wages or job losses.[12]

Another problem stems from the required reporting of public corporations being limited to financial matters. Under the view that we signal what is important by what we measure, a number of corporate law scholars have called for an expansion of the reporting requirements of corporations. Kent Greenfield is typical of this view:

> Even though a company's narrow-gauged financial reports are often popularly cited as a measure of the company's worth, they do not, of course, come close to reporting a company's true value. Instead, companies should be measured on more than their finances, and because externalities count, we should count them, too. Moreover because external benefits count, we should try to count them as well. At present, company financial reports do not indicate the value of the company to its workers or to the communities in which it does business. . . . Because public policy requires corporations to report only on finances, corporate decision makers will accordingly make decisions as if the financial aspect of the company is their only concern. But if public policy required corporations to make a more extensive accounting of their activities, corporate decision makers would likely take a broader view of their responsibilities. But as the structure stands, corporate decision makers are urged to focus only on shareholder return, so inevitably they will continue to make decisions different from ones they would make if they were forced to take account of broader goals and measures.[13]

---

[12] David Leonhardt, Opinion, *We're Measuring the Economy All Wrong*, N.Y. TIMES (Sept. 14, 2018), https://www.nytimes.com/2018/09/14/opinion/columnists/great-recession-economy-gdp.html [https://perma.cc/2S2M-XJBY] ("When television commentators drone on about the Dow, they're not talking about a good measure of most people's wealth.").

[13] KENT GREENFIELD, THE FAILURE OF CORPORATE LAW: FUNDAMENTAL FLAWS AND PROGRESSIVE POSSIBILITIES 129 (2006).

II. Harm to Workers

The countries in Europe balance the interests of labor and shareholders much better than we do in the United States. As explained in the previous chapter, cultural differences between the European Union and the United States are an important cause of that. There is a strain of individualism in the United States not present in Europe. Our myths tell stories of individuals who succeeded on their own, like the lone cowboy who cleans up a town or the Horatio Alger story of the person who pulls himself up by the bootstraps to success. I think this individualism manifests itself in the prevalent desire for gun ownership, showing a desire to provide one's own protection rather than relying on the government. A lack of willingness to protect workers is consistent with this sense of individualism: workers should be able to protect themselves and so do not need the protection of the government.

A. Disparity of Income and Wealth

Just as the culture toward labor needs to be changed, the public perception of the legitimization of greed needs to be changed because it leads to an acceptance of serious harm to other people. An acceptance of shareholder and management primacy affects how U.S. workers are treated even when they do not lose their jobs. According to the Organisation for Economic Co-operation and Development, the research group for the advanced industrialized nations, the United States suffers the highest incidence of low pay for workers among the member nations.[14] A quarter of workers earn less than two-thirds of the median wage.[15] In addition, workers who start with low wages more often maintain them for a long time because mobility has been declining.[16]

Economists who study mobility have pointed out that upward mobility in the United States has been declining for decades:

Absolute mobility declined starkly across birth cohorts: On average, 92% of children born in 1940 grew up to earn more than their parents. In contrast,

---

[14] *Wage Levels (Indicator)*, ORG. ECON. COOPERATION & DEV. (2020), https://data.oecd.org/earnwage/wage-levels.htm [https://perma.cc/WDU4-4YHX].

[15] *Id.*

[16] Eduardo Porter, *Reviving the Working Class without Building Walls*, N.Y. TIMES (Mar. 8, 2016), https://www.nytimes.com/2016/03/09/business/economy/a-few-solutions-to-the-working-class-revolt.html [https://perma.cc/K33N-Q39R].

only 50% of children born in 1984 grew up to earn more than their parents. The downward trend in absolute mobility was especially sharp between the 1940 and 1964 cohorts. The decline paused for children born in the late 1960s and early 1970s, whose incomes at age 30 were measured in the midst of the economic boom of the late 1990s. Absolute mobility then continued to fall steadily in the remaining birth cohorts.[17]

The people in the 1964 cohort, which experienced a sharp decline in mobility, would have been at a prime working age when the mergers and outsourcing began to take a toll on labor. Without a realistic prospect at upward mobility, there is little left of the American Dream.

The increasing disparity in wealth in the United States is partially a consequence of the lack of competition described in Chapter 3. One economic study of the current state of the economy reached these conclusions:

> The increase in market power also has implications for income inequality. With higher pure profits, workers receive a lower share of output and capitalists a higher share. Since individuals with higher incomes receive a larger percentage of their income as capital income, and the poorest individuals generally do not hold financial assets, this mechanism will tend to increase income inequality. There is also a potential interaction of inequality with changes in labor bargaining power. Although it is unclear that the overall level of labor bargaining power has decreased, there is some evidence that with the fall of unionization and the rise of outsourcing the bargaining power of the poorest workers has decreased. Meanwhile, the bargaining power of the highest educated superstars and CEOs may have increased. If CEOs are taking a larger portion of the profits and workers a smaller portion, this would also tend to increase income inequality. An increase in monopoly rents also has implications for wealth inequality. We have seen how an increase in pure profits leads to a boom in stock prices, since equities hold the residual rights to corporate profits. Since those with the highest level of wealth tend to hold a greater fraction in equities, and those with lower wealth tend to hold a greater portion in housing, an increase in monopoly rents would tend to increase wealth inequality.[18]

[17] Raj Chetty et al., *The Fading American Dream: Trends in Absolute Income Mobility since 1940*, 356 SCIENCE 398, 401 (2017).

[18] Gauti B. Eggertsson et al., *Kaldor and Piketty's Facts: The Rise of Monopoly Power in the United States* 40 (Nat'l Bureau of Econ. Research, Working Paper No. 24,287, 2018), http://www.nber.org/papers/w24287 [https://perma.cc/D3VT-BZE9].

According to Mark Rank, a professor of social work who studies income inequality, the economic well-being of the middle class has been stagnant. In 1973, the inflation-adjusted median income of men working full time was $54,030, while it was $51,640 in 2016, a decrease of about $2,400 in forty-three years.[19] The richest 1 percent have seen their share of national income roughly double from 11 percent in 1980 to 20 percent in 2014. Among the developed countries, only Russia has seen a larger increase, from 3 percent to 20 percent in that same span. For a comparison, both Britain and China have increased from 6 percent to 14 percent, while France increased from 8 percent to 11 percent.[20]

In addition to the disparity in income, the disparity in wealth in the United States has increased dramatically. In 2016, the top 1 percent of families owned 40 percent of all household wealth, while the next 9 percent owned an additional 39 percent. That left 21 percent of household wealth to be divided between the remaining 90 percent of the population.[21] Using another accepted measure of inequality, the Gini coefficient for the United States rose from 43 in 1992 to 49 in 2018.[22] The lower the number, the more equal the distribution. That coefficient ranks the United States as having greater inequality than all the countries in the European Union and Canada. For example, the United Kingdom has a coefficient of 32.4, Canada 32.1, and France 29.3.[23]

We could argue that workers indirectly benefit from the savings in labor cost through their stock ownership or investment in pension plans. However, many workers do not benefit from higher stock prices. Only about 50 percent of all workers in private industry participate in pension plans. The participation rate among the lower paid workers is significantly below average.[24]

---

[19] Patricia Cohen, *Bump in U.S. Incomes Doesn't Erase 50 Years of Pain*, N.Y. TIMES (Sept. 16, 2017), https://www.nytimes.com/2017/09/16/business/economy/bump-in-us-incomes-doesnt-erase-50-years-of-pain.html [https://perma.cc/FQL4-UC5X].

[20] Jonathan Rothwell, *Myths of the 1 Percent: What Puts People at the Top*, N.Y. TIMES: UPSHOT (Nov. 20, 2017), https://www.nytimes.com/2017/11/17/upshot/income-inequality-united-states.html [https://perma.cc/NM9H-GV3N].

[21] Christopher Ingraham, *Household Net Worth Falls by Largest Amount since the Great Recession, New Fed Data Shows*, WASH. POST (Mar. 7, 2019), https://www.washingtonpost.com/us-policy/2019/03/07/household-net-worth-falls-by-largest-amount-since-great-recession-new-fed-data-show/ [https://perma.cc/Y874-L2XA].

[22] Erin Duffin, *U.S. Household Income Distribution from 1990 to 2018 (by Gini-Coefficient)*, STATISTA (Sept. 24, 2019), https://www.statista.com/statistics/219643/gini-coefficient-for-us-individuals-families-and-households/ [https://perma.cc/MXJ5-2LK3].

[23] *Gini Coefficient by Country 2020*, WORLD POPULATION REV. (Feb. 17, 2020), http://worldpopulationreview.com/countries/gini-coefficient-by-country/ [https://perma.cc/7D5U-NA97].

[24] According to Labor Department statistics, only 49 percent of workers in private industry participated in pension plans in March 2016. The participation rate of the lowest 25 percent of wage earners was only 22 percent. This shrunk to 14 percent for the lowest 10 percent. In addition, 35 percent of

Laid-off workers' income from stock ownership comes nowhere near to making up for their lost wages.

We have ignored the harm to labor for a number of reasons. Part of the cause is the increase in size of manufacturing firms. When senior management shared the same campus as workers, many officers knew the workers firsthand. They knew their parents and their children. When workers were laid off, the managers saw the pain of the people who were affected. In many firms today, workers are just numbers on a spreadsheet to many managers, who do not see firsthand the personal consequences of their actions. The disregard of the damage done to workers may also have resulted from the belief that this was a normal consequence of a market economy, something we have to accept as part of our economic way of life. Europe has shown that the great loss of jobs is not inherent in a market economy. We can maintain our system of capitalism while being kinder to workers.

B. Unemployment Rates

Perhaps well-meaning people have overlooked the harm to workers because they never knew the magnitude of the problem. It is strange that the government has chosen not to record the actual job losses from mergers and outsourcing, which has resulted in conflicting estimates of the magnitude of the problem. However, it is clear now that the amount of job losses this century was greater than anything our country has seen since the Great Depression. Economic theory treats labor like other factors of production, with the assumption that unemployed workers will move to places where there are jobs. When economists theorized about the movement of unemployed labor, they surely never contemplated the magnitude of workers who lost their jobs this century. In addition, labor is nowhere near as mobile as other factors of production. The geographic mobility rate of workers is the lowest it has been since the U.S. Census Bureau started measuring mobility in 1948.[25] Unlike

---

U.S. stocks are foreign owned. Patricia Cohen, *A Tax Cut That Lifts the Economy? Opinions Are Split*, N.Y. TIMES (Nov. 2, 2017), https://www.nytimes.com/2017/11/02/business/economy/corporate-tax-economists.html [https://perma.cc/V6FF-JQLKs]. Ten percent of the population owns 84 percent of all the stock. Paul Krugman, Opinion, *Apple and the Fruits of Tax Cuts*, N.Y. TIMES (May 3, 2018), https://www.nytimes.com/2018/05/03/opinion/apple-tax-cuts.html [https://perma.cc/V62P-SBLL].

[25] Sabrina Tavernise, *Frozen in Place: Americans Are Moving at the Lowest Rate on Record*, N.Y. TIMES (Nov. 20, 2019), https://www.nytimes.com/2019/11/20/us/american-workers-moving-states-.html

other input factors, people have attachments to families and geographic regions. With a strong preference for a hometown and ties to families, many workers are not mobile. Plus many jobs themselves are not mobile. If firms in Silicon Valley need workers, they rarely open facilities in places in the Midwest where jobs are needed.

Perhaps some people may have found job losses acceptable out of a belief that they were temporary. In the aftermath of the Great Recession, the unemployment rate was near 10 percent, the worst since the Great Depression. By 2019, it had fallen to about 3.6 percent, the lowest unemployment rate in fifty years.[26] This might make it seem that the job losses from mergers and outsourcing are only a temporary phenomenon. However, that low unemployment rate is misleading. The calculation of the unemployment rate is based on the number of unemployed workers who say they are looking for jobs. It excludes people who are not actively looking for work.[27] According to the Bureau of Labor Statistics, about 37 percent of people who could work are unemployed and not seeking work, a percentage that has been relatively steady since 2013.[28] Based on this labor market participation rate, the Economic Policy Institute estimates that 1.5 million workers were not counted in the unemployment rate in June 2017. The vast majority of the missing workers are between forty-five and sixty-four years old.[29] According to Gregory Mankiw, only 4 percent of prime-age men were not working or looking for work in 1950, while that number grew to 11 percent in 2018.[30] I suspect that these missing workers include a significant share of manufacturing workers who lost jobs from mergers or outsourcing.

[https://perma.cc/M9ZB-YX6W]; David Ihrke, *United States Mover Rate at a New Record Low*, CENSUS BLOGS (Jan. 23, 2017), https://www.census.gov/newsroom/blogs/random-samplings/2017/01/mover-rate.html [https://perma.cc/C5NN-4JGS].

[26] *US Unemployment Rate by Year*, MULTPL, https://www.multpl.com/unemployment/table/by-year [https://perma.cc/R7KY-BUWP].

[27] *Labor Force Statistics from the Current Population Survey*, U.S. BUREAU OF LABOR STATISTICS (Feb. 21, 2020), https://www.bls.gov/web/empsit/cpseea01.htm [https://perma.cc/SV2K-G47A].

[28] *Labor Force Statistics from the Current Population Survey*, U.S. BUREAU OF LABOR STATISTICS, https://data.bls.gov/timeseries/LNS11300000 [https://perma.cc/5TLF-2LBW]; Jim Chappelow, *Labor Force Participation Rate*, INVESTOPEDIA (Jan. 29, 2020), https://www.investopedia.com/terms/p/participationrate.asp [https://perma.cc/65JG-VBWN].

[29] ECON. POLICY INST., MISSING WORKERS: THE MISSING PART OF THE UNEMPLOYMENT STORY (July 7, 2017), https://www.epi.org/publication/missing-workers/ [https://perma.cc/8GRQ-VHG6].

[30] N. Gregory Mankiw, *Why Aren't More Men Working?*, N.Y. TIMES (June 15, 2018), https://www.nytimes.com/2018/06/15/business/men-unemployment-jobs.html [https://perma.cc/9HTU-EMJC].

In addition to laid-off workers who are not reflected in the unemployment rate, many laid-off workers re-entered the workforce in jobs with much lower pay and poorer benefits. Studies show that many displaced workers remain persistently underemployed and underpaid years after their job separation.[31] In 2014, the National Employment Law Project found that most of the job gains have been in the low-wage sector, which includes food services, retail, and administrative and support services. There has also been a significant increase in part-time jobs, which often come without health insurance and other benefits. The weakest growth in jobs has been in manufacturing, which still has not recovered all the jobs lost this century.[32] Workers formerly earning a middle-class wage have been forced to accept low-paying or minimum-wage jobs. For example, in St. Louis, more workers in 2008 "toiled in factories than in bars and restaurants. A decade later, waiters and bartenders outnumber manufacturing workers."[33] Over that period, the job growth has been in business services, healthcare, and day-care centers. An economist at the St. Louis Federal Reserve Bank saw strong gains at the top of the income distribution and modest gains at the bottom. "There is a disparity in gains," he said. "In the middle is where we see most of the struggles."[34] Similarly, a study of workers who lost their jobs when an auto factory closed in Janesville, Wisconsin, showed that the absence of other manufacturing opportunities in the region resulted in people taking jobs in hospitals, jails, and distribution centers.[35] The author of that study wrote:

> So, seven and a half years after the Great Recession technically ended, how is Janesville faring? Surprisingly well, or not, depending on how you measure.

[31] Benjamin G. Hyman, *Can Displaced Labor Be Retrained? Evidence from Quasi-Random Assignment to Trade Adjustment Assistance* 1 (Nov. 5, 2018), https://papers.ssrn.com/sol3/papers.cfm?abstract_id=3155386 [https://perma.cc/48RY-XLP6].

[32] ANNETTE BERNHARDT & MIKE EVANGELIST, NAT'L EMP. LAW PROJECT, THE LOW-WAGE RECOVERY: INDUSTRY EMPLOYMENT AND WAGES FOUR YEARS INTO THE RECOVERY (Apr. 2014), https://s27147.pcdn.co/wp-content/uploads/2015/03/Low-Wage-Recovery-Industry-Employment-Wages-2014-Report.pdf [https://perma.cc/2K6H-KRYU]; Michael Collins, *Where Have All the Good Paying Jobs Gone?*, INDUSTRY WK. (Mar. 4, 2016), https://www.industryweek.com/the-economy/public-policy/article/22007276/where-have-all-the-good-paying-jobs-gone [https://perma.cc/Y6MN-LLEF].

[33] David Nicklaus, *A Decade Later, the Recession Has Caused Big Changes in St. Louis*, ST. LOUIS POST-DISPATCH (Dec. 24, 2017), https://www.stltoday.com/business/columns/david-nicklaus/a-decade-later-the-recession-has-caused-big-changes-in/article_c6be3164-49a1-50fd-b24b-23b8607b3962.html [https://perma.cc/PG2T-543X].

[34] *Id.*

[35] AMY GOLDSTEIN, JANESVILLE: AN AMERICAN STORY 309 (2017) (survey of effects from losing job).

By the most recent count, unemployment in Rock County has slid remarkably to just under 4 percent, the lowest level since the start of the century. As many people are working now as just before the Great Recession; distribution centers have arrived. Beloit plants such as ones for Frito-Lay and Hormel Foods have been hiring, and some people are working further away. Good news. But not everyone who now has a job is earning enough for the comfortable life they expected. Real wages in the county have fallen since the assembly plant shut down. And while factory jobs have been appearing lately in some parts of the United States, Rock County is not one of those places. The county had about 9,500 manufacturing jobs in 2015—almost one forth fewer than in 2008 and nearly 45 percent fewer than in 1990.[36]

C. Retraining

Perhaps some people have overlooked the harm to workers out of a belief that retraining will solve the problem. The one long-standing federal program designed to help workers harmed by outsourcing is the Trade Adjustment Assistance (TAA) program, which began in 1962 while John F. Kennedy was president.[37] The program was designed to provide assistance to workers "who lose their jobs or whose hours of work and wages are reduced as a result of increased imports or shift in production out of the United States."[38] The program provides financial support for up to three years of retraining, job counseling, and increased unemployment insurance.[39] It is essential that the government try to help displaced workers, but it no easy task to retrain low-skilled workers who are middle-aged or older, especially if the workers need to learn new and different skills after years of mechanical work in factories. A good number of these displaced workers are decades away from the end of their formal education. Most have no college degree; some, not even a high school degree. An even greater hurdle comes from the lack of jobs that pay as much as the ones that were lost. It is absurd to expect a factory worker to be satisfied with a job as an orderly in a hospital at half his former salary or working two part-time jobs without insurance benefits. Again, a

---

[36] Id. at 292–93.
[37] Trade Expansion Act of 1962, tit. III, Pub. L. 87-794, 76 Stat. 872, 883.
[38] Hyman, supra note 31, at 7.
[39] Id. at 7–8.

reluctance to move to where a new job would be available hinders the success of retraining.

There are few studies of the effectiveness of the TAA program. In May 2017, a literature review of studies made between 1981 through 2012 reached these conclusions: two studies "found that workers under TAA experienced lower reemployment rates and greater earnings losses 36 months after they lost their jobs."[40] Another study determined that there was little evidence that TAA improved wages after three years of displacement.[41] A fourth study "found that TAA workers had lower wages compared with workers with similar demographic characteristics who did not receive TAA benefits [although] they were significantly more likely to find reemployment."[42] Another study concluded that "the program had largely neutral effects on labor force participation, employment, and earnings at four years."[43]

These kinds of studies face difficult methodological hurdles in matching workers who went through training with those who did not. The two categories of workers have different demographic and other personal characteristics; plus the features of the jobs often differ. In 2018, another study developed a new methodology to try to better overcome these difficulties and found more positive results:

> I find evidence of large initial returns to TAA. Workers inferred to take up benefits forego roughly $10,000 in income while training, yet ten years later have approximately $50,000 higher cumulative earnings relative to all-the-equal workers that do not retrain. I estimate that 33% of these returns are driven by higher wages—a sizeable share which suggests that TAA-trained workers are not only compensated through greater labor force participation or higher priority in job queues. Rather TAA workers also appear to

[40] JOANNE GUTH & JEAN LEE, U.S. INT'L TRADE COMM'N, EVALUATIONS OF THE TRADE ADJUSTMENT ASSISTANCE PROGRAM FOR WORKERS: A LITERATURE REVIEW (2017), https://www.usitc.gov/publications/332/executive_briefings/ebot_taaevaluationsguthlee.pdf [https://perma.cc/GL6V-S8DB] (citing WALTER CORSON ET AL., INTERNATIONAL TRADE AND WORKER DISLOCATION: EVALUATION OF THE TRADE ADJUSTMENT ASSISTANCE PROGRAM (1993)).

[41] GUTH & LEE, supra note 40; Leah E. Marcal, Does Trade Adjustment Assistance Help Trade-Displaced Workers?, 19 CONTEMP. ECON. POL'Y 59 (2001).

[42] GUTH & LEE, supra note 40; Kara M. Reynolds & John S. Palatucci, Does Trade Adjustment Assistance Make a Difference?, 30 CONTEMP. ECON. POL'Y 43 (2012).

[43] GUTH & LEE, supra note 40; RONALD D'AMICO & PETER Z. SCHOCHET, Mathematica Pol'y Research, The Evaluation of the Trade Adjustment Assistance Program: A Synthesis of Major Findings (2012), https://www.mathematica.org/our-publications-and-findings/publications/the-evaluation-of-the-trade-adjustment-assistance-program-a-synthesis-of-major-findings [https://perma.cc/G2KF-BSJB].

be paid a premium for their newly acquired human capital. But these large relative gains also decay over time, such that annual incomes among TAA and non-TAA workers fully converge after ten years.[44]

Another positive finding of the study is that TAA-trained workers are more willing to move to find a new job.[45]

The Janesville study included an examination of the effectiveness of the retraining programs for the autoworkers laid off in Janesville. The results raised questions about the worth of the retraining programs for displaced workers in the local community college, which specialized in vocational education. The study found that workers who had retraining were less likely to have a job after they retrained than those who did not undergo retraining. For the laid-off workers who found steady work, a higher proportion had no retraining. "Worse still, more of those who retrained were not earning any money at all."[46] Displaced workers who went to school earned less afterward than those who did not. Age was a relevant factor—older students had a bigger drop in earnings. The study also examined a special program at the college designed to teach skills in occupations that seemed the most promising for new jobs. These included associate degree programs for information technology and clinical laboratory technicians and shorter certificate programs in certified nursing assistance, welding, and business. The students in those programs had no better success in finding jobs than the students in other programs.[47]

It would be comforting to know that the TAA program ameliorated the economic problems caused displaced workers. Although there is no reason to cease the retraining programs, they appear not to help anywhere as much as we would wish. One cause of the lack of success is the lack of employment available to laid-off workers, whether or not they are retrained. A similar problem occurred after the end of the Cold War, when Murray Weidenbaum, who was the first Economic Adviser for President Ronald Reagan, had hoped that firms that produced swords would be able to convert to producing plowshares and thereby keep their workers employed. However, there was no demand for the nondefense products to be produced by these defense firms,

---

[44] Hyman, *supra* note 31, at 2.
[45] *Id.* at 3.
[46] GOLDSTEIN, *supra* note 35, at 314.
[47] *Id.* at 311–16.

and converting production was not easy in practice.[48] Frustrated at this process, Weidenbaum told this author that the best that could be done was to make severance payments to the laid-off workers and realize that they would have a very difficult time finding alternative employment.

Losing an income that can support a middle-class lifestyle is only the beginning of the harm caused by the loss of jobs. Most people need work to provide fulfillment to their lives. It is satisfying if you believe in your company and believe that what you do benefits society. In addition, many people need to have a reason to get up in the morning. Even for jobs that are repetitive, many workers find enjoyment in the camaraderie of their fellow workers. Oren Cass has explained the broad social benefits of having a job:

> For the individual, work imposes structure on each day and on life in general. It offers the mundane but essential disciplines of timeliness and reliability and hygiene as well as the more complex socialization of collaboration and paying attention to others. It requires people to interact and forges shared experiences and bonds. It promotes goal setting and long-term planning. True, other pursuits can provide these kinds of benefits—for example, raising children, keeping a home, or volunteering in the community. But sleeping, couch-surfing, or, pace *Reason*, playing video games does not. And for out-of-work men in particular, such idle activities tend to fill up their time.
>
> Work (again, especially for men) helps establish and preserve families. Where fewer men work, fewer marriages form. Unemployment doubles the risk of divorce, and male joblessness appears the primary culprit. These outcomes likely result from the damage to both economic prospects and individual well-being associated with being out of work. . . .
>
> Work is both a nexus of community and a prerequisite for it. Work relationships represent a crucial source of social capital, establishing a base from which people can engage in the boarder community—whether it is playing on a softball team, organizing a fund-raising drive, or hosting a field trip for the local preschool. This dimension of employment is especially relevant outside of urban centers; in such settings, the workplace can become a central meeting point. Communities that lack work, by contrast,

---

[48] Murray Weidenbaum, *Conversion and the Future Direction of Defence Contractors, in* ECONOMIC ISSUES OF DISARMAMENT: CONTRIBUTIONS FROM PEACE ECONOMICS AND PEACE SCIENCE 97 (Jurgen Brauer & Manas Chatterji eds., 1993).

suffer maladies that degrade social capital and lead to persistent poverty. Crime and addiction increase, their participants in turn becoming ever less employable; investments in housing and communal assets decline; a downward spiral is set in motion.[49]

Without a job, self-esteem declines and a sense of helplessness increases, leading for many to too much television, drug use, and depression.[50] These are people who not only lost their income but also a purpose in life.

III. The Experience of Two Towns

Unemployed workers are not the only ones who suffer. The suffering extends to their families and their communities. Two books poignantly describe the suffering caused by massive layoffs in Janesville, Wisconsin (mentioned earlier), and in Lancaster, Ohio. A General Motors assembly plant closed in Janesville, while investment bankers rolled over the Anchor Hocking glass company in Lancaster for more than twenty years. Neither plant closing was the direct result of mergers or outsourcing. However, what those towns experienced is an example of what towns affected by large job losses from mergers and outsourcing experience. Both towns declined, with the massive layoffs followed by increased poverty, drug use, and crime. In both cases, the unions were powerless to stop the layoffs.

In 2008, before the Great Recession exploded, General Motors decided to help its ailing financial difficulties by eliminating 30,000 jobs. When GM announced that it was closing the Janesville plant as part of its restructuring, government leaders tried to get GM to choose Janesville for the production of the next-generation of subcompact cars. However, competition for that production led to a bidding war. Ultimately, GM chose to produce the new car in Orion Township, Michigan, rather than in Janesville. Orion had offered GM $779 million in tax breaks, while Janesville had only offered $195 million in incentives. In addition, the union at the Orion plant agreed that workers could be paid $14 per hour, half of the standard wage of $28 per

---

[49] OREN CASS, THE ONCE AND FUTURE WORKER: A VISION FOR THE RENEWAL OF WORK IN AMERICA 48–50 (2018).

[50] Id. at 31; BRIAN ALEXANDER, GLASS HOUSE: THE 1% ECONOMY AND THE SHATTERING OF THE ALL-AMERICAN TOWN 199 (2017); GOLDSTEIN, supra note 35, at 309; Alan B. Krueger, Where Have All the Workers Gone? An Inquiry into the Decline of the US Labor Force Participation Rate, 2017 BROOKINGS PAPERS ON ECON. ACTIVITY 1 (2017).

hour, while engines would be made in Mexico and many parts in Korea.[51] Even though the Janesville plant was GM's oldest, beginning production in 1923, GM closed the plant in December 2008, thereby eliminating about 7,000 jobs, with another 2,000 lost in local companies that supplied parts and services to the GM plant.

Compounding the workers' problems, GM closed the plant right after the financial and real estate markets crashed in the Great Recession. Janesville saw many foreclosures and a spurt in the growth of payday lenders. Many in the middle class dropped into poverty, which hurt the poor since they now had to compete with laid-off workers for jobs like those at Walmart and McDonald's. The number of homeless children in Janesville increased con- siderably.[52] Some people fell into depression; drug use and addiction grew. Even the number of suicides increased.[53] Displaced workers swamped the local community college for retraining, but as explained earlier, that was not helpful for most of the workers. Many people took jobs at much lower wages, while others were in and out of jobs, without steady income or health insur- ance. As is typical with many massive layoffs, a group of workers used their transfer rights to work in GM plants. These "GM gypsies" took jobs in Kansas City, Missouri, Fort Wayne, Indiana, and Arlington, Texas.[54] Many of their families did not want to leave Janesville, so these workers headed home as soon as their Friday shift ended to spend the weekend with their families. To give you a sense of their lack of attachment to their new homes, some workers keep the clocks in their cars on Janesville time instead of local time.[55]

Not surprisingly, a backlash against unions developed. Although Janesville was an old union town, the loss of so many union jobs from the shuttered factory and supplier companies resulted in twice as many former union members as active members. Opinion was divided over whether unions helped the economy or hurt it.[56] There was less division over the disdain for the union for public employees, however. "In a community in which so many had lost so much, some people were starting to regard public workers, including the city's teachers, as fat cats by comparison."[57] They were "over- paid and overindulged at taxpayer expense."[58] Economic problems were

---

[51] GOLDSTEIN, *supra* note 35, at 62–69.
[52] *Id.* at 131.
[53] *Id.* at 231 ff.
[54] *Id.* at 105.
[55] *Id.* at 307.
[56] *Id.* at 158.
[57] *Id.*
[58] *Id.*

changing political views in Janesville. Throughout the upper Midwest, displaced workers, their families, and supporters were part of the movement that elected President Trump.

In Lancaster, Ohio, there was not a complete shutdown of the entire plant, but there were still massive layoffs. In the late 1960s, Anchor Hocking was the world's largest manufacturer of tableware and the second largest of glass containers, employing 5,000 workers in a town of about 29,000 residents. By 2017, it employed only about 1,000 people in Lancaster. Beginning with Carl Ichan in 1982, who tried to loot the company, a series of private equity firms bought and sold the company, causing it to incur massive debts and go through two bankruptcies. They closed some of the factories, cut staff, reduced wages, got more wage concessions, cut back on pensions and medical insurance, and deferred maintenance of the plant for years. Summing up his study of the economic decline in Lancaster, Brian Alexander wrote:

> For decades, politicians—Republicans and Democrats both—and pundits had been spewing empty platitudes of praise for the "the heartland," "real America," and "small-town values." Then, with shameless hypocrisy, they supported the very policies that helped destroy thriving small towns.
>
> Corporate elites said they needed free-market agreements, so they got them. Manufacturers said they needed tax breaks and public-money incentives in order to keep their plants operating in the United States, so they got them. Banks and financiers needed looser regulations, so they got them. Employers said they needed weaker unions—or no unions at all—so they got them. Private equity firms said they needed carried interest and secrecy, so they got them. Everybody, including Lancastrians themselves, said they needed lower taxes, so they got them. What did Lancaster and a hundred other towns like it get? Job losses, slashed wages, poor civic leadership, social dysfunction, drugs.[59]

It is a tragedy that we as a society tolerate so much harm to hundreds of thousands, perhaps millions, of workers. And for what reason? If the primary beneficiaries are owners of capital and managers, I think it speaks poorly of our society. I know that there must be some benefit to consumers from some mergers and from outsourcing. The price of goods should be lower, but we

---

[59] ALEXANDER, *supra* note 50, at 291.

have to guess at the aggregate gain to consumers. I am skeptical that the gain is anywhere enough to justify this kind of harm.

I also know that many readers will remain skeptical of my conclusions. Part of that is the result of their fundamental beliefs about how our society works. The next chapter discusses how hard it is to change these deeply held beliefs.

8

Belief Systems and Confirmation Bias

We all see the world through slightly different glasses. In the latter stages of his long career, the Nobel laureate and economic historian Douglass C. North emphasized the importance of recognizing that we all have different belief systems, which change how we perceive things.[1] As a result of our upbringing, education, and life experiences, we are prone to find some things more believable than others.[2] As a result of different perspectives than mine, I am sure that some readers will remain skeptical of the conclusions in this book. Part of the reason for that is the underlying skepticism by many economists and a good portion of the public some about government regulation, which they see as always worse than the market.

For decades, Republican politicians have criticized the ineffectiveness of government.[3] They have claimed that we need to "get the fat out of the government." They have criticized taxation as just feeding a bloated government.[4] This message has hit home with many, fueling the skepticism about government regulation doing any good. In addition, we all have seen examples of ineffective government actions, whether it is at the federal, state, or local level. It is too easy to extrapolate from these instances to a general conclusion that government is ineffective. Polls of the public's perception of the government regularly show that this view of the government is part of the belief systems of many people in the United States.[5]

I have tried to show that competitive constraints are lacking in many markets, including in the market for low-skilled and semiskilled labor, and that government regulation of these markets is a desirable alternative.

---

[1] DOUGLASS C. NORTH, UNDERSTANDING THE PROCESS OF ECONOMIC CHANGE 2 (2005).

[2] Id. 48–64.

[3] DONALD T. CRITCHLOW, THE CONSERVATIVE ASCENDANCY: HOW THE GOP RIGHT MADE POLITICAL HISTORY (2007).

[4] Eric Cantor, A Year of Living Dangerously, in YOUNG GUNS: A NEW GENERATION OF CONSERVATIVE LEADERS 39, 51 (Eric Cantor et al. eds., 2010) (criticizing the stimulus as "a bloated grab bag of taxpayer-funded government gifts to special interests").

[5] Trust in Government, GALLUP, https://news.gallup.com/poll/5392/trust-government.aspx [https://perma.cc/CR2B-M4K4].

Rethinking Market Regulation. John N. Drobak, Oxford University Press. © Oxford University Press 2021.
DOI: 10.1093/oso/9780197578957.003.0008

However, it is an extremely difficult task to convince people who are locked into a contrary view of how the world works.

I. Underlying Fundamental Premises

Three fundamental propositions are important to understanding why people develop and retain beliefs: (1) it is often difficult to identify the "truth" of a claim, (2) the belief systems of individuals and society have a tremendous influence on the receptivity of new information, and (3) the "nonrational" character of human decision-making also affects the processing of new information. These three premises will be explained in order.

A. The Difficulty of Determining the Truth

Much of what people know is learned from other people. We begin to learn from our parents in infancy, we learn from our teachers, and we spend our lives learning from others. For the most part, we trust the people who teach us, so we believe them without any need for verification. Of course, there is knowledge gained directly from our senses. No one needs to teach us that the sun is in the sky every day, nor that gravity makes things fall down, not up. If need be, we can verify these beliefs by testing. However, most of us did not perform tests to be sure that these beliefs are true. We were taught that by our teachers, who probably also taught us that physical truths have been demonstrated experimentally. The same holds for historical facts. We believe that George Washington was the first president of the United States without needing to examine any historical documents. Not only did we learn this from our teachers, historical knowledge is part of the culture that is passed on from generation to generation. Everyone speaks as if these historical facts are true, and we also know that earlier generations believed them. We believe physical and historical truths firmly, even if a few outliers occasionally try to convince us otherwise.

There is another type of knowledge, however, that is not verifiable or clearly supported by historical record. Theories about how the world works fit into that category. Some theoretical explanations are debatable because our knowledge and processing abilities are limited. As Thráinn Eggertsson has explained,

Theories of social systems which explicitly recognize that actors live in a world of scare information confront three types of information issues: (i) scarce data and knowledge; (ii) the limited mental capacity of actors to absorb and process data and to make decisions; and (iii) the propensity of actors to economize on scarce data, limited knowledge, and limited mental capacity by making simple and inaccurate models of their environment. I refer to these three issues as incomplete data, incomplete processing, and incomplete models.[6]

There is another, just as serious, problem with the acceptance by the public of theoretical knowledge. Sometimes even theories supported by a strong consensus of experts nonetheless appear to many people to be only opinion. This type of knowledge is more susceptible to be changed by contrary opinion in the minds of some people notwithstanding what experts say. The disbelief in the theory of evolution or in global warming are but two examples of this.

Determining the truth has become more difficult over the past few years with the rise of "alternative facts" and false information on the internet.[7] When President Trump lied or embellished facts, many people believed him. One example was his constant claim that President Obama was not born in the United States, which made Obama legally ineligible to be president. This is a refutation of a historic fact, which should be relatively easy to determine. Likewise, when President Trump expressed a disbelief in global warming, people believed him. This is a refutation of a theory, which is harder to prove than a fact. Misinformation from government leaders is compounded by members of the media and websites that put forth false information as the truth. The fake news websites that proliferated during the 2016 presidential election are well-known examples of this. All of this makes the determination of the truth much more difficult for many.

B. Belief Systems

The world is too complex for people to rationally analyze every question that faces them. As a result, we create mental models of the world that simplify

---

[6] Thráinn Eggertsson, *The Old Theory of Economic Policy and the New Institutionalism*, 25 WORLD DEV. 1187, 1191 (1997).

[7] FAKE NEWS: UNDERSTANDING MEDIA AND MISINFORMATION IN THE DIGITAL AGE (Melissa Zimdars & Kembrew McLeod eds., 2020).

decisions for us, and we use heuristics and rules of thumb to help us derive answers to problems.[8] Eggertsson has pointed out that "[p]eople (scientists included) respond to complexity by creating simple mental constructs of their worlds. The models are incomplete, sometimes misleading, and actors are often not even aware of relevant information sets."[9] Moreover, people "are often unaware that they lack the necessary knowledge."[10]

What people know is the result of the inputs from our five senses, which is then sent to the brain for processing where our belief systems control how we analyze the inputs and make decisions. As Douglass North has explained:

> the world we . . . are trying to understand is a construction of the human mind. It has no independent existence outside the human mind; thus our understanding is unlike that in the physical sciences, which can employ reductionism to understand and expand comprehension of, the physical world. Physical scientists, when they seek a greater understanding of some puzzle in the physical world, can build from the fundamental unit of their science to explore the dimensions of the problem they seek to comprehend. The social sciences do not have anything comparable to genes, protons, neutrons, elements to build upon. The whole structure that makes up the foundation of human interaction is a construct of the human mind and has evolved over time in an incremental process. . . . It is essential to remember that the constructs humans create are a blend of "rational" beliefs and "non-rational" ones (superstitions, religions, myths, prejudices) that shape the choices that are made.[11]

Eggertsson has referred to belief systems as "people's subjective models of reality."[12] These belief systems develop from life experiences with a myriad of influences—from parents and family, peers, teachers, religious authorities, government leaders, public commentators, and so on. The shared belief systems of a society are passed on from generation to generation as part of the

---

[8] Thráinn Eggertsson, *Knowledge and the Theory of Institutional Change*, 5 J. INSTITUTIONAL ECON. 137, 147 (2009) ("An individual's social model contains a set of assumptions and relationships—theories—that he or she uses to interpret a complex environment.").

[9] *Id.* at 143.

[10] Thráinn Eggertsson, *Mapping Social Technologies in the Cultural Commons*, 95 CORNELL L. REV. 711, 713 (2009).

[11] North, *supra* note 1, at 83.

[12] THRÁINN EGGERTSSON, NORMS IN ECONOMICS: WITH SPECIAL REFERENCE TO ECONOMIC DEVELOPMENT 93 (1999); *see* Eggertsson, *Knowledge and the Theory of Institutional Change, supra* note 8, at 149 ("[S]ubjective models guide all types of actors.").

society's cultural heritage.[13] Our minds do not reproduce reality; rather, they attempt to interpret the very complex relationships in what are always theories. We may know all the facts and numbers possible about a particular set of events, but to order them and to explain them requires theory, and that theory, obviously, is a construction of the mind.

This does not mean that all results are subjective. Obviously, what we try to do is to test the theories we have against the evidence so that we can arrive at rough, very rough, estimates of the reliability of such theories. But it does mean that all the theories we have are subjective; they are just imperfect and incomplete.

Eggertsson has noted that "individuals with comparable experience and interests usually have faith in similar social models and social institutions: these models cluster."[14] This clustering of individual models leads to "[s]ocial groups shar[ing] symbols, models, and collective memories of historical events, such as ethnic strife, that people use for filtering data and interpreting current events."[15] As a result, a society's culture that is passed down to the next generation includes the shared mental models.

Individuals from different backgrounds will interpret the same evidence differently and in consequence make different choices. Individuals have different systems of beliefs that create different filters through which they perceive the world and its problems and also create different theories to explain the world and devise solutions for the problems. As Eggertsson has written, "mental models and expectations guide the organizations and households when they approach new rules and systems of enforcement."[16]

In any society, there are large variations in the belief systems among people.[17] As a result, some people see problems and solutions very differently than other people. For example, both private industry and the U.S. government contributed to the housing bubble that led to the Great Recession. The federal government tried to increase homeownership and so subsidized

[13] DOUGLASS C. NORTH, INSTITUTIONS, INSTITUTIONAL CHANGE AND ECONOMIC PERFORMANCE 37 (1990) (quoting ROBERT BOYD & PETER J. RICHERSON, CULTURE AND THE EVOLUTIONARY PROCESS 2 (1985)) ("Culture can be defined as the transmission from one generation to the next, via teaching and imitation, of knowledge, values and other factors that influence behavior.").

[14] THRÁINN EGGERTSSON, IMPERFECT INSTITUTIONS: POSSIBILITIES AND LIMITS OF REFORM 39 (2005).

[15] Id. at 95.

[16] Eggertsson, supra note 10, at 724; see id. at 727 ("[T]he final outcome of major social experiments depends on the content of mental models or theories at all levels, the evolution of these models, and how they are eventually coordinated.").

[17] EGGERTSSON, NORMS IN ECONOMICS, supra note 12, at 93.

housing through Fannie Mae and Freddie Mac. This led to people owning homes they could not afford. Concurrently, some private mortgage firms tried to get anyone possible to buy a house and obtain a mortgage, regardless of their financial abilities. Those mortgage firms bore no risk from risky mortgages and earned their fees just by processing the mortgages. Investment firms fueled the fire for mortgages because they needed them to back their derivative instruments. Without a doubt, both private industry and the federal government played major roles in creating the subprime mortgage crisis. Yet opponents of government blame the government and never mention private industry, and vice versa, others blame private industry and never acknowledge the government's role.

C. Nonrational Human Decision-Making

All of social science is based on the assumption that people act rationally, in a logical, unemotional fashion. This is true for all disciplines in social science, including both economics and law. Neoclassical price theory assumes that producers and consumers are rational actors, while the "reasonable person" in law is the rational cousin of the economic actor. As Eggertsson has explained, "rational expectations theory assumes that all actors share common beliefs, without explaining the origins of those beliefs and how they are shared; the problem of knowledge is assumed away."[18] Today, a large and growing body of scholarship exhibits a willingness to modify the rationality assumption by using cognitive science, behavioral psychology, and experimental economics.

That human decision-making is not as described by rational choice theory has relevance for understanding the transmission of information to people. There is every reason to believe that people are not open to receive new information and to update their knowledge in light of the new information. That computer-like conduct is too rational to be true. Add into the mix the difficulty of achieving agreement on theories and well-formed belief systems that are resistant to new information, and we should expect information to mean less than social science assumes. It is well established that all of us act with conformation bias. We are prone to accept as the gospel truth information that confirms our prior beliefs and reluctant to put much

---

[18] Eggertsson, *Knowledge and the Theory of Institutional Change*, *supra* note 8, at 141.

stock in information that is inconsistent with our beliefs.[19] There probably is a difference in the receptivity of information by laypeople and educated professionals, with professionals taught to be open to certain types of information, ideas, and arguments. Nonetheless, even policymakers are limited by their belief systems and nonrational behavior.

II. Economists' Faith in the Market

Economists are highly educated people who spend their lives thinking about the economic system. I think that, in general, the belief systems of economists center on an abiding preference for the unregulated or slightly regulated market over government regulation. This belief colors the way they view economic issues. Economists are educated, beginning in their Econ 1 course, that competitive markets are the norm and that monopolies and oligopolies are the exception. During their education, they are taught that what they are studying is relevant to real-world markets because markets are competitive. It is hard for them to believe otherwise: if markets are not competitive, their discipline is truly just an academic enterprise. Their long period of education is a socialization process that ingrains in them a belief in the existence of competitive markets. Once they become professors, their career concerns reinforce the orthodoxy of the profession. One economist, who sees the constraints of the profession resulting in a kind of "capture" of research and perspective, has written:

> An academic career is mostly determined by a person's ability to publish in peer reviewed journals and to have her articles cited. . . . Hence the ability to publish is mostly determined by editors and referees. Editors have probably the greatest power in deciding whether to publish a paper or not. They choose the referees, who are very predictable in their taste, and reserve the right to overrule them. I am very confident that editors receive no form of direct pressure to publish articles that reflect more pro-business interests. Yet this does not mean that the publication process is free from biases and that academic careers are completely free of any outside influence.[20]

[19] The study of confirmation bias goes back at least to the seminal article by Albert H. Hastorf & Hadley Cantril, *They Saw a Game; a Case Study*, 49 J. ABNORMAL & SOC. PSYCHOL. 129 (1954).

[20] Luigi Zingales, *Preventing Economists' Capture, in* PREVENTING REGULATORY CAPTURE: SPECIAL INTEREST INFLUENCE AND HOW TO LIMIT IT 124, 132–33 (Daniel Carpenter & David A. Moss eds., 2014).

Senior economists with great faith in competitive markets pass that belief on to their juniors.

Over fifty years ago, George Stigler noted that the professional training of economists made them conservative, with a preference for "most economic activity to be conducted by private enterprise" and with a belief that "efficiency and progress [will] usually be provided by forces of competition."[21] I think that is as true today as it was when Stigler wrote. Douglass North used to poke fun at the effects of economic education by noting a study of how people around the world in various cultures play the Ultimatum Game. The game involves two players, with one being given a sum of money, say $20, and the other nothing. The person with the money is then told to share as much as he or she desires with the other person. If the person accepts the split of the proceeds, both parties get to keep the money. If the person rejects the offer, neither gets the money. The study showed that virtually all people offer a reasonable share of the pot to the other party, often one-half or something near half.[22] This shows the similar norms of sharing throughout the world. However, North would point out that only two groups play the game like *homo economicus* (by making a very low offer under the view that even a penny makes the other person better off): a tribe in the Amazon and economics graduate students. This is a lesson that training in economics students socializes economists to look at the world as if it actually operates according to the assumptions of economic theory.

The belief systems of many economists lead them at times to exaggerate the theoretical foundations for their claims about the effectiveness of a market in circumstances in which economic theory does not fit well. They sometimes present conclusions as driven by economic theory, extolling the benefits of a limited "market," when they are really making normative statements based on their own philosophy or social theory. Although this is only their belief, many people take their conclusion to be factually correct. Some economists do this unknowingly. Others do this with an implicit recognition that the market is far from perfect, but they prefer the known imperfect economic consequences over uncertain results that could come with government regulation. Opposition to government regulation in many noncompetitive markets, including limits on the compensation of corporate officers and rent control, probably also reflects a fear that government will

[21] GEORGE J. STIGLER, ESSAYS IN THE HISTORY OF ECONOMICS 52–54, 59 (1965).
[22] Lynn A. Stout, *Social Norms and Other-Regarding Preferences, in* NORMS AND THE LAW 13, 19 (John N. Drobak ed., 2006).

continue to intervene in additional markets (including competitive ones) once it intervenes in a few. This is a "slippery slope" argument that government will not be able to limit its tendency to regulate once it gets into the habit. Worse consequences from government action and a slippery slope of regulation may be valid reasons for opposing government intervention in markets, but they are not arguments derived from economic theory. Compounding the problem is the difficulty of really determining if markets are competitive. As this book has shown, the methodology is imprecise, and results are often debatable.

III. The Public's Faith in the Market

Much social science theory assumes that voters process the information they receive as if they were rational actors, but as I explained earlier, people often do not make decisions that way. Established belief systems can make the reception of new information very difficult. To illustrate this point, Douglass North has used the example of the inability of the leaders of the Soviet Union to accept the information that showed the failing of the Soviet economic system. He explains the phenomenon as follows:

> This is a story about the perceptions of reality held by human beings. Those perceptions of reality are translated into beliefs. . . . Actually, if we consider in greater detail what happened in the Soviet Union during the Brezhnev era, we observe that there were two failures of feedback. One of them is that the failures of the Soviet Union—as in agriculture, for example—never could penetrate the top echelon of the Soviet leaders. The second problem is that such information was antithetical to fundamental Marxist tenets about the nature of property. It was widely known in the late 1970s, although not officially admitted, that the one acre private plots in Uzbekistan made up one percent of the arable land and produced about twenty percent of total soviet agricultural output.[23]

The difficulty of conveying political information is compounded by the tendency of many people to put little time and effort into learning about issues

---

[23] Douglass C. North, *Cognitive Science and the Study of the "Rules of the Game" in a World of Uncertainty, in* NORMS AND THE LAW 48, 53–54 (John N. Drobak ed., 2006).

and candidates. Walter Lippman reminded us in *The Phantom Public*, a book published more than seventy-five years ago, that most people are too busy with the routine needs of life to have the time to become educated about political issues.[24] It is natural for people to be more interested in their families, religion, sports, hobbies, and the other aspects of ordinary life. Not surprisingly, many people care more about a reality television personality or a sports star than whether markets in the United States are competitive. As a result, the vast majority of the ordinary public has only a casual understanding of and interest in economic and political issues. Another scholar has suggested that the problem is more than inattention. He suggests that "[i]t is by now a commonplace belief that the mass of Americans do not have a sophisticated conceptual organization by which politics may be understood."[25] Rather,

> [for that to happen,] a person must: 1) have cognitive skills which allow him to see linkages between ideas and events. Such linkages determine the amount of constraint in his belief system. 2) Have a developed morality which allows him to evaluate consistently the ethical meanings of political events.[26]

There are a number of studies of voting behavior in the United States that suggest that beliefs systems and nonrational action affect the way people form political opinions. Although this type of survey data provides only rough measures of information and is therefore subject to considerable disagreement on some effects, there is enough evidence to draw some plausible, tentative conclusions about how people form opinions on political issues.

Many studies show that political views are strongly influenced by events during childhood and then through secondary school and college. Taken as a whole, the literature on childhood political socialization suggests that the party affiliation of one's parents is largely predictive of one's own party affiliation, though parents' beliefs on specific issues are not predictive of their children's beliefs on the same issues.[27] Of course, political ideologies

---

[24] WALTER LIPPMAN, THE PHANTOM PUBLIC: A SEQUEL TO PUBLIC OPINION 24–27 (1927). Richard Fallon gently refers to "the public's relative lack of attentiveness." Richard H. Fallon Jr., *Legitimacy and the Constitution*, 118 HARV. L. REV. 1787, 1830 (2004); *see also* Walter F. Murphy & Joseph Tanenhaus, *Publicity, Public Opinion, and the Court*, 84 NW. U. L. REV. 985, 990 (1989) (small portion of public have sophisticated understanding of the Court).

[25] Richard M. Merelman, *The Development of Political Ideology: A Framework for the Analysis of Political Socialization*, 63 AM. POL. SCI. REV. 750, 750 (1969).

[26] *Id.* at 753.

[27] Richard G. Niemi & Barbara I. Sobieszek, *Political Socialization*, 3 ANN. REV. SOC. 209 (1977). Some studies they cited suggested that parents and children have extremely high correlations on all

are a function of more than just family political affiliation and structure. Prevailing community sentiments also help direct children's political worldviews. Children in ethnic—or racial—minority communities develop different political sensibilities than White children, suggesting that views that are widely held within a community do filter down to children.[28] Education also influences the political views of many young people. The end of adolescence is not the end of political development. It is accepted that adults rarely switch from one political party to another, but they do move from party affiliation to independent status.[29] In addition, adults may change their political attitudes when confronted with new events for which neither childhood nor adulthood prepared them adequately. These new challenges can cause "considerable change in sociopolitical attitudes and behaviors as individuals are confronted with new conditions and contingencies."[30] For example, adults who join the military might find that they are socialized to dedicate themselves to "the nation . . . ahead of family and even self."[31] People who acclimate to such an environment would necessarily restructure their political views. It is a change in the adult's own personal experience, rather than an open-minded reading of the news, that causes the holder to change their narrative. Similarly, job pressure, continued exclusion or oppression, or prosperity can all cause an adult to reformulate their political ideas to accommodate their economic or social position.[32]

By adulthood, the vast majority of people have developed a belief system that allows for easy processing of new political information. As adults, citizens accumulate political information through the filter of their previously existing political outlook. Instead of first understanding facts, considering available information, and then making political choices, we "choose what

political views, whereas others suggested the matching was relatively minimal. They concluded that the most sound research showed high levels of correlation for party and voting preferences, with quite small (though positive) correlations for opinions on specific opinions. Parental politics are apparently strongly predictive of children's party, but not very predictive of children's views on issues.

[28] *See* Niemi & Sobieszek, *id.* at 212–13 (describing how White children tend to believe that political leaders "know more than anyone" and "almost never make mistakes," whereas Mexican or Black children tend to have very negative views of the political system as a whole.)

[29] *Id.* at 226.

[30] Roberta S. Sigel, *Conclusion: Adult Political Learning—A Lifelong Process, in* POLITICAL LEARNING IN ADULTHOOD: A SOURCEBOOK OF THEORY AND RESEARCH 458, 458 (Roberta S. Sigel ed., 1988).

[31] William M. Lafferty, *Work as a Source of Political Learning among Wage-Laborers and Lower-Level Employees, in* POLITICAL LEARNING IN ADULTHOOD: A SOURCEBOOK OF THEORY AND RESEARCH 89, 91 (Roberta S. Sigel ed., 1989).

[32] *Id.*

we like, and only after we have decided what to do, we retroactively try to rationalize our decision."[33] This method of decision-making presents a significant challenge to democracy because "most American voters lack sufficient information or interest" to rationally evaluate political choices.[34] Instead of relying on facts, events, and careful deliberation, citizens rely on "heuristic cues" to guide their experience of political events. These cues provide "simple pieces of information that can lead citizens to make the same choices that many, complex pieces of information do."[35] These cues often take the form of party affiliation—voters who hold liberal viewpoints will be predisposed to agree with ideas propagated by a source they know to be liberal. Once a citizen is presented with a narrative from what they consider to be a credible source, the citizen will normally accept that viewpoint. Repetition of a narrative leads the citizen to instinctively agree with it more and more, creating a cascading effect.[36] Presenting a citizen with unexpected facts about a topic— even facts that cast doubt upon the basis of the citizen's belief—is unlikely to alter the citizen's position.[37] Even if the narrative is conclusively shown to be inaccurate, informing the citizen of its falseness can serve to engrain the idea even deeper, because revealing its falseness "require[s] repetition of the false proposition."[38] Behavioral economists have demonstrated these phenomena with their studies of confirmation bias.

This narrative may paint a dismal picture of voters in the United States, but it not a new picture. "Since the 1940's, when social scientists began measuring it, political ignorance has remained virtually unchanged."[39] While voters appear to be no less informed than they used to be, there is no reason to believe

[33] Jeremy N. Sheff, *The Myth of the Level Playing Field: Knowledge, Affect, and Repetition in Public Debate*, 75 Mo. L. Rev. 143, 158 (2010).

[34] *Id.* at 165.

[35] Michael S. Kang, *Democratizing Direct Democracy: Restoring Voter Competence through Heuristic Cues and "Disclosure Plus,"* 50 UCLA L. Rev. 1141, 1149–50 (2002) (quoting Arthur Lupia, *Dumber Than Chimps? An Assessment of Direct Democracy Voters, in* DANGEROUS DEMOCRACY?: THE BATTLE OVER BALLOT INITIATIVES IN AMERICA 66, 67 (Larry Sabato et al. eds., 2001).

[36] Sheff, *supra* note 33, at 162. Cass Sunstein has noted the danger of zealots constantly reinforcing views over the internet. He is concerned that "enclave deliberation" can lead to "crippling epistemology," and "in the extreme case . . . may even put social stability at risk." CASS R. SUNSTEIN, REPUBLIC.COM 2.0, at 76, 78 (2007) (quoting Russell Hardin, *The Crippled Epistemology of Extremism, in* POLITICAL EXTREMISM AND RATIONALITY 3, 16 (Albert Breton et al. eds., 2002)).

[37] Sheff, *supra* note 33, at 176–77 (stating that "[v]oters have a tendency to discount information that conflicts with their worldview and to accept uncritically information that confirms that worldview").

[38] Sheff, *supra* note 33, at 162–63; *see also* Norbert Schwarz et al., *Metacognitive Experiences and the Intricacies of Setting People Straight: Implications for Debiasing and Public Information Campaigns*, 39 ADVANCES EXPERIMENTAL SOC. PSYCHOL. 127 (2007).

[39] Michael Schudson, *America's Ignorant Voters*, WILSON Q., Spring 2000, at 16, 18.

that modern voters are significantly more rational than their predecessors. After all, voters then and now are people. This means that data and logical analysis will not convince most people that many markets in the United States are uncompetitive and that corporations should take the interests of workers and communities into account. Changing people's attitudes requires a change in culture. A consistent narrative by economists, public officials, and social commentators has a chance of getting people to accept these two propositions. That is impossible today with the common presumption in favor of limited regulation of markets. Another way is through political action that leads to social change. The campaigns of Donald Trump and Bernie Sanders and the rise of the populist movement in the 2016 presidential campaign raised the visibility of the problems of U.S. labor. This has not yet resulted in any changes to benefit labor or to enhance competition, but at least it is a start in the right direction.

9
Recommendations

It would be ideal if the United States has seen the last of the outsourcing of manufacturing jobs. If this turns out to be true, part of what I have written is just history. But the outsourcing of jobs may continue, not just for manufacturing workers but also for white collar jobs. In addition, there is no sign of the merger mania abating, with its attendant job losses. So what can be done to help with this type of unemployment? Experience has shown that we cannot rely on market competition to protect labor. Self-restraint, religious precepts, and norms have had no impact. In his early months in office, President Trump tried to use the power of the bully pulpit to get firms to limit layoffs, plant closings, and outsourcing. This followed in the footsteps of President Kennedy, who was able to get the steel companies to roll back a price increase in 1962.[1] President Trump has had only very limited success. With no real constraints on business, there needs to be legal limits if things are to change.

First, the government needs to gather data on the amount of lost jobs. It is astonishing to me that we need to rely on estimates from scholars who study these issues and reporters who scour press releases and corporate reports. It is difficult to deal with a problem when we have to make educated guesses about the degree of the problem. It is as if we are hiding our heads in the sand hoping that the problem is not so bad. The government needs to keep track of layoffs on a regular basis, indicating the cause of the displacements, whether it is a merger, outsourcing, or some other cause. This proposal should not be controversial. The Bureau of Labor Statistics in the Department of Labor compiled some of this data until curtailed by budget cuts in 2013. That

---

[1] Milton Friedman, *Monopoly and the Social Responsibility of Business and Labor, in* MONOPOLY POWER AND ECONOMIC PERFORMANCE: THE PROBLEM OF INDUSTRIAL CONCENTRATION 105, 114 (Edwin Mansfield ed., 1964). *See* John F. Kennedy, *Attack on the Steel Price Increase (Apr. 11, 1962), in* MONOPOLY POWER AND ECONOMIC PERFORMANCE: THE PROBLEM OF INDUSTRIAL CONCENTRATION 87 (Edwin Mansfield ed., 1964); *recording at Press Conference, 11 April 1962*, JOHN F. KENNEDY PRESIDENTIAL LIBRARY & MUSEUM, https://www.jfklibrary.org/asset-viewer/archives/JFKWHA/1962/JFKWHA-086/JFKWHA-086 [https://perma.cc/U3YS-4AS3].

Rethinking Market Regulation. John N. Drobak, Oxford University Press. © Oxford University Press 2021.
DOI: 10.1093/oso/9780197578957.003.0009

agency could easily gather and compile the data needed to understand the amount of jobs lost from outsourcing and from mergers.

Second, the size of unemployment benefits paid by corporations to their displaced workers needs to be increased greatly. Not only would this help the displaced workers financially, it would create a financial disincentive for laying off workers. Companies should bear some cost to account for the costs they impose on their former workers. To put this in economic terms, we would be internalizing, to some degree, the costs the firms impose on their workers. The size of these benefits is debatable, but I think that two years' salary and benefits would be fair compensation. I'm sure that this proposal would face opposition from the corporations that would incur these higher costs, but it should not be too controversial since unemployment benefits are an accepted part of our government programs.

Third, we should follow the lead of Germany with its codetermination for workers and put serious representation of labor on the board of directors. As stakeholders of the corporation, workers need to participate in the company's decision-making, including plans for outsourcing and mergers. In Germany, the amount of labor representation varies from one-third of the board to one-half, depending on the size of the corporation. This major change in the way U.S. corporations are governed would be highly controversial and face strong opposition. For at least the last forty years, a few corporate law scholars have made this proposal without any success.[2] Overcoming the opposition to this idea requires a cultural change in the way we as a society perceive workers. We need to see workers as partners in the production process, not just inputs to production. The need for this type of cultural change is also true for the proposals that follow.

Fourth, we need to stop relying on the assumption that both outsourcing and mergers serve the public interest. There needs to be serious review of these actions to be sure that the harm they cause is justified by the benefits. Some people have proposed that merger review be modified to take into account the merger's impact on labor. I don't think that it is feasible to change the merger review process. It is a process based on an economic analysis of competitiveness, which does not lend itself to a consideration of social issues. Plus, this limited review of competitiveness is too imbedded to change. It would be better to establish a new board to review mergers based on an

---

[2] KENT GREENFIELD, THE FAILURE OF CORPORATE LAW: FUNDAMENTAL FLAWS AND PROGRESSIVE POSSIBILITIES 149–50, 265 n.38 (2006).

assessment of the likely harm to workers and their communities and the expected benefits to consumers, not just to shareholders. It may be that outsourcing has run its course, so trying to limit its harm to workers would be like shutting the barn door after the horse has bolted. However, just in case a second round of outsourcing is around the corner, the board that reviews mergers should also review outsourcing. The burden should be on the businesses to demonstrate a high probability of consumer benefit that would outweigh the harm. Both benefits and harm would be predictions, so it is essential that the board require predictions based on the best evidence available. It would be sensible to compare the proposals to comparable mergers and past instances of outsourcing. As done for some mergers, the board should be able to award conduct remedies. If a corporation claims that a merger will reduce costs, the board should have the authority to order a reduction in price for some time period, assuming no drastic increases in the cost of production. As the FTC has done with its merger retrospective studies, the board should examine how the predictions panned out. Without a doubt, this proposal would be controversial and face significant opposition.

Fifth, it would be helpful to analyze the usefulness of the education we provide people who become low- and middle-skilled workers, many of whom are undereducated.[3] Having an education should make retraining easier for displaced workers. Some firms have identified a shortage of workers with skills they need, especially in high-tech industries. It is likely that the education some people receive does not prepare them for the kind of jobs that are available. As done in Germany, it may help to expand a vocational track in high school and to develop apprenticeship programs. However, educational reform is a huge and controversial task, something that is not on the near horizon.

Sixth, none of these proposals is feasible unless the influence of business on Congress is diminished. It was business interests that prevented the passage of any law that would have affected outsourcing; it was business interests that turned back the tide on the unions' ability to get Congress to enact laws

[3] In 2017, about 15 percent of students failed to graduate from high school in four years, which was an all-time low. Laura Baker, Data, *U.S. Graduation Rates by State and Student Demographics*, Educ. Wk. (Dec. 7, 2017), https://www.edweek.org/ew/section/multimedia/data-us-graduation-rates-by-state-and.html [https://perma.cc/5Q27-V7J9]. By age twenty-four, the percentage of students who have not graduated from high school or obtained a GED is down to 6 percent. *Key Facts About High School Dropout Rates*, Child Trends Databank (2018), https://www.childtrends.org/indicators/high-school-dropout-rates [https://perma.cc/L3Y6-DRDF]. Concerning college, the six-year graduation rate in 2011 was 60 percent. *Fast Facts: Graduation Rates*, Nat'l Center for Educ. Statistics (2019), https://nces.ed.gov/fastfacts/display.asp?id=40 [https://perma.cc/2QXE-UCTQ].

benefiting labor. It is not just Republicans who have refused to legislate for workers; Democrats have done the same. At this time, it seems to be impossible to limit the influence of business through lobbying and campaign contributions. To the extent that members of Congress have been influenced by theory, my hope is that this book and other similar writings will help change perceptions about the existence of competitive markets, the harms of little or no regulation, and the need to help displaced workers. However, I am pessimistic about any change taking place in Congress until the public takes up the cause of labor.

The countries of Western Europe have economies and political systems similar to ours. Their success should show us that we do not need to harm workers and limit regulation of labor issues in order to have a productive economy. Of course, we can point to excessive protection of workers that makes for inefficiencies in Europe, but many of those economies are still very successful. Doesn't this teach us that our way is not the only way to have a vibrant economy? In moving ahead, we have a choice as a society that is not binary; it is not just an unregulated market versus a heavily regulated one. A little bit of what the countries in Europe do to help their workers would go a long way in the United States.

It will be a hard task to move closer to what the countries in Europe do. Accomplishing this requires a change in fundamental beliefs toward labor, something that usually takes generations. When communism ended in the former Iron Curtain countries, one common saying was that it takes six months to change a political system, six years to change an economic system, and sixty years to change the hearts and minds of the people.[4] With hindsight, it did not take sixty years in some of these countries, but it still took generations. To make the kind of changes I am proposing, people's attitudes need to change before the government will change. To do this, the opinion makers—scholars, government leaders, and the media—need to advocate change. However, as long as people are bombarded by statements that government interference in the markets is unwise and even un-American, the country will not change. In the days of President Kennedy, most of the public saw the government as doing good. That has changed over the decades for many reasons, starting with the distrust of the government by the baby boomers during the Vietnam War. If there was any hope

---

[4] RALF DAHRENDORF, REFLECTIONS ON THE REVOLUTION IN EUROPE: IN A LETTER INTENDED TO HAVE BEEN SENT TO A GENTLEMAN IN WARSAW 99–100 (1990).

for a greater government role in society, President Reagan squelched that. He popularized the notion that the federal government was bloated, much too large, and unnecessary. And he helped spread the idea that taxes— nearly all taxes—were bad. Of course, a government needs taxes to operate, so less tax revenue means a smaller government. Today's conservatives have carried on that mantra.

We need to deal with the problem of displaced labor out of compassion for workers, families, and communities. But there is another reason to respond to this problem. Economic issues eventually become political ones. In the presidential campaigns of President Trump and Bernie Sanders in 2016, laid-off workers found voice to their concerns, resulting in a new populist movement formed by labor and people who are sympathetic to their cause. Many of the Republican voters for President Trump were high-school-educated members of the working class.[5] The positive side of this movement is the mobilization of government to focus on real jobs for workers and to give people hope that they can achieve a middle-class life. There is a dark side, however, because disgruntled labor has played a role in nationalistic and fascistic movements during the twentieth century. It would be a tragedy if the situation worsened so badly that it fueled a violent movement. For both economic and political reasons, there needs to be a change.

Part of the political support for Donald Trump came from voters who were influenced by feelings of anti-elitism. Government leaders and politicians have disregarded the problems of the working class for decades. Many workers view elites as the wealthy who care about social issues but not economic ones. These people live in affluent urban areas often on the coasts, like the Boston to D.C. metroplex, Silicon Valley, and Hollywood. They care about same-sex marriage, discrimination, and immigration, but not about lost jobs. They are well-off financially, so they see no need to concern themselves with economic issues. Plus, they are thought to have a disdain for the working class, viewing them as people with limited education and little self-initiative. To Trump supporters, Hillary Clinton epitomized these elites. She and her husband used their political careers to become wealthy, taking advantage of their connections with New York bankers

---

[5] David Brooks, Opinion, *What the Working Class Is Still Trying to Tell Us*, N.Y. Times (Nov. 8, 2018), https://www.nytimes.com/2018/11/08/opinion/midterms-working-class-labor.html [https://perma.cc/5YVF-AJ5V].

and billionaires around the world, while having done nothing to help workers retain their jobs. Her claim that Trump supporters were a "basket of deplorables" was viewed as disdain for the working class.[6] As others have noted, this is a socially divisive attitude that needs to change.[7] Even more important, the general public's perception of the worth of working-class labor must change.

[6] Morgan Winsor & David Caplan, *Clinton's "Deplorables" Comment Show Disdain for Working People, Trump Camp Says*, ABC NEWS (Sept. 10, 2016), https://abcnews.go.com/Politics/hillary-clinton-half-donald-trumps-supporters-basket-deplorables/story?id=41993204 [https://perma.cc/3VE4-CNLS].

[7] *See, e.g.*, JOAN C. WILLIAMS, WHITE WORKING CLASS: OVERCOMING CLASS CLUELESSNESS IN AMERICA (2017).

10

Postscript

This book has been about two economic claims: (1) U.S. markets are competitive, and (2) the primary responsibility of corporations is to make money for its shareholders. I showed in Chapter 3 that the first is a mistaken belief because many markets are not competitive. I showed in Chapter 5 that the second is a normative statement that is not only wrong but also harmful. People take these statements by economists to be absolute truths, even though they are only opinions, albeit drawn from theory. Believe it or not, there was a time when economists were not so well thought of as policymakers. When William McChesney Martin was the head of the Federal Reserve, he told a visitor that he had a small staff of economists he kept in the basement. He said that they "were in the building because they asked good questions. They were in the basement because 'they don't know their own limitations.'"[1] To many people today, economists rule. However, as I explained earlier, many of the positions taken by economists come out of mathematics and laboratory experiments where the assumptions do not mirror reality. Some of their positions are helpful guides to regulation; others are not. We need to take economists' recommendations with a little skepticism and judge whether their prescriptions actually work in the real world.

Economics is a serious discipline, with research that strives to be scientific. However, when economic theories are transported from the laboratory to the real world, to the world of policy, human nature makes it impossible for the theories to be unaffected by existing beliefs and ideology. As a result, the theories are distorted and given a life beyond the academy that fits the interest of policymakers. It may be that policymakers use economic theories to justify positions they espouse even if they do not care if the theories are correct or if the theories are appropriate for the problems at hand. I assume that many policymakers are not hypocritical and do believe the economic theories

---

[1] Binyamin Appelbaum, Opinion, *Blame Economists for the Mess We're In*, N.Y. Times (Aug. 30, 2019), https://www.nytimes.com/2019/08/24/opinion/sunday/economics-milton-friedman.html [https://perma.cc/J8X4-P2FP].

Rethinking Market Regulation. John N. Drobak, Oxford University Press. © Oxford University Press 2021.
DOI: 10.1093/oso/9780197578957.003.0010

they use. Those people, like all of us, are affected by confirmation bias, as I explained in Chapter 8. Subconsciously, they see the theories supporting their prior beliefs.

John Quiggin calls these imperfect economic prescriptions "zombie economics" because they are "dead ideas [that] still walk among us."[2] What I have written about in this book is only a small part of a much larger problem. I want to use this postscript to give the reader a sense of the problem of zombie economics that still drive public policy for some.

I. Trickle-Down Economics

Trickle-down economics is easy pickin's. This is the theory, or rather narrative, that cutting taxes, particularly among the wealthy, will increase productivity among businesses and workers who will work harder and invest more because they get to keep more of their income. The legend has it that the economic growth created by this boost in productivity will lead to increased jobs, wages, and even increase tax revenues. That means that a decrease in tax rates will lead to higher tax revenues, so the budget deficit will not worsen from the tax cut. Almost no mainstream economist buys such a theory today, but this theory remains incredibly popular among conservative policymakers due to its narrative power.

Rather than focusing on increasing demand to stimulate economic growth, it may be true that increasing productivity from the supply side will sometimes also increase economic growth. The early history of Massachusetts subsidizing business is an example of that.[3] However, just decreasing taxes as a way to stimulate growth raises serious problems. The story is that the tax reduction theory was born in the 1970s when economist Art Laffer famously drew a curve mapping the relationship between tax rate and total revenues on a napkin.[4] On the Laffer curve, at 0 percent and at 100 percent tax rates there is no revenue. There is no tax revenue at a tax rate of 100 percent because businesses will lose their incentive to earn income and people will have

[2] JOHN QUIGGIN, ZOMBIE ECONOMICS: HOW DEAD IDEAS STILL WALK AMONG US (2012).

[3] OSCAR HANDLIN & MARY FLUG HANDLIN, COMMONWEALTH: A STUDY OF THE ROLE OF GOVERNMENT IN THE AMERICAN ECONOMY: MASSACHUSETTS, 1774–1861 (1969).

[4] Scott Horsley, *From a Napkin to a White House Medal—The Path of a Controversial Economic Idea*, NPR: MORNING EDITION (June 19, 2019), https://www.npr.org/2019/06/19/733779337/from-a-napkin-to-a-white-house-medal-the-path-of-a-controversial-economic-idea [https://perma.cc/5QG4-Q7ZT].

no incentive to work. Between the extremes, there is a tax rate that optimizes the tax revenue. As the tax rate rises from 0, the increasing taxes will continue to raise tax revenue. Once the optimal tax rate is reached, increasing the rate even further will decrease tax revenues because people will work less. The result is that if the current tax rate is higher than the optimal tax rate, the government should decrease the tax rate in order to raise tax revenues. Then, the narrative continues, the lower tax rate will increase productivity, which will lead to the higher tax revenues. Economists accept that there is a relationship between tax rates and tax revenue; that part of the theory is uncontroversial. Where most economists and supply-siders disagree, however, is over the shape of the curve and where the optimal point lies. Supply-siders tend to believe that most state and national income tax rates are already too high and so tax rates should be reduced, while most economists tend to think that the maximization point is at a much higher tax rate. One study estimated that the revenue maximizing point was at about 70 percent and that the United States and most of Europe had tax rates significantly lower.[5] Additionally, economists have found that lowering the tax rate for the wealthiest will have little impact on productivity. The people in the wealthiest top 10 percent have better tactics when it comes to avoiding top tax rates, so decreasing those rates only impacts the extent to which they seek loopholes, rather than increasing their productivity and job creation.[6]

The link between increased revenues for firms from reduced taxes and enhanced economic productivity is unclear. Ideally, the "rising tide lifts all boats," so workers will benefit as well as shareholders.[7] But the evidence is to the contrary: the tax reductions have worsened the divergence between the wealthy and the working class in the United States. Economists have also diverged with trickle-down policymakers because of a lack of empirical support for their claims about economic growth.

This theory remains popular among conservative policymakers despite failures at both the state and national level. This popularity is partly due to the economic growth experienced during the Reagan presidency when Reagan himself espoused supply-side arguments and policies. However, rather than

[5] Mathias Trabandt & Harald Uhlig, *The Laffer Curve Revisited*, 58 J. MONETARY ECON. 305, 319 (2011).
[6] Emmanuel Saez et al., *The Elasticity of Taxable Income with Respect to Marginal Tax Rates: A Critical Review*, 50 J. ECON. LITERATURE 3 (2012); Owen Zidar, *Tax Cuts for Whom? Heterogeneous Effects of Income Tax Changes on Growth and Employment*, 127 J. POL. ECON. 1437 (2019).
[7] QUIGGIN, *supra* note 2, at 137 (attributing the quote to President Kennedy).

balancing the budget, the federal debt tripled during Reagan's presidency.[8] Realizing the drastic budgetary effects of the initial cut, Reagan actually increased taxes eleven subsequent times, which undid about half of the initial cut.[9] David Stockman, Reagan's budget director, later lamented after discovering that the math for supply-side economics failed to work in the real world and even went as far as to call the whole approach a "Trojan horse" to lower the top rate for the wealthy.[10] It is, however, undeniable that the economy grew during the 1980s under this tax policy, which partly explains the popularity of this tax policy today. But a number of economists have concluded that the economic growth of this period was unrelated to the tax cuts and was merely part of the natural boom-bust cycle expected by Keynesianism.[11]

Perhaps no better example demonstrates the failure of this economic ideology than tax reform in Kansas in 2013. That year, Republican Governor Sam Brownback signed into law sweeping tax cuts designed to spur economic growth, with no corresponding spending cuts to public services.[12] The resulting budget deficits were almost immediate. In 2014, only a year after the cuts had been enacted, Moody's downgraded Kansas's credit rating from AA+ to AA.[13] The legislature later had to scramble to make drastic cuts to infrastructure and education spending.[14] Despite these cuts, the budget deficit had ballooned to $280 million by 2017.[15] Unlike President Reagan's tax cuts,

---

[8] *Federal Debt Held by the Public*, FED. BANK OF ST. LOUIS, U.S. DEP'T OF TREAS., https://fred. stlouisfed.org/graph/?g=k977 [https://perma.cc/YYJ9-Z74M].

[9] Bruce Bartlett, *Reagan's Forgotten Tax Record*, 130 TAX NOTES 965, 966 (2011). *See also* Scott Horsley, *Ronald Reagan's Legacy Clouds Tax Record*, NPR: MORNING EDITION (Feb. 4, 2011), https:// www.npr.org/2011/02/04/133489113/Reagan-Legacy-Clouds-Tax-Record [https://perma.cc/ PJ9R-V7DP].

[10] William Greider, *The Education of David Stockman*, ATLANTIC (Dec. 1981), https://www. theatlantic.com/magazine/archive/1981/12/the-education-of-david-stockman/305760/ [https:// perma.cc/CH9Y-CQQY].

[11] QUIGGIN, *supra* note 2, at 143; Nouriel Roubini, *Supply Side Economics: Do Tax Rate Cuts Increase Growth and Revenues and Reduce Budget Deficits? Or Is It Voodoo Economics All Over Again?*, STERN SCH. OF BUS. (1997), http://people.stern.nyu.edu/nroubini/SUPPLY.HTM [https://perma.cc/ EHG4-DEJ8].

[12] Brad Cooper, *Brownback Signs Big Tax Bill in Kansas*, KAN. CITY STAR (May 23, 2012), https:// www.kansascity.com/latest-news/article303137/Brownback-signs-big-tax-cut-in-Kansas.html [https://perma.cc/Z9FN-59T2].

[13] Steve Kraske, *Gov. Sam Brownback Suffers a Political Brownout*, KAN. CITY STAR (May 2, 2014), https://www.kansascity.com/sports/spt-columns-blogs/article348571/Gov.-Sam-Brownback-suffers-a-political-brownout.html [https://perma.cc/S8KN-HV3T].

[14] Jonathan Shorman, *Kansas Legislature Approves Budget Deal after Lawmakers Deliver Blistering Critiques of State's Finances*, TOPEKA CAP.-J. (May 2, 2016), https://www.cjonline.com/news/2016-05-02/kansas-legislature-approves-budget-deal-after-lawmakers-deliver-blistering-critiques?page=2 [https://perma.cc/P3V2-F99D].

[15] Howard Gleckman, *The Great Kansas Tax Cut Experiment Crashes and Burns*, FORBES (June 7, 2017), https://www.forbes.com/sites/beltway/2017/06/07/the-great-kansas-tax-cut-experiment-crashes-and-burns/#1e2e2aa45508 [https://perma.cc/9ATE-RCYB].

however, Governor Brownback's tax cuts did not accompany increased economic growth. Instead, what Kansas experienced was well below the national average economic growth during this period.[16]

In 2017, as Kansas was rolling back Brownback's cuts, President Trump rolled out similar sweeping tax cuts on the federal level. While rates were slashed across the board, wealthy individuals and corporations saw the most savings.[17] The Trump administration, unsurprisingly, claimed that the growth created by the tax cuts would increase revenue and decrease the federal deficit.[18] Just like in Kansas, however, the deficit exploded, and ten months into 2018, it had already increased by 20 percent.[19] While the economy was growing at a solid rate before the tax cut, the cut did not have a noticeable effect on economic growth.[20] Some companies did raise salaries, while others made one-time payments to their workers. By two years after the tax cuts, Paul Krugman concluded that business investment in manufacturing had actually declined.[21] One result of the tax cuts has been a huge increase in the repurchasing of stock by corporations.[22] Part of the cause of that is the lack of profitable investment opportunities for businesses. If a firm has a profitable investment opportunity, it usually can find ways to finance that investment. It does not need additional cash from a tax cut in order to make that investment. "Some companies now have extra cash but no ideas to spend it on. For them, the best response is to return the money to shareholders, through higher dividends and stock buybacks."[23]

It is bad enough that these kinds of tax cuts do not stimulate the economy while increasing the budget deficit. Even worse, trickle-down economics

[16] *Id.*

[17] Tony Nitti, *What Will the Trump Tax Cuts Mean for Your Wallet?*, FORBES (July 13, 2017), https://www.forbes.com/sites/anthonynitti/2017/07/13/what-will-the-trump-tax-cuts-mean-for-your-wallet/ [https://perma.cc/7MY4-S8CY].

[18] Niv Elis, *Federal Deficit Jumps 20 Percent after Tax Cuts, Spending Bill*, HILL (Aug. 8, 2018), https://thehill.com/policy/finance/400876-federal-deficit-jumps-20-percent-after-tax-cuts-spending-bill [https://perma.cc/XA3W-8E6T].

[19] *Id.*

[20] Noah Smith, Opinion, *Trump's Tax Cuts Failed to Deliver*, BLOOMBERG (June 7, 2019), https://www.bloomberg.com/opinion/articles/2019-06-07/trump-s-tax-cuts-failed-to-deliver-the-promised-boom [https://perma.cc/YT7K-X4GQ].

[21] Paul Krugman, Opinion, *Manufacturing Ain't Great Again. Why?*, N.Y. TIMES (Oct. 31, 2019), https://www.nytimes.com/2019/10/31/opinion/manufacturing-trump.html   [https://perma.cc/XQY2-E2ZH].

[22] Matt Phillips, *Trump's Tax Cuts in Hand, Companies Spend More on Themselves Than on Wages*, N.Y. TIMES (Feb. 26, 2018), https://www.nytimes.com/2018/02/26/business/tax-cuts-share-buybacks-corporate.html [https://perma.cc/64JS-FA6S].

[23] Justin Wolfers, *How to Think about Corporate Tax Cuts*, N.Y. TIMES (Mar. 30, 2018), https://www.nytimes.com/2018/03/30/business/how-to-think-about-corporate-tax-cuts.html [https://perma.cc/PXQ7-AW9Z].

contributes to the increasing disparity of wealth in the United States. The tax cuts make the rich much richer with doing little to help the middle class. John Quiggin's explanation of trickle-down economics as zombie economics focuses on this consequence.[24] With income and wealth disparity a serious problem, the last kind of regulation we need is a tax cut that makes the disparity even worse.

Trickle-down economics shows that even when economists correctly reject a theory due to its practical and theoretical defects, policymakers may not do the same. As an editor of the *Wall Street Journal* put it, "Economists still ridicule the Laffer Curve, but policymakers pay it careful heed."[25] Part of the reason for that is confirmation bias; policymakers want to believe that trickle-down economics really works. However, I cannot help but believe that at least some people speak in favor of this narrative because they want to benefit the wealthy and they need a "theory" to justify that.

Unlike the near-universal rejection of trickle-down tax policy, there are other economic ideas that are not very useful to resolving real-world problems, but nonetheless are put forth as gospel by some economists. Remedying a country's fiscal problems through austerity is one of them.

II. Austerity

Austerity is a type of "voluntary deflation in which the economy adjusts through the reduction of wages, prices, and public spending to restore competitiveness, which is (supposedly) best achieved by cutting the state's budget, debts, and deficits."[26] Similar to the claims in support of trickle-down economics, proponents of austerity claim that fiscal contraction will lead to economic growth.[27] In his book *Austerity: The History of a Dangerous Idea*, Mark Blyth criticizes the use of austerity to deal with the effects of the Great Recession. As he explains:

Austerity is a zombie economic idea because it has been disproven time and again, but it keeps coming. Partly because the commonsense notion that

---

[24] QUIGGIN, *supra* note 2, at 146–73.
[25] Robert L. Bartley, *Introduction* to JUDE WANNISKI, THE WAY THE WORLD WORKS xiii (3d ed. 1989).
[26] MARK BLYTH, AUSTERITY: THE HISTORY OF A DANGEROUS IDEA 2 (2013).
[27] *Id.* at 61.

"more debt doesn't cure debt" remains seductive in its simplicity, and partly because it enables conservatives to try (once again) to run the detested welfare state out of town, it never dies. In sum, austerity is a dangerous idea for three reasons: it doesn't work in practice, it relies on the poor paying for the mistakes of the rich, and it rests upon the absence of a rather large fallacy of composition that is all too present in the modern world.[28]

Most economists reject the automatic use of austerity as a way to respond to a financial crisis and stimulate a county's economy.[29] Their consensus is to use stimulus policies to restart an economy in most cases, recognizing that some form of austerity may make sense in some circumstances. Unlike the nearly uniform rejection by economists of trickle-down tax policy, however, there are some economists who do support austerity as a general policy.[30]

The Great Recession of 2008 was caused by a private credit–led speculative boom, not by lax public spending. But then the bailout of the banks in the United States and in Europe led to huge government debt. The response to the sovereign debt crisis in some countries then led to austerity policies. In the European countries that turned to austerity policies (Greece, Ireland, Italy, Portugal, and Spain), their budgets shrunk, debt loads got bigger, and interest payments shot up.[31] These policies in turn put most of the burden on the middle and lower classes, greatly worsening the disparity in wealth between them and the wealthy. Thus policies of austerity hurt millions of people.

In his book, Blyth compared the different responses of various E.U. countries to the crisis and showed that austerity measures did not work. For example, as a result of the banking bailout in Ireland, "[g]overnment debt increased by 320 percent to over 110 percent of GDP as the government spent some 70 billion euros to shore up the banking system. Meanwhile, unemployment rose to 14 percent by mid-2011, a figure that would have been higher had it not been for emigration."[32] Similar problems resulted in the other E.U. countries that embraced austerity. According to Blyth, austerity only works when there is a country that massively imports from the country

---

[28] *Id.* at 10.

[29] *Id.* at 212–16; *e.g.*, Robert Boyer, *The Four Fallacies of Contemporary Austerity Policies: The Lost Keynesian Legacy*, 36 CAMBRIDGE J. ECON. 283 (2012).

[30] Blyth centers the modern support for austerity starting in the Bocconi University of Milan. BLYTH, *supra* note 26, at 165–67.

[31] *Id.* at 4.

[32] *Id.* at 66.

practicing austerity in an amount sufficient to overcome the effects of the cuts.[33] That did not happen after the Great Recession, with so many countries experiencing their own financial crisis.

Just as a lack of attention to the problems of laid-off workers in the United States led to the rise of populism and the election of President Trump, Blyth sees similar political consequences resulting from austerity:

> Austerity is, then, a dangerous idea because it ignores the externalities it generates, the impact of one person's choices on another person's choices, especially for societies with highly skewed income distribution. . . . In sum, when those at the bottom are expected to pay disproportionately for a problem created by those at the top, and when those at the top actively eschew any responsibility for that problem by blaming the state for their mistakes, not only will squeezing the bottom not produce enough revenues to fix things, it will produce an even more polarized and politicized society in which the conditions for a sustainable politics of dealing with more debt and less growth are undermined. Populism, nationalism, and calls for the return of "God and gold" in equal doses are what unequal austerity generates, and no one, not even those at the top, benefits. In such an unequal and austere world, those who start at the bottom of the income distribution will stay at the bottom, and without the possibility of progression, the "betterment of one's condition" as Adam Smith put it, the only possible movement is a violent one.[34]

Thankfully we have not seen violence in the United States as a result of displaced workers, but we have seen the rise of a new populism, a resurgence of nationalism, and the divisiveness of a more polarized and politicized society. This is not the only parallel between austerity and the topics of this book. The embrace of austerity grew from the notion in economic theory that government's role in the economy should be as limited as possible.[35] Just as an aversion to regulation justifies the noninterference with layoffs from mergers

---

[33] *Id.* at 10.

[34] *Id.* at 14–15 (quoting ADAM SMITH, AN INQUIRY INTO THE NATURE AND CAUSES OF THE WEALTH OF NATIONS 341 (R.H. Campbell & A.S. Skinner eds., Liberty Fund 1981) (1776)).

[35] Blyth traces the intellectual development of austerity back to John Locke's view of the importance of private property and the need to protect it from an avaricious government, to David Hume's and Adam Smith's fear of large public debt, then to the Austrian economists personified by Friedrich Hayak, Ludwig von Mises, and Joseph Schumpeter, and finally to the German ordoliberalists, whose influence still drives the German view on deficits. *Id.* at 104–52.

and outsourcing, an aversion to government stimulus of a sagging economy leads to austerity. Both stem from the fear of government. This takes us back to one of the underlying questions raised throughout this book: How much should the government be involved in the market?

III. Privatization

John Quiggin includes privatization as part of zombie economics. In a way, it is a strange issue to view as a dead idea that will not go away. In some circumstances, it makes sense to have private rather than public ownership of a business. Different countries frequently make different choices about the type of ownership for the same kind of industry, with similar results. What Quiggin is referring to, however, is the simple-minded notion that everything is better off being privatized. Privatize utilities, like electric, gas, and railroad companies; privatize roads; privatize the educational system; privatize jails; even privatize Social Security. This embrace of privatization was part of the Washington Consensus, just as was austerity. The Washington Consensus, authored by the British economist John Williamson in 1989, was the blueprint used by the World Bank and the International Monetary Fund to aid development in the countries who sought the help of those institutions.[36]

Natural monopolies, markets in which it makes sense to have one firm supply the entire market, make for a good comparison of the benefits of private versus public ownership. Private ownership requires some form of government regulation to prevent the private monopoly from charging monopoly prices. Notwithstanding the costs of regulation, many economists prefer private ownership because they believe that private firms will be more efficient than public ones. To the extent that politicians hand out jobs in public utilities as patronage, the risk of inefficiency is high. However, the vast majority of public utilities in the United States have been operated professionally. In fact, studies of the efficiency of utilities have found no significant difference between public and private ownership.[37] That makes sense

---

[36] *Id.* at 161–62.

[37] Paul M. Hayashi et al., *An Analysis of Pricing and Production Efficiency of Electric Utilities by Mode of Ownership, in* REGULATING UTILITIES IN AN ERA OF DEREGULATION 111, 112 (Michael A. Crew ed., 1987); Scott E. Atkinson & Robert Halvorsen, *The Relative Efficiency of Public and Private Firms in a Regulated Environment: The Case of US Electric Utilities*, 29 J. PUB. ECON. 281, 293 (1986); Robert A. Meyer, *Publicly Owned Versus Privately Owned Utilities: A Policy Choice*, 57 REV. ECON. & STAT. 391, 398 (1975); Donn R. Pescatrice & John M. Trapani III, *The Performance and Objectives of Public and Private Utilities Operating in the United States*, 13 J. PUB. ECON. 259, 259–60, 274–75 (1980) (finding

because people who work in either type of utility respond in the same ways to supervision, salaries, and motivation.

Dissatisfaction with a company's performance can lead to changes in the type of ownership. For example, "New York City shifted its water supply system back and forth between private and public ownership, beginning with a private company in the late 1700s, then shifting to public control in the 1830s, then trying a private firm again in the early 20th Century, before putting the system firmly in the city's hands thereafter."[38] In the early 1980s, Margaret Thatcher acted on her neoliberal philosophy and began massive privatization of many types of enterprises then under public ownership in the United Kingdom: telecommunications, electricity, water, and transportation. Australia and New Zealand followed suit. Australia sold off Quantas Airways and the publicly owned Commonwealth Bank. Likewise, New Zealand sold off Air New Zealand and the Bank of New Zealand. Privatizations of airlines and banks should not be surprising because many countries have privately owned airlines and banks. New Zealand went even further than Australia when it sold New Zealand Rail. However, private ownership was not a panacea. Dissatisfaction with some aspects of these privatized companies led to the United Kingdom retaking ownership of the railroad network, including track maintenance, early this century, but not the railroad companies themselves. Australia re-entered the telecom industry by building a national broadband network. New Zealand undid the privatization of its national airline and its railroads also early this century.

Other than the belief in the superiority of private enterprise, there really is no economic theory for deciding whether to privatize. Just as I believe that the dealmakers—investment bankers, M&A specialists, and corporate lawyers—play an important role today in pushing firms to merge, Quiggin believes that the "power of the financial sector" drove the wave of privatizations in the late twentieth century.[39] That some professionals make lots of money from market restructuring is not a valid justification for either mergers or privatizations.

---

significant differences). For studies of the efficiency of utilities in other countries, *see* MICHAEL G. POLLITT, OWNERSHIP AND PERFORMANCE IN ELECTRIC UTILITIES: THE INTERNATIONAL EVIDENCE ON PRIVATIZATION AND EFFICIENCY 21–22 (1995); Johan Willner, *Ownership, Efficiency, and Political Interference*, 17 EUR. J. POL. ECON. 723 (2001).

[38] Carol M. Rose, *Privatization-the Road to Democracy?*, 50 ST. LOUIS L.J. 691, 708 (2005).
[39] QUIGGIN, *supra* note 2, at 183.

IV. Belief in the Market and Mistrust of Government

Trickle-down tax policy, austerity, and privatization all share a strong preference for the market rather than the government. Both tax-reduction and austerity policies result in reduced revenues for the government, an impetus for government shrinkage. Proponents of those policies argue that each policy will actually increase government revenues, but experience has shown that not to be true. Both austerity and privatization express a preference for market activities rather than government conduct. Austerity cuts government spending, while privatization moves activities from the public to the private sector. The one constant among these three economic ideas is a distrust in the government. That constant also runs through many of the issues I discuss in this book—a belief that the U.S. economy is competitive; a reliance on the benefits of competition as a way to minimize government regulation; a desire to keep merger regulation limited to competitive issues; a decision to not regulate the outsourcing of jobs; and a preference to let the market, rather than the government, resolve the problems caused by job losses. This strong preference for the market over the government makes it difficult to enact regulations that would help millions of workers.

Early in the book, I explained how European economists who feared a creeping socialism in Europe after World War II still influence policy today even though there is zero risk that the United States will become a socialist country. Mark Blyth has noted that the economists' fear of government actually goes back much further, to a fear of the power of kings:

> Liberal economics grew up in reaction to the state. Not the state as we know it today—(usually) a representative democracy with large-scale spending ambitions—but the state personified by sovereigns: vicious, capricious, untrustworthy monarchs who would as soon steal wealth as look at you. The state was therefore something to be avoided, minimized, bypassed, curtailed, and above all, not trusted. The market, in contrast, emerged in liberal thought as the intellectual and institutional antidote to the confiscation politics of the king. In such a world, if prices and merchants were set free, the wealth of nations (note, not "kingdoms") would multiply.[40]

[40] BLYTH, *supra* note 26, at 99.

An important lesson of confirmation bias is that initial beliefs are extremely important. Once they become imbedded, they are difficult to change. People mostly see the things that confirm their initial beliefs. That is why ideas born out of a fear of monarchs and socialism remain so powerful today. When people develop strong beliefs in the wonder of competitive markets and the ills of regulation, those beliefs are hard to shake. This is true for the economists and other social scientists, the reporters and pundits, and the politicians and regulators who believe in the market. This makes the education of young people about economic ideas crucial. Whether the education comes from parents, family, peers, high school teachers, university professors, media members, or politicians, mistaken beliefs can last a lifetime. Even when economists make it clear that their theories ideas are limited in their application to real-world problems, or when economists modify their theories, the precision of their views is hard to get to the public. Commentators who are not trained in economics often miss the limitations or the subtle aspects of a theory, so the public only gets simplified information. A preference for the market over the government is a simple idea easily grasped by the public. However, people need to get over their fear of government and to understand the good that regulation can do. They need to understand the harm done to workers, their families, and their communities by mergers and outsourcing. They need to understand and overcome the power of business if they are to get Congress to act in the interest of workers. These are hard things to accomplish, but they are necessary if we are to have a better society.

Profitability of the Four Major Airlines

I. Operating Margin

There are three common measures of profitability: gross margin, operating margin, and net margin. Operating margin is viewed as the best measure of the profitability of a firm's operations because it shows the percentage of revenue a company generates that can be used to pay the company's investors.

As a measure of profitability, operating margin is calculated by dividing a company's operating income by total revenue. Operating income equals total revenue minus cost of goods sold and operating expenses incurred in the normal course of business. Therefore, expenses not directly related to a company's core business operations and one-time or unique expenses are typically not considered.[1]

Operating margin shows how efficiently a company controls its costs and expenses associated with business operating. Therefore, the higher the operating margin, the more profitable a company's core business is. However, because each industry is unique and companies within the same industry generally follow the same accounting principles, it is more meaningful to compare operating margins of businesses within the same industry.[2]

Figure 1 shows the operating margins of the four major airlines in the United States from 2008 to 2017.

II. Residual Income

Residual income is a managerial accounting concept used to evaluate the profitability of different companies.[3] Unlike gross margin, which measures accounting profit, residual income measures economic profit, which is a more realistic measure of profit. The formula for calculating residual income is as follows:

Residual Income = Operating Income − (Cost of Capital * Operating Assets)

Operating assets are assets acquired by a company to use in its ongoing operations to generate revenue.[4] For example, cash, prepaid expenses, accounts receivable, inventory, fixed

---

[1] *See* Jim Wilkinson, *Operating Profit Margin Ratio*, Strategic CFO (July 24, 2013), https://strategiccfo.com/operating-profit-margin-ratio/ [https://perma.cc/ZTZ3-JR7H]; *Operating Margin*, Investing Answers (Oct. 1, 2019), https://investinganswers.com/dictionary/o/operating-margin [https://perma.cc/5SF7-XYGW].

[2] Investing Answers, *supra* note 1.

[3] For a definition of residual income, *see* Will Kenton, *Residual Income*, Investopedia (Nov. 27, 2019), https://www.investopedia.com/terms/r/residualincome.asp [https://perma.cc/4RCK-HX6D]; *Residual Income (Ri)*.

[4] SeeSteven Bragg, *Operating Assets*, Accounting Tools (2019), https://www.accountingtools.com/articles/what-are-operating-assets.html [https://perma.cc/YCS6-68PJ]. Although most of the

Figure 1 Operating Margins of Four Major Airlines in the United States from 2008 to 2017[a]

	Operating Margins									
	2008	2009	2010	2011	2012	2013	2014	2015	2016	2017
Delta Airlines	5.3%	5.8%	8.4%	10.9%	11.5%	14.1%	14.4%	27.8%	25.4%	22.9%
United Airlines	3.6%	17.9%	7.1%	6.5%	3.7%	4.6%	7.2%	14.5%	13.6%	9.7%
American Airlines	12.2%	14.5%	1.4%	−1.2%	2.2%	7.4%	11.9%	17.6%	15.0%	11.0%
Southwest Airlines	18.9%	2.5%	8.2%	5.3%	4.7%	7.7%	12.6%	21.0%	18.4%	16.6%

[a] The data in Figure 1 is taken from *Morningstar. Delta Air Lines Inc DAL: Financials, Key Ratios,* MORNINGSTAR, http://financials.morningstar.com/ratios/r.html?t=DAL [https://perma.cc/X9KD-X9RL]; *United Airlines Holdings Inc UAL: Financials, Key Ratios,* MORNINGSTAR, http://financials.morningstar.com/ratios/r.html?t=UAL [https://perma.cc/4V6X-9EL9]; *Southwest Airlines Co LUV: Financials, Key Ratios,* MORNINGSTAR, http://financials.morningstar.com/ratios/r.html?t=LUV [https://perma.cc/YA99-NDEA]; *American Airlines Group Inc AAL: Financials, Key Ratios,* MORNINGSTAR, http://financials.morningstar.com/ratios/r.html?t=AAL [https://perma.cc/6TKN-35Y8]. These databases were accessed in June 2018.

assets, and certain intangible assets are operating assets. The cost of capital is sometimes referred to as the weighted-average cost of capital (WACC).[5] It is calculated by combining a weighted average of the required return of the shareholders and the cost of net financial debt. The weights are given by the relative value of the equity and debt in the value of the firm.

Residual income considers a company's net operating income or the amount of profit that exceeds its minimum required rate of return. When different companies have similar profitability, the company with lower residual income usually requires more assets to produce the same amount of income. In addition, since the calculation of WACC, especially the cost of equity, is somewhat subjective and there is no publicly available industry benchmark for residual income, it is difficult to reliably compare residual income across companies within the same industry.[6] In comparison, accounting profit is more readily available and comparable because it is calculated according to generally accepted accounting principles. Overall, residual income is a better performance measure because it is an absolute measure in terms of money.

Figures 2 and 4 show the residual income of the four major airlines from 2013 to 2017 using two different sources for WACC. Figure 3 shows the residual income of the four major airlines prior to 2013.

operating assets are similarly titled by different airlines, the numbers are not perfect comparisons. They should be considered together with the notes in the annual statements filed with the Securities and Exchange Commission.

[5] *See* Steven Bragg, *Cost of Capital Formula,* ACCOUNTING TOOLS (May 27, 2019), https://www.accountingtools.com/articles/2017/5/13/cost-of-capital-formula [https://perma.cc/S52R-5GDD]. WACC can be very different from one period to another for cyclical companies like airlines.

[6] For the same company, different sources (like Bloomberg, GuruFocus, and Yahoo Finance) may give different betas. Beta, a key figure used to calculate cost of equity, represents the volatility of a stock relative to the market. Therefore, cost of equity is almost always subjective.

Figure 2 Residual Income of Four Major Airlines in the United States from 2013 to 2017 Using Bloomberg WACC[a]

	Residual Income (in millions)				
	2013	2014	2015	2016	2017
Delta Airlines	$(910)	$(2,602)	$3,575	$2,687	$1,338
American Airlines	N/A	$1,061	$2,857	$2,427	$965
United Airlines	$(1,418)	$(616)	$2,308	$1,515	$280
Southwest Airlines	$(75)	$681	$2,391	$1,948	$1,402

[a] The values of operating income are quoted directly from the airlines' annual reports filed with the Securities and Exchange Commission. The operating income of United Continental Holdings, Inc. and American Airlines Group Inc. is used instead of that of United Airlines and American Airlines. The values of operating assets are selected from the airlines' annual reports filed with the Securities and Exchange Commission, and the selection is based on whether a certain type of assets is used in the company's core business to generate operating revenue. The cost of capital is obtained from Bloomberg's WACC analyses (not all years are available). A positive residual income indicates that the company is creating shareholder wealth, while a negative residual income indicates that the company is depleting shareholder wealth.

Figure 3 Residual Income of Four Major Airlines in the United States from Years Prior to 2013 Using Bloomberg WACC[a]

	Residual Income (in millions)				
	2007	2008	2009	2010	2011
Delta Airlines	$(1,968)	$(11,746)	$(4,226)	(1,700)	$(201)
	2000	2001	2002	2003	2007
American Airlines	$(96)	$(4,591)	$(4,784)	$(2,447)	$(564)
	2009	2010	2011	2012	
United Airlines	$(929)	$(1,148)	$(282)	$(1,895)	
	2007	2008	2009	2010	2011
Southwest Airlines	$(431)	$(541)	$(795)	$(245)	$(437)

[a] The values of operating income are quoted directly from the airlines' annual reports filed with the Securities and Exchange Commission. The operating income of United Continental Holdings, Inc. and American Airlines Group Inc. is used instead of that of United Airlines and American Airlines. The values of operating assets are selected from the airlines' annual reports filed with the Securities and Exchange Commission, and the selection is based on whether a certain type of assets is used in the company's core business to generate operating revenue. The cost of capital is obtained from Bloomberg's WACC analyses (not all years are available).

Figure 4 Residual Income of Four Major Airlines in the United States from 2013 to 2017 Using GuruFocus WACC[a]

	Residual Income (in millions)				
	2013	2014	2015	2016	2017
Delta Airlines	$(3,417)	$(2,396)	$3,686	$3,504	$2,747
American Airlines	$1,399	$4,249	$6,204	$1,231	$1,268
United Airlines	$(717)	$969	$2,576	$2,211	$1,037
Southwest Airlines	$(14)	$1,248	$2,333	$2,135	$1,581

[a] The values of operating income are quoted directly from the airlines' annual reports filed with the Securities and Exchange Commission. The values of operating assets are selected from the airlines' annual reports filed with the Securities and Exchange Commission, and the selection is based on the whether a certain type of assets is used in the company's core business of operation to generate operating revenue. The cost of capital is obtained from GuruFocus's WACC analyses. https://www.gurufocus.com/term/wacc/NYSE:DAL/WACC-/Delta-Air-Lines-Inc, https://www.gurufocus.com/term/wacc/LUV/WACC-/Southwest-Airlines-Co, https://www.gurufocus.com/term/wacc/NAS:AAL/WACC-/American-Airlines-Group-Inc, https://www.gurufocus.com/term/wacc/UAL/WACC-/United-Continental-Holdings-Inc.

Methods to Determine Concentration

One determination that can affect the concentration measure is the choice of which market or industry to use. The method of measuring concentration itself can also have an impact on the analysis. Additionally, there are various sources that provide data to help the public and researchers when analyzing market concentration. This appendix discusses the different methods for determining market and industry, the concentration measurement, and the data available.

I. Market/Industry

Before determining whether a market is concentrated, one has to first define the industry or market. There are a couple of different ways researchers and economists have defined the industry, including: Standard Industrial Classification (*SIC*), North American Industry Classification System (NAICS), and Text-Based Network Industry Classifications. The *SIC* "was originally developed in the 1930's to classify establishments by the type of activity in which they are primarily engaged and to promote the comparability of establishment data describing various facets of the U.S. economy."[1] The *SIC* uses a four-digit code to identify industries. It had been updated in 1967, 1972, and 1987 to include new industries, but has since been replaced with the NAICS.

The NAICS replaced the *SIC* in 1997.[2] The NAICS was developed to be "the standard for use by the Federal statistical agencies in classifying business establishments for the collection, tabulation, presentation, and analysis of statistical data describing the U.S. economy."[3] The NAICS reorganized the coding of different industries.[4] The NAICS uses a two- to six-digit code to identify industries. "Each digit in the code is part of a series of progressively narrower categories, and the more digits in the code signify greater classification detail."[5] Specifically, "the first two digits designate the economic sector, the third digit designates the subsector, the fourth digit designates the industry group, the fifth digit designates the NAICS industry, and the sixth digit designates the national industry."[6] The *SIC* and NAICS were used in the Economic Census data.[7] Comparing data obtained using *SIC* classifications with data obtained using NAICS classifications is not possible. The *SIC*

---

[1] *History of the NAICS Code*, N. Am. Indus. Classification Sys. Ass'n, https://www.naics.com/history-naics-code/ [https://perma.cc/S57N-9PSY].

[2] *North American Industry Classification System: Frequently Asked Questions*, U.S. Census Bureau, https://www.census.gov/eos/www/naics/faqs/faqs.html [https://perma.cc/GC32-JFVD].

[3] *Id.*

[4] *Id.*

[5] *Id.*

[6] *Id.*

[7] *SIC and NAICS Codes*, Wash. State Dep't of Revenue, https://dor.wa.gov/about/statistics-reports/sic-and-naics-codes [https://perma.cc/QE9S-URNS].

codes do not directly convert to NAICS codes because "a firm that may have fallen under a particular code may now be classified under a different NAICS code."[8]

Economists Gerard Hoberg and Gordon Phillips created the Text-Based Network Industry Classifications because they believe there are limitations with the *SIC* and NAICS industry measures.[9] Hoberg and Phillips "develop new time-varying industry classifications using text-based analysis of firm product descriptions filed with the Securities and Exchange Commission."[10] They specifically used the business description section of the Form 10-K, which businesses are required to file yearly, which they accessed on the SEC Edgar web-site from 1996 to 2008.[11] They "process[ed] the text in these business descriptions to form new industry classifications based on the strong tendency of product market vocabulary to cluster among firms operating in the same market."[12] They believe this classification is better than the *SIC* or the NAICS because the "new classifications are based on the products sold by firms that arise from underlying consumer preferences and demand."[13]

Definitions of markets have two main components: "identifying the relevant product or service market and then identifying the relevant geographic area."[14] Therefore, the def-inition of industry is important in defining a market because once the industry has been established, all that needs to be defined is the geographic area.

II. Concentration

After defining the market, one can determine whether the market is concentrated. Again, there are different methods one can use to determine concentration. These methods in-clude: the k-firm ratio, the Herfindahl-Hirschman Index (HHI), and the inverse HHI. First, consider the k-firm ratio. The k-firm ratio was used extensively in early studies on market concentration and is still used today.[15] The k-firm ratio represents the sum of the shares of the largest number of firms, where k represents the number of firms.[16] Most studies and researchers use the four-firm concentration ratio; however, the eight-firm ratio is another possibility.[17] Next, consider HHI. HHI "is calculated by summing the squares of the individual market shares of all the participants."[18] Instead of reflecting just

---

[8] U.S. Census Bureau, *supra* note 2.

[9] Gerard Hoberg & Gordon Phillips, *Text-Based Network Industries and Endogenous Product Differentiation*, 124 J. Pol. Econ. 1423 (2016). The limitations they found with the *SIC* and NAICS classifications include: "First, neither reclassifies firms significantly over time as the product market evolves. Second, neither can easily accommodate innovations that create entirely new product markets.... Third, *SIC* and NAICS impose transitivity even though two firms that are rivals to a third firm might not be rivals. Finally, they do not provide continuous measures of similarity both within and across industries." *Id.* at 1427.

[10] *Id.* at 1424.

[11] *Id.* at 1429–30.

[12] *Id.* at 1424.

[13] *Id.*

[14] Lawrence A. Sullivan & Warren S. Grimes, The Law of Antitrust: An Integrated Handbook 64 (2d ed. 2006).

[15] V. Hovhannisyan & M. Bozic, *The Effects of Retail Concentration on Retail Dairy Product Prices in the United States*, 99 J. Dairy Sci. 4928, 4931 (2016).

[16] Sullivan & Grimes, *supra* note 14, at 71.

[17] *Id.*

[18] U.S. Dep't of Justice & Fed. Trade Comm'n, Horizontal Merger Guidelines 13 (1997), https://www.justice.gov/sites/default/files/atr/legacy/2007/07/11/11251.pdf   [https://perma.cc/B2UL-YA7E].

the market shares of the top four firms, this method "reflects both the distribution of the market shares of the top four firms and the composition of the market outside the top four firms."[19] Typically HHIs that are below 1500 are considered unconcentrated, HHIs between 1500 and 2500 are moderately concentrated, and HHIs above 2500 are highly concentrated.[20] (Until 2010 the comparable cut-off numbers were 1000 and 1800.) The inverse of HHI can also be used when describing concentration and competition. The advantage of an inverse HHI is that it is easier to visualize the number of equivalent firms with equal market shares that are competing in the market.[21] The inverse HHI is calculated by dividing 10,000 by the HHI.[22] The number produced is always 1.00 or greater, as 1.00 "is the equivalent of only one [firm] competing."[23]

III. Data Available to Help

Besides the methods for determining industry and concentration, there are various groups that provide data researchers can use to analyze concentration. These groups can be broken down into those that make the data publicly available, such as the U.S. Census Bureau and economists Hoberg and Phillips, and data purchased from commercial suppliers. S&P Global Market Intelligence, S&P Compustat data, and the Center for Research in Security Prices (CRSP) are examples of commercially provided data.

A. Publicly Available Data

The Economic Census is published by the federal government and provides information about different industries across the United States. It is an "official count" that "serves as the foundation for the measurement of U.S. businesses and their economic impact."[24] The U.S. Census Bureau sends forms out to American businesses that have employees in almost all industries.[25] The census "collects reliable business statistics that are essential to understanding the American economy."[26] One of the statistics the Economic Census

---

[19] *Id.* at 14.

[20] *Id.*

[21] Marvin E. Prater et al., *Rail Competition Changes since the Staggers Act*, 49 J. Transp. Res. F. 111, 118 (2010).

[22] *Id.*

[23] *Id.*

[24] *About the Economic Census*, U.S. Census Bureau (Dec. 23, 2019), https://www.census.gov/programs-surveys/economic-census/about.html [https://perma.cc/CM4H-FAV3].

[25] The Economic Census does not cover the following industries: Agriculture, Forestry, Fishing and Hunting; Rail Transportation; Postal Service; Funds, Trusts, and Other Financial Vehicles; Elementary and Secondary Schools; Junior Colleges; Colleges, Universities, and Professional Schools; Religious Organizations; Labor Unions and Similar Labor Organizations; Political Organizations; Private Households; or Public Administration. Additionally, the Economic Census does not include government-owned establishments. *NAICS Codes & Understanding Industry Classification Systems*, U.S. Census Bureau (Apr. 5, 2018), https://www.census.gov/programs-surveys/economic-census/guidance/understanding-naics.html#par_textimage [https://perma.cc/EBR4-G5ZC].

[26] *The Economic Census: How It Works for You*, U.S. Census Bureau (Jan. 2012), https://www2.census.gov/programs-surveys/economic-census/2012/program-management/outreach-partnerships/factsheets/ec-brochure.pdf [https://perma.cc/U7FY-3B2U].

provides, among others, is industry concentration and competitiveness.[27] The Economic Census collects information every five years and releases the information once collected and analyzed.[28] The most recent collection of data occurred in 2017. While some of the collected information has been released, not all the information is available for this census. Some concentration data for the manufacturing sector is available from the 2012 census. The information provided by the Economic Census is publicly available and used by agencies in the federal government, as well as researchers.

Economists Hoberg and Phillips also provide data to the public for free online.[29] They used the text-based network industries approach to define industries and then calculated HHI scores for the different industries. Because they used the text-based network approach, the information was limited to public companies, as public companies are required to file Form 10-K annually.[30] They have made the data available to the public and other researchers.

B. Commercially Provided Data

S&P Global Market Intelligence is a division of McGraw Hill Financial which provides "financial and industry data, research, news and analytics to investment professionals, government agencies, corporations, and universities worldwide."[31] Subscribers can get information about "2.5 million companies in 10 sectors, 24 industry groups, 67 industries, and 156 sub-industries."[32] S&P also provides Compustat data. The Compustat data represents "98 percent of the world's total market capitalization."[33] The data provides a variety of information about industries, indexes, and companies. Additionally, the data can be used to "conduct event studies, industry comparisons, backtesting, transfer pricing and valuation."[34] Note that there are criticisms of using just the Compustat data to calculate industry concentration.[35]

The CRSP, which is part of the University of Chicago Booth School of Business, also provides research data to subscribers. They provide data to "academicians whose research

---

[27] *Id.*

[28] The Economic Census collects information in years ending in 2 and 7. *Economic Census*, U.S. Census Bureau, https://www.census.gov/programs-surveys/economic-census.html.

[29] Gerard Hoberg & Gordon Phillips, *Hoberg-Phillips Data Library*, (Dec. 15, 2016), https://hobergphillips.tuck.dartmouth.edu/industryconcen.htm [https://perma.cc/LD46-RS4Q].

[30] Gerard Hoberg & Gordon Phillips, *Readme File Describing TNIC HHI and Total Similarity Data* (Dec. 15, 2016), https://hobergphillips.tuck.dartmouth.edu/idata/Readme_tnic3HHIData.txt [https://perma.cc/2BET-KQ5Q].

[31] Press Release, *S&P Capital IQ and SNL Unveils New Division Name: S&P Global Market Intelligence* (Feb. 8, 2016), https://www.prnewswire.com/news-releases/sp-capital-iq-and-snl-unveils-new-division-name-sp-global-market-intelligence-300216420.html [https://perma.cc/Z53S-554K].

[32] *Id.*

[33] *Standard & Poor's Compustat: Products & Services for the Academic Community*, Standard & Poor's (Jan. 7, 2009), http://fccee.ugr.es/pages/facultad/vicedecanatos/vicedecanato-de-investigacion-y-posgrado/documentos/bases-de-datos/compustat-for-academics/! [https://perma.cc/XUT9-RW9G].

[34] *Id.*

[35] There are limitations of industry concentration measures constructed with Compustat data. Specifically, researchers have stated, "[o]ur empirical evidence indicates that Compustat-based industry concentration measures are poor proxies for actual industry concentration. The correlation between the Compustat and U.S. Census-based Herfindahl indexes is only 13 percent." Ashiq Ali et al., *The Limitations of Industry Concentration Measures Constructed with Compustat Data: Implications for Finance Research*, 22 Rev. Fin. Stud. 3839, 3840 (2008). They argue, "only when U.S. Census-based industry concentration measures are used are the results consistent with

and publications must withstand rigorous analysis for accuracy."[36] One of the products which researchers use is the CRSP/Compustat Merged Database, which combines the CRSP and Compustat data. The "CRSP US Stock Databases contain daily and monthly market and corporate action data for over 32,000 active and inactive securities with primary listing on the NYSE, NYSE American, NASDAQ, NYSE Arca and Bats exchanges and include CRSP broad market indexes."[37]

theoretical predictions that more concentrated industries that should be more oligopolistic are populated by fewer and larger firms that enjoy higher price-cost margins due to their greater market power." *Id.*

[36] *Research Data*, CTR. FOR RESEARCH IN SEC. PRICES, http://www.crsp.org/products/research-products [https://perma.cc/63PW-3X2X].
[37] *CRSP US Stock Databases*, CTR. FOR RESEARCH IN SEC. PRICES, http://www.crsp.org/products/research-products/crsp-us-stock-databases.

Results of Concentration Studies

Researchers have used a variety of different methods and pulled from various sources of data in order to analyze market concentration. This appendix discusses what researchers have found when using the various sources and data available.

I. Text-Based Network Industries and HHI

The *Wall Street Journal* analyzed the HHI data generated by Gerard Hoberg and Gordon Phillips. The *Journal* found that "[i]n nearly a third of industries, most U.S. companies compete in markets that would be considered highly concentrated under current federal antitrust standards, up from about a quarter in 1996."[1] Additionally the *Journal* found "among more than 1,700 public companies operating in 1996 and 2013, 62 percent had a bigger share of the markets in which they competed at the end of the period than at the beginning."[2] The article provided the example of the "consumer staples sector," which "in 2013 had an HHI for their products above 2,893 up from 2,661 in 1996."[3]

II. K-Firm

Dean Corbae and Pablo D'Erasmo have researched market concentration of banks.[4] They considered data from the Consolidated Report of Condition and Income that insured banks submit to the Federal Reserve each quarter. They used this data to generate the k-firm ratio. For the U.S. loan and deposit market, "in 1976 the four largest banks (when sorted by loans) had 11 and 10 percent of the banking industry's loans and deposits respectively while by 2010 these shares had grown to 38 to 37 percent."[5] These researchers argue "[t]he high degree of concentration in the banking industry is the reflection of the presence of a large number of small banks and only a few large banks."[6]

Martin Gaynor, Kate Ho, and Robert Town studied the healthcare markets.[7] They compiled other studies on the industrial organization of healthcare markets. Some of the

---

[1] Theo Francis & Ryan Knutson, *Wave of Megadeals Tests Antitrust Limits in U.S.*, WALL ST. J. (Oct. 18, 2015), https://www.wsj.com/articles/wave-of-megadeals-tests-antitrust-limits-in-u-s-1445213306 [https://perma.cc/XH9A-2MMX].

[2] *Id.*

[3] *Id.*

[4] Dean Corbae & Pablo D'Erasmo, *A Quantitative Model of Banking Industry Dynamics* (Mar. 21, 2013), https://02e278dc-a-62cb3a1a-s-sites.googlegroups.com/site/deancorbae/research/bank032113.pdf [https://perma.cc/L8L8-4RUC].

[5] *Id.* at 12.

[6] *Id.* at 14.

[7] Martin Gaynor et al., *The Industrial Organization of Health Care Markets* (Nat'l Bureau of Econ. Research, Working Paper No. 19800, 2014), https://www.nber.org/papers/w19800.pdf [https://perma.cc/8NUG-Q98G].

studies on which they reported used the four-firm ratio for explaining the concentration in health insurance. When discussing health insurance, they reported "the median four firm concentration ratio increased from 79 to 90 percent."[8]

Additionally, using NAICS classification of industry and the four-firm concentration ratio to measure concentration, researchers John Bellamy Foster, Robert W. McChesney, and R. Jamil Jonna find an increase in concentration from 1997 to 2007.[9] They find this increase specifically in the food and beverage stores, health and personal care stores, general merchandise stores, supermarkets, bookstores, and computer and software sales.[10] Foster, McChesney, and Jonna additionally find "[c]oncentration is also proceeding apace in most other sectors of the economy, aside from manufacturing, such as retail trade, transportation, information, and finance."[11] Furthermore, "in 1995 the six largest bank holding companies . . . had assets equal to 17 percent of U.S. GDP. By the end of 2006, this had risen to 55 percent and by 2010 (Q3) to 64 percent."[12] They explain, "[t]he evidence we have provided with respect to the U.S. economy suggests that economic concentration is greater today than it has ever been, and it has increased sharply over the past two decades."[13]

III. Census Data and K-Firm

Although the Economic Census is conducted every five years, the most recent available concentration data available is from the 2012 census; however, this data was not released until August 18, 2015. As a result, few of the studies include this data, but rather use the data from the 2007 Economic Census.

Researchers Jason Furman and Peter Orszag used the data available from the 2007 Economic Census.[14] They determined that "[t]he Census Bureau's data on market consolidation shows a clear trend of consolidation in the nonfarm business sector."[15] Consolidation is slightly different from concentration; consolidation is defined as "the shift to fewer and larger firms."[16] Additionally, they note, "in three-fourths of the broad sectors for which Census Bureau data is available, the 50 largest firms gained revenue share between 1997 and 2007."[17] If other firms do not replace the recently consolidated firms, a smaller number of firms would control most of the sales.

The *Wall Street Journal* article that was previously mentioned also uses the Economic Census to support the idea there is increased concentration. The *Journal* explains, "Census data suggest . . . the grocery business was growing more concentrated through at least

---

[8] *Id.* at 7.

[9] John Bellamy Foster et al., *Monopoly and Competition in Twenty-First Century Capitalism*, MONTHLY REV., Apr. 2011, at 1.

[10] *Id.* at 5.

[11] *Id.*

[12] *Id.*

[13] *Id.* at 8.

[14] Jason Furman & Peter Orzag, A Firm-Level Perspective on the Role of Rents in the Rise in Inequality, Presentation at "A Just Society" Event at Columbia University (Oct. 16, 2015), http://gabriel-zucman.eu/files/teaching/FurmanOrszag15.pdf [https://perma.cc/9QNG-T5RZ].

[15] *Id.* at 11.

[16] DENNIS A. SHIELDS, CONG. RESEARCH SERV., CONSOLIDATION AND CONCENTRATION IN THE U.S. DAIRY INDUSTRY, RL41224 1 (2010).

[17] Furman & Orszag, *supra* note 14, at 11.

2007.... That year, the four biggest grocers accounted for 31 percent of U.S. sales, up from 20 percent in 1997."[18]

Researchers at the Congressional Research Service used Economic Census data and considered the four-firm concentration ratio to study concentration in the U.S. dairy industry.[19] They found concentration has been increasing and that "[n]early all segments of the dairy industry have become more concentrated over time."[20] The study further states, "[c]oncentration trends in the dairy processing and manufacturing industry are not unlike those in other food processing sectors."[21] In terms of different industries, they explain the four-firm concentration ratio "was 35 percent for cheese processing and 43 percent for fluid milk processing. These figures compare with a mean industry concentration ratio of 49 percent for nine selected food processing industries. Several industries were substantially more concentrated than dairy, including meatpacking (59 percent) and soybean processing (80 percent)."[22] This study was published in 2010 so the most recent census data that had been published was from 2002.[23]

The Council of Economic Advisers used the Economic Census and considered the change in market concentration share by sector for the fifty largest firms.[24] The k-firm ratio for the fifty largest firms in transportation and warehousing sector increased by 11.4 percent between 1997 and 2012, increased for retail trade by 11.2 percent, increased for finance and insurance by 9.9 percent, increased for wholesale trade by 7.3 percent, increased for real estate rental and leasing by 5.4 percent, increased for utilities by 4.6 percent, increased for educational services by 3.1 percent, increased for professional, scientific, and technical services by 2.6 percent, increased for administrative/support services by 1.6 percent, and increased for accommodation and food services by .1 percent.[25] The k-firm ratio for the fifty largest firms in other services (nonpublic administration) decreased by 1.9 percent, decreased for arts, entertainment, and recreation by 2.2 percent, and decreased for healthcare and assistance by 1.6 percent.[26]

IV. Commercially Provided Data and K-Firm

The *Wall Street Journal* also used S&P Global Market Intelligence Data when discussing concentration. Specifically, when discussing the trend in the grocery business, the article looked to S&P Capital IQ data and noted, "[i]n 1996, 40 publicly traded companies operated food retailers.... As of this year, only 18 do."[27]

---

[18] Francis & Knutson, *supra* note 1.

[19] Shields, *supra* note 16.

[20] *Id.* at 6.

[21] *Id.* at 12.

[22] *Id.*

[23] *Id.*

[24] Exec. Office of the President, Council Econ. Advisers, Benefits of Competition and Indicators of Market Power 4 (2016), https://obamawhitehouse.archives.gov/sites/default/files/page/files/20160414_cea_competition_issue_brief.pdf [https://perma.cc/CS72-XZL3].

[25] *Id.*

[26] *Id.*

[27] Francis & Knutson, *supra* note 1. S&P Capital IQ has rebranded to S&P Global Market Intelligence. *See* Gaynor et al., *supra* note 7.

V. HHI

The Federal Trade Commission (FTC) analyzed HHI in the ethanol industry. The FTC found "HHIs are substantially unchanged from a year ago, with three of the four HHIs for 2015 slightly lower . . . than in 2014."[28] Additionally, the report found "each of the 2015 HHIs indicates that the industry is unconcentrated."[29]

The Federal Communications Commission (FCC) analyzed HHI in the mobile wireless services industry.[30] It found that at the end of 2013, the HHI "for the mobile wireless services industry was 3,027, a small increase from 2,966 at the end of 2012, which in turn was an increase from 2,874 at the end of 2011."[31] Based on the government's definitions, this industry would be highly concentrated.[32]

The Consumer Federation of America recently conducted a study about the special access service market.[33] They used HHI and publicly available data, specifically FCC local competition reports, to conduct their analysis of the concentration.[34] They found the HHI for special access is between 7,000 and 8,300, which is much greater than 2,500, the level indicated as highly concentrated by the Department of Justice.[35]

The American Action Forum (AAF) analyzed concentration among all industries in the United States.[36] It tried to use national figures on HHI, but "[o]verall HHI data, however, are limited and frequently AAF had to calculate the HHI index using data on market shares."[37] AAF found "[a]cross the industries that became more concentrated, the average HHI index increased by more than 22 percent from 2008 to 2014."[38] AAF did find that "[t]he auto industry became slightly less concentrated, with a 13 percent decrease in HHI."[39] AAF also points out "almost every industry above [including hospitals, health

---

[28] FED. TRADE COMM'N, REPORT ON ETHANOL MARKET CONCENTRATION 2 (Dec. 14, 2015), https://www.ftc.gov/system/files/documents/reports/federal-trade-commission-report-congress-ethanol-market-concentration-december-2015/2015ethanolreport.pdf [https://perma.cc/H6PZ-HCFA].

[29] Id.

[30] Seventeenth Mobile Wireless Competition Report, 29 FCC Rcd. 15311 (19) (2014), https://www.fcc.gov/document/17th-annual-competition-report [https://perma.cc/9YCD-CM5B].

[31] Id. at 17.

[32] Id.

[33] MARK COOPER, CONSUMER FED'N OF AM., THE SPECIAL PROBLEM OF SPECIAL ACCESS: CONSUMER OVERCHARGES AND TELEPHONE COMPANY EXCESS PROFITS 2 (Apr. 2016), https://consumerfed.org/wp-content/uploads/2016/04/4-16-The-Special-Problem-of-Special-Access.pdf [https://perma.cc/8HLN-BVYX]. Special access is the nonswitched transport of voice and data over a dedicated transmission line between two or more designated points. For example, wireless providers use high-capacity special access lines to send voice and data from cell towers to their mobile switching center where the call is then switched to the sender's intended recipient. Data Collection Small Entity Compliance Guide, 29 FCC Rcd. 12702 (16) (2014), 3, https://docs.fcc.gov/public/attachments/DA-14-1521A1.pdf [https://perma.cc/2EZY-BFPM]. Special access is used by, for example, many "[i]ndividual consumers, small businesses, government offices, hospitals, medical offices, schools, libraries, ATMs and credit card readers use special access to either connect to a dedicated network or to an Internet service provider for the completion of the transmission via the Internet." Id.

[34] COOPER, supra note 33, at 2.

[35] Id.

[36] Sam Batkins et al., Market Concentration Grew During Obama Administration, AM. ACTION F. (Apr. 7, 2016), https://www.americanactionforum.org/print/?url=https://www.americanactionforum.org/research/market-concentration-grew-obama-administration/ [https://perma.cc/5FKW-CUU9].

[37] Id. at 1.

[38] Id.

[39] Id.

insurance, banking, telecom, airlines, auto industry, and energy] has observed significant mergers . . . in 2014 there were 95 hospital mergers following 98 mergers in 2013 . . . the HHI index in this industry grew from 2,556 to 2,840."[40] AAF found that the health insurance industry is one of the most concentrated, with HHI near 4,000 and up to 8,000 in some states.[41] The HHI index increased by 31 percent during the Obama administration for this industry.[42] AAF also found an increase of 41 percent between 2008 and 2014 in the HHI for the airline industry and 32 percent increase in HHI for the banking industry.[43]

Some of the studies on which Gaynor, Ho, and Town reported also used HHI in order to study concentration. They reported that the hospital markets are highly concentrated, with concentration increasing over time.[44] Specifically, "[i]n 1987, the mean HHI was 2,340 and by 2006 the HHI was 3,161."[45] They state that "[t]he market for physician services is generally unconcentrated, but there is meaningful variation across geography . . . 10 percent of cardiology and orthopedic patients are treated in markets where the HHI is greater than 2,200."[46] In terms of the health insurers, they reported "that 21 percent of counties have HHI below 1,800, 55 percent had HHIs between 1,800 and 3,600 and 24 percent had HHIs above 3,600."[47]

VI. Inverse HHI

Marvin Prater et al. studied concentration among railroads for agricultural producers. They analyzed concentration by using the inverse HHI along with USDA Crop Reporting Districts (CRD).[48] With the inverse HHI analysis, they found "the level of rail-to-rail competition for grains and oilseeds decreased significantly between 1985 and 2007."[49] They additionally found "[t]he number of competing lines decreased in 70 percent of the CRDs and increased in only 24 percent. The CRDs served by only one railroad increased from 10 percent in 1985 to 15 percent by 2007."[50]

VII. Compustat and Census Data

Using the CRSP-Compustat merged dataset, the Economic Census, and NAICS industry classifications, one study analyzed concentration levels in various industries.[51] It noted

---

[40] *Id.* at 3.

[41] *Id.*

[42] *Id.*

[43] *Id.*

[44] Gaynor et al., *supra* note 7, at 5.

[45] *Id.* at 6.

[46] *Id.*

[47] *Id.* at 7.

[48] Marvin E. Prater et al., *Rail Competition Changes since the Staggers Act*, 49 J. Transp. Res. F. 111 (2010). Similar to the Economic Census, the USDA publishes a census that is "[a] comprehensive summary of agricultural activity and for each state. Includes number of farms by size and type, inventory and values of crops and livestock, operator characteristics, and much more." U.S. Dep't of Agriculture, *Census of Agriculture* (May 2, 2014), https://www.nass.usda.gov/Publications/ AgCensus/2012/ [https://perma.cc/ZYB7-WJYD]. Crop Reporting Districts are set by the USDA and used to collect data for the census.

[49] Prater et al., *supra* note 48, at 126.

[50] *Id.*

[51] Gustavo Grullon, Yelena Larkin, & Roni Michaely, *Are US Industries Becoming More Concentrated?*, 23 Rev. Fin. 697 (2019).

that the number of U.S. firms on the NYSE, AMEX, and NASDAQ markets decreased from more than 7,500 in 1997 to under 4,000 in 2013, a level that is lower than the number of publicly traded firms in the 1970s.[52] The authors found "that the number of publicly traded firms has significantly declined in most industries. Out of seventy-one industries, sixty-six have experienced a negative change between 1997 and 2014. Moreover, the largest portion of the distribution is concentrated in the extreme range, indicating that 73 percent of the industries have lost over 40 percent of their publicly traded peers."[53] The authors also examined the market share of the four largest firms in various industries, finding that the increase in the four firms' market share increased more than 40 percent in twenty-one out of sixty-five industries.[54] Mergers were a primary cause of the disappearance of so many publicly traded firms and the increased concentration in the industries. In examining the effect of concentration on profits, the authors wrote "that sustained increased concentration subsequently exhibit increases in profitability proportionate to the relevant increase in industry concentration. We also find that increased profits are driven primarily by wider operating margins rather than by higher operational efficiency, in line with the increased market-power explanation. Additionally, and consistent with this hypothesis, we show that related mergers are more profitable when markets are more likely to become highly concentrated. Finally, our third contribution entails the finding that increase in profitability stemming from increased market power has been transferred to investors by generating higher abnormal returns."[55]

[52] *Id.* at 701 & 702, Fig. 1B.
[53] *Id.* at 706–7.
[54] *Id.* at 706.
[55] *Id.* at 700.

Congressional Bills Regulating Outsourcing

Overview: Congress has continually attempted to create laws limiting the outsourcing of American jobs, sometimes introducing the same bills year after year. Most congressional attempts to limit outsourcing—from requiring governmental overview of outsourcing practices to limiting federal contracts and tax deductions for businesses that engage in outsourcing—have failed.

I. 108th Congress (2003–2004)

In 2004, the "American Jobs Creation Act" (H.R. 4520) became law and prohibited federal government work from being outsourced, with a few exceptions.[1]

The "Outsourcing Information Act of 2004" (S. 2962) was referred to the Committee on Banking, Housing, and Urban Affairs where no report was made. The bill instructed the Secretary of Commerce to collect information on foreign operations of U.S. corporations and certain foreign investments.[2]

II. 109th Congress (2005–2006)

In 2005, the "Commission on Americans Jobs Act" (H.R. 828) proposed to collect data on the outsourcing of jobs and brainstorm ideas to prevent outsourcing. This bill was referred to the House Education and the Workforce Subcommittee on Employer-Employee Relations and no report was made.[3]

III. 111th Congress (2009–2010)

The "Aviation Job Outsourcing Prevention Act" (H.R. 4788) was introduced in March 2010 and was referred to the House Transportation and Infrastructure Subcommittee on Aviation where no reports were made. This law would have required the Secretary of Transportation to approve of any agreement between domestic and foreign air carriers.[4]

---

[1] American Jobs Creation Act of 2004, Pub. L. No. 108-357, 118 Stat. 1418 (Codified in Scattered Sections of 26 U.S.C.), https://www.congress.gov/bill/108th-congress/house-bill/4520/ [https://perma.cc/HK4E-FCNS].

[2] Outsourcing Information Act of 2004, S. 2962, 108th Cong. (2004), https://www.congress.gov/bill/108th-congress/senate-bill/2962 [https://perma.cc/53FC-3QBN].

[3] Commission on American Jobs Act, H.R. 828, 109th Cong. (2005), https://www.congress.gov/bill/109th-congress/house-bill/828 (previously introduced as H.R. 3878, 108th Cong. (2004)).

[4] Aviation Jobs Outsourcing Prevention Act, H.R. 4788, 111th Cong. (2010), https://www.congress.gov/bill/111th-congress/house-bill/4788/.

IV. 113th Congress (2013–2014)

In 2013, Senator Barbara Mikulski sponsored the "American Family Economic Protection Act of 2013" (S. 388). This bill was never referred to a committee. It attempted to regulate outsourcing by not allow deductions for outsourcing-related expenses incurred by businesses.[5]

The "Keeping Jobs in America Act" (S. 2681) was introduced in July 2014 and sent to the Senate Committee on Finance where no reports were made. This bill would have denied tax deductions for expenses incurred while outsourcing by businesses and would have required an increase in the taxpayer's employment of full-time employees in the United States in order to claim the tax credit for insourcing expenses.[6]

V. 114th Congress (2015–2016)

In July 2015, the "Bring Jobs Home Act" (H.R. 2963, S. 1737) was introduced and referred to the House Committee on Ways and Means and the Senate Committee on Finance. This bill, which had first been proposed in 2012, attempted to do the same thing as the "Keeping Jobs in America Act" and would have denied tax deductions for expenses incurred while outsourcing by businesses and would have required an increase in taxpayer's employment of full-time employees in the United States in order to claim the tax credit for insourcing expenses. No reports were issued.[7]

House Bill 3812, entitled "Stop Outsourcing and Create American Jobs Act of 2015," was introduced in October 2015. While the bill was assigned to the House Oversight and Government Reform Committee, no reports were made. This bill would have given priority of federal contracts to contractors that did not engaged in outsourcing.[8]

At the same time, in October 2015, House Bill 3811, entitled "Outsourcing Accountability Act of 2015," was introduced and referred to the House Committee on Financial Services. No reports were made. This proposal would have required registered securities issues to list the number of employees they had who work in the United States and those who work in other countries.[9]

---

[5] American Family Economic Protection Act of 2013, S. 388, 113th Cong., https://www.congress.gov/bill/113th-congress/senate-bill/388/.

[6] Keeping Jobs in America Act, S. 2681, 113th Cong. (2014), https://www.congress.gov/bill/113th-congress/senate-bill/2681.

[7] Bring Jobs Home Act, H.R. 2963, 114th Cong. (2015), https://www.congress.gov/bill/114th-congress/house-bill/2963; Bring Jobs Home Act, S. 1737, 114th Cong. (2015), https://www.congress.gov/bill/114th-congress/senate-bill/1737 (previously introduced in the 112th Cong. as H.R. 5542, H.R. 6152, S. 2284, S. 3364; in the 113th Cong. as H.R. 851, S. 2562, S. 2569; and subsequently in the 115th Cong. as H.R. 2963, H.R. 685, S. 1737, S. 247).

[8] Stop Outsourcing and Create American Jobs Act of 2015, H.R. 3812, 114th Cong., https://www.congress.gov/bill/114th-congress/house-bill/3812 (previously introduced as H.R. 5622, 111th Cong. (2010); H.R. 3338, 112th Cong. (2011); H.R. 2740, 113th Cong. (2013)).

[9] Outsourcing Accountability Act of 2015, H.R. 3811, 115th Cong., https://www.congress.gov/bill/114th-congress/house-bill/3811 (previously introduced as H.R. 3875, 112th Cong. (2012); S. 3392, 112th Cong. (2012); H.R. 790, 113th Cong. (2013)).

Appendix Bibliography

Ashiq Ali et al., *The Limitations of Industry Concentration Measures Constructed with Compustat Data: Implications for Finance Research*, 22 REV. FIN. STUD. 3839 (2008).

American Airlines Group Inc., *Annual Reports (Form 10-K)*, https://www.sec.gov/cgi-bin/browse-edgar?action=getcompany&CIK=0000006201&type=10-k&dateb=&owner=exclude&count=40 [https://perma.cc/VL6B-2BQC].

American Airlines Group Inc AAL: Financials, Key Ratios, MORNINGSTAR, http://financials.morningstar.com/ratios/r.html?t=AAL [https://perma.cc/6TKN-35Y8].

American Family Economic Protection Act of 2013, S. 322, 113th Cong., https://www.congress.gov/bill/113th-congress/senate-bill/388/.

American Jobs Creation Act of 2004, Pub. L. No. 108-357, 118 Stat. 1418 (Codified in Scattered Sections of 26 U.S.C), https://www.congress.gov/bill/108th-congress/house-bill/4520/ [https://perma.cc/HK4E-FCNS].

Aviation Jobs Outsourcing Prevention Act, H.R. 4788, 111th Cong. (2010), https://www.congress.gov/bill/111th-congress/house-bill/4788/.

Sam Batkins et al., *Market Concentration Grew During Obama Administration*, AM. ACTION F. (Apr. 7, 2016), https://www.americanactionforum.org/print/?url=https://www.americanactionforum.org/research/market-concentration-grew-obama-administration/ [https://perma.cc/5FKW-CUU9].

Steven Bragg, *Cost of Capital Formula*, ACCOUNTING TOOLS (May 27, 2019), https://www.accountingtools.com/articles/2017/5/13/cost-of-capital-formula [https://perma.cc/S52R-5GDD].

Steven Bragg, *Operating Assets*, ACCOUNTING TOOLS (2019), https://www.accountingtools.com/articles/what-are-operating-assets.html [https://perma.cc/YCS6-68PJ].

Bring Jobs Home Act, H.R. 2963, 114th Cong. (2015), https://www.congress.gov/bill/114th-congress/house-bill/2963.

Bring Jobs Home Act, S. 1737, 114th Cong. (2015), https://www.congress.gov/bill/114th-congress/senate-bill/1737.

CTR. FOR RESEARCH IN SEC. PRICES, *CRSP US Stock Databases*, http://www.crsp.org/products/research-products/crsp-us-stock-databases.

CTR. FOR RESEARCH IN SEC. PRICES, *Research Data*, http://www.crsp.org/products/research-products [https://perma.cc/63PW-3X2X].

Commission on American Jobs Act, H.R. 828, 109th Cong. (2005), https://www.congress.gov/bill/109th-congress/house-bill/828.

MARK COOPER, CONSUMER FED'N OF AM., THE SPECIAL PROBLEM OF SPECIAL ACCESS: CONSUMER OVERCHARGES AND TELEPHONE COMPANY EXCESS PROFITS (Apr. 2016), https://consumerfed.org/wp-content/uploads/2016/04/4-16-The-Special-Problem-of-Special-Access.pdf [https://perma.cc/8HLN-BVYX].

Dean Corbae & Pablo D'Erasmo, *A Quantitative Model of Banking Industry Dynamics* (Mar. 21, 2013), https://02e278dc-a-62cb3a1a-s-sites.googlegroups.com/site/deancorbae/research/bank032113.pdf [https://perma.cc/L8L8-4RUC].

Data Collection Small Entity Compliance Guide, 29 FCC Rcd. 12702 (16) (2014), https://docs.fcc.gov/public/attachments/DA-14-1521A1.pdf [https://perma.cc/2EZY-BFPM].

Delta Airlines Inc., *Annual Reports (Form 10-K)*, https://www.sec.gov/cgi-bin/browse-edgar?action=getcompany&CIK=0000027904&type=10-k&dateb=&owner=exclude&count=100 [https://perma.cc/Q2SK-7LYR].

Delta Air Lines Inc DAL: Financials, Key Ratios, MORNINGSTAR, http://financials. morningstar.com/ratios/r.html?t=DAL [https://perma.cc/X9KD-X9RL].

EXEC. OFFICE OF THE PRESIDENT, COUNCIL ECON. ADVISORS, BENEFITS OF COMPETITION AND INDICATORS OF MARKET POWER (2016), https://obamawhitehouse.archives.gov/ sites/default/files/page/files/20160414_cea_competition_issue_brief.pdf   [https:// perma.cc/CS72-XZL3].

FED. TRADE COMM'N, REPORT ON ETHANOL MARKET CONCENTRATION (Dec. 14, 2015), https://www.ftc.gov/system/files/documents/reports/federal-trade-commission-report-congress-ethanol-market-concentration-december-2015/2015ethanolreport. pdf [https://perma.cc/H6PZ-HCFA].

John Bellamy Foster et al., *Monopoly and Competition in Twenty-First Century Capitalism*, MONTHLY REV., Apr. 2011, at 1.

Theo Francis & Ryan Knutson, *Wave of Megadeals Tests Antitrust Limits in U.S.*, WALL ST. J. (Oct. 18, 2015), https://www.wsj.com/articles/wave-of-megadeals-tests-antitrust-limits-in-u-s-1445213306 [https://perma.cc/XH9A-2MMX].

Jason Furman & Peter Orzag, *A Firm-Level Perspective on the Role of Rents in the Rise in Inequality*, Presentation at "A Just Society" Event at Columbia University (Oct. 16, 2015), http://gabriel-zucman.eu/files/teaching/FurmanOrszag15.pdf [https://perma. cc/9QNG-T5RZ].

Martin Gaynor et al., *The Industrial Organization of Health Care Markets* (Nat'l Bureau of Econ. Research, Working Paper No. 19800, 2014), https://www.nber.org/papers/ w19800.pdf [https://perma.cc/8NUG-Q98G].

Gustavo Grullon, Yelena Larkin, & Roni Michaely, *Are US Industries Becoming More Concentrated?*, 23 REV. FIN. 697 (2019).

Gerard Hoberg & Gordon Phillips, *Hoberg-Phillips Data Library* (Dec. 15, 2016), https://hobergphillips.tuck.dartmouth.edu/industryconcen.htm   [https://perma.cc/ LD46-RS4Q].

Gerard Hoberg & Gordon Phillips, *Readme File Describing TNIC HHI and Total Similarity Data* (Dec. 15, 2016), https://hobergphillips.tuck.dartmouth.edu/idata/Readme_ tnic3HHIData.txt [https://perma.cc/2BET-KQ5Q].

Gerard Hoberg & Gordon Phillips, *Text-Based Network Industries and Endogenous Product Differentiation*, 124 J. POL. ECON. 1423 (2016).

V. Hovhannisyan & M. Bozic, *The Effects of Retail Concentration on Retail Dairy Product Prices in the United States*, 99 J. DAIRY SCI. 4928 (2016).

Keeping Jobs in America Act, S. 2681, 113th Cong. (2014), https://www.congress.gov/bill/ 113th-congress/senate-bill/2681.

Will Kenton, *Residual Income*, INVESTOPEDIA (Nov. 27, 2019), https://www.investopedia. com/terms/r/residualincome.asp [https://perma.cc/4RCK-HX6D].

N. AM. INDUS. CLASSIFICATION SYS. ASS'N, *History of the NAICS Code*, https://www.naics. com/history-naics-code/ [https://perma.cc/S57N-9PSY].

Operating Margin, INVESTING ANSWERS (Oct. 1, 2019), https://investinganswers.com/ dictionary/o/operating-margin [https://perma.cc/5SF7-XYGW].

Outsourcing Accountability Act of 2015, H.R. 3811, 115th Cong., https://www.congress. gov/bill/114th-congress/house-bill/3811.

Outsourcing Information Act of 2004, S. 2962, 108th Cong. (2004), https://www.con-gress.gov/bill/108th-congress/senate-bill/2962 [https://perma.cc/53FC-3QBN].

Marvin E. Prater et al., *Rail Competition Changes since the Staggers Act*, 49 J. TRANSP. RES. F. 111 (2010).

Press Release, *S&P Capital IQ and SNL Unveils New Division Name: S&P Global Market Intelligence* (Feb. 8, 2016), https://www.prnewswire.com/news-releases/

sp-capital-iq-and-snl-unveils-new-division-name-sp-global-market-intelligence-300216420.html [https://perma.cc/Z53S-554K].

Seventeenth Mobile Wireless Competition Report, 29 FCC Rcd. 15311 (19) (2014), https://www.fcc.gov/document/17th-annual-competition-report [https://perma.cc/9YCD-CM5B].

DENNIS A. SHIELDS, CONG. RESEARCH SERV., CONSOLIDATION AND CONCENTRATION IN THE U.S. DAIRY INDUSTRY, RL41224 (2010).

Southwest Airlines Co., *Annual Reports (Form 10-K)*, https://www.sec.gov/cgi-bin/browse-edgar?action=getcompany&CIK=0000092380&type=10-k&dateb=&owner=exclude&count=40 [https://perma.cc/YKY7-MEQ8].

Southwest Airlines Co LUV: Financials, Key Ratios, MORNINGSTAR, http://financials.morningstar.com/ratios/r.html?t=LUV [https://perma.cc/YA99-NDEA].

Standard & Poor's Compustat: Products & Services for the Academic Community, STANDARD & POOR'S (Jan. 7, 2009), http://fccee.ugr.es/pages/facultad/vicedecanatos/vicedecanato-de-investigacion-y-posgrado/documentos/bases-de-datos/compustat-for-academics/! [https://perma.cc/XUT9-RW9G].

Stop Outsourcing and Create American Jobs Act of 2015, H.R. 3812, 114th Cong., https://www.congress.gov/bill/114th-congress/house-bill/3812.

LAWRENCE A. SULLIVAN & WARREN S. GRIMES, THE LAW OF ANTITRUST: AN INTEGRATED HANDBOOK (2d ed. 2006).

United Airlines Holdings Inc., *Annual Reports (Form 10-K)*, https://www.sec.gov/cgi-bin/browse-edgar?action=getcompany&CIK=0000100517&type=10-k&dateb=&owner=exclude&count=40 [https://perma.cc/HD9X-FP94].

United Airlines Holdings Inc UAL: Financials, Key Ratios, MORNINGSTAR, http://financials.morningstar.com/ratios/r.html?t=UAL [https://perma.cc/4V6X-9EL9].

U.S. CENSUS BUREAU, *About the Economic Census* (Dec. 23, 2019), https://www.census.gov/programs-surveys/economic-census/about.html [https://perma.cc/CM4H-FAV3].

U.S. CENSUS BUREAU, *Economic Census*, https://www.census.gov/programs-surveys/economic-census.html.

U.S. CENSUS BUREAU, *The Economic Census: How It Works for You* (Jan. 2012), https://www2.census.gov/programs-surveys/economic-census/2012/program-management/outreach-partnerships/factsheets/ec-brochure.pdf [https://perma.cc/U7FY-3B2U].

U.S. CENSUS BUREAU, *NAICS Codes & Understanding Industry Classification Systems* (Apr. 5, 2018), https://www.census.gov/programs-surveys/economic-census/guidance/understanding-naics.html#par_textimage [https://perma.cc/EBR4-G5ZC].

U.S. CENSUS BUREAU, *North American Industry Classification System: Frequently Asked Questions*, https://www.census.gov/eos/www/naics/faqs/faqs.html [https://perma.cc/GC32-JFVD].

U.S. Dep't of Agriculture, *Census of Agriculture* (May 2, 2014), https://www.nass.usda.gov/Publications/AgCensus/2012/ [https://perma.cc/ZYB7-WJYD].

U.S. DEP'T OF JUSTICE & FED. TRADE COMM'N, HORIZONTAL MERGER GUIDELINES (1997), https://www.justice.gov/sites/default/files/atr/legacy/2007/07/11/11251.pdf [https://perma.cc/B2UL-YA7E].

WASH. STATE DEP'T OF REVENUE, *SIC and NAICS Codes* https://dor.wa.gov/about/statistics-reports/sic-and-naics-codes [https://perma.cc/QE9S-URNS].

Jim Wilkinson, *Operating Profit Margin Ratio*, STRATEGIC CFO (July 24, 2013), https://strategiccfo.com/operating-profit-margin-ratio/ [https://perma.cc/ZTZ3-JR7H].

Bibliography

Reed Abelson, *CVS Health and Aetna $69 Billion Merger Is Approved with Conditions*, N.Y. TIMES (Oct. 10, 2018), https://www.nytimes.com/2018/10/10/health/cvs-aetna-merger.html [https://perma.cc/3FKY-JMXT].

Reed Abelson, *Merger of Cigna and Express Scripts Gets Approval from Justice Dept.*, N.Y. TIMES (Sept. 17, 2018), https://www.nytimes.com/2018/09/17/health/cigna-express-scripts-merger.html [https://perma.cc/EJ6R-6V64].

Daron Acemoglu et al., *Import Competition and the Great US Employment Sag of the 2000s*, 34 J. LAB. ECON. S141 (2016).

Matthew D. Adler & Eric A. Posner, *Rethinking Cost-Benefit Analysis*, 109 YALE L.J. 165 (1999).

Azam Ahmed & Elisabeth Malkin, *For Commerce Pick Wilbur Ross, "Inherently Bad" Deals Paid Off*, N.Y. TIMES (Feb. 25, 2017), https://www.nytimes.com/2017/02/25/world/americas/wilbur-ross-trump-commerce-secretary.html [https://perma.cc/BP65-FZ3F].

BRIAN ALEXANDER, GLASS HOUSE: THE 1% ECONOMY AND THE SHATTERING OF THE ALL-AMERICAN TOWN (2017).

Raquel Alexander et al., *Measuring Rates of Return on Lobbying Expenditures: An Empirical Case Study of Tax Breaks for Multinational Corporations*, 25 J.L. & POL. 401 (2009).

Anheuser-Busch Cos., *Quarterly Report (Form 10-Q)* (Nov. 6, 2008), https://www.sec.gov/Archives/edgar/data/310569/000095013708013472/c47434e10vq.htm [https://perma.cc/44Z2-2WRV].

Binyamin Appelbaum, Opinion, *Blame Economists for the Mess We're In*, N.Y. TIMES (Aug. 30, 2019), https://www.nytimes.com/2019/08/24/opinion/sunday/economics-milton-friedman.html [https://perma.cc/J8X4-P2FP].

Apple Inc., *Annual Report (Form 10-K)* (Sept. 30, 2017), https://www.sec.gov/Archives/edgar/data/320193/000032019317000070/a10-k20179302017.htm#s65EBF38841D3591FA44752CC48FB0D37 [https://perma.cc/YAY4-NQRS].

Tali Arbel & Marcy Gordon, *T-Mobile's $26.5b Sprint Deal Ok'd Despite Competition Fears*, ASSOCIATED PRESS (July 26, 2019), https://apnews.com/7cd71d5aae224188a93d679ac74d24d7 [https://perma.cc/8TY3-GB9C].

KENNETH J. ARROW, SOCIAL CHOICE AND INDIVIDUAL VALUES (1963).

Benito Arruñada, *Coase and the Departure from Property*, in THE ELGAR COMPANION TO RONALD H. COASE 305 (Claude Menard & Elodie Bertrand eds., 2016).

Orley Ashenfelter et al., *Did Robert Bork Understate the Competitive Impact of Mergers? Evidence from Consummated Mergers*, 57 J.L. & ECON. S67 (2014).

Scott E. Atkinson & Robert Halvorsen, *The Relative Efficiency of Public and Private Firms in a Regulated Environment: The Case of US Electric Utilities*, 29 J. PUB. ECON. 281 (1986).

David H. Autor et al., *The China Shock: Learning from Labor-Market Adjustment to Large Changes in Trade*, 8 ANN. REV. ECON. 205 (2016).

Laura Baker, Data, *U.S. Graduation Rates by State and Student Demographics*, EDUC. WK. (Dec. 7, 2017), https://www.edweek.org/ew/section/multimedia/data-us-graduation-rates-by-state-and.html [https://perma.cc/5Q27-V7J9].

Liana B. Baker & Anjali Athavaley, *Sprint, T-Mobile Call Off Merger after Months of Talks*, REUTERS (Nov. 4, 2017), https://www.reuters.com/article/us-sprint-corp-m-a-t-mobile-us/sprint-t-mobile-call-off-merger-after-months-of-talks-idUSKBN1D40RY [https://perma.cc/8TFZ-7RXK].

Brooks Barnes, *Disney Heiress Escalates Attack on Company's Pay Practices*, N.Y. TIMES (Apr. 23, 2019), https://www.nytimes.com/2019/04/23/business/media/disney-heiress-attacks-pay-practices.html [https://perma.cc/B6XT-Q4CV].

Bruce Bartlett, *Reagan's Forgotten Tax Record*, 130 TAX NOTES 965 (2011).

Robert L. Bartley, *Introduction* to JUDE WANNISKI, THE WAY THE WORLD WORKS (3d ed. 1989).

YORAM BARZEL, ECONOMIC ANALYSIS OF PROPERTY RIGHTS (1989).

Sam Batkins et al., *Market Concentration Grew During Obama Administration*, AM. ACTION F. (Apr. 7, 2016), https://www.americanactionforum.org/print/?url=https://www.americanactionforum.org/research/market-concentration-grew-obama-administration/ [https://perma.cc/5FKW-CUU9].

BEN BEACHY, *NAFTA's 20-Year Legacy and the Fate of the Trans-Pacific Partnership*, PUB. CITIZEN (Feb. 2014), https://www.citizen.org/wp-content/uploads/migration/nafta-at-20-embargoed.pdf [https://perma.cc/VV98-N5KA].

Marie Beaugureau, *Here's Why Insulin Is So Expensive—And What You Can Do About It*, GOODRX (Feb. 8, 2018), https://www.goodrx.com/blog/heres-why-insulin-is-so-expensive-and-what-you-can-do-about-it/ [https://perma.cc/H3Y3-7FU8].

ADOLF A. BERLE, THE TWENTIETH-CENTURY CAPITALIST REVOLUTION (1954).

ADOLF A. BERLE & GARDINER C. MEANS, THE MODERN CORPORATION AND PRIVATE PROPERTY (1991) (1932).

ANNETTE BERNHARDT & MIKE EVANGELIST, NAT'L EMP'T LAW PROJECT, THE LOW-WAGE RECOVERY: INDUSTRY EMPLOYMENT AND WAGES FOUR YEARS INTO THE RECOVERY (Apr. 2014), https://s27147.pcdn.co/wp-content/uploads/2015/03/Low-Wage-Recovery-Industry-Employment-Wages-2014-Report.pdf [https://perma.cc/2K6H-KRYU].

Betriebsverfassungsgesetz [Betrvg] [Works Constitution Act], Sept. 25, 2001, BGBl I at 2518, § 1 (Ger.), https://www.gesetze-im-internet.de/englisch_betrvg/englisch_betrvg.pdf.

Sanjai Bhagat et al., *Hostile Takeovers in the 1980s: The Return to Corporate Specialization*, 1990 BROOKINGS PAPERS ON ECON. ACTIVITY 1 (1990).

Henry Blodget, *This One Tweet Reveals What's Wrong with American Business Culture and the Economy*, BUS. INSIDER (July 31, 2013), https://www.businessinsider.com/business-and-the-economy-2013-7 [https://perma.cc/5M48-ATYK].

MARK BLYTH, AUSTERITY: THE HISTORY OF A DANGEROUS IDEA (2013).

ROBERT H. BORK, THE ANTITRUST PARADOX: A POLICY AT WAR WITH ITSELF (1978).

ROBERT BOYD & PETER J. RICHERSON, CULTURE AND THE EVOLUTIONARY PROCESS (1985).

Robert Boyer, *The Four Fallacies of Contemporary Austerity Policies: The Lost Keynesian Legacy*, 36 CAMBRIDGE J. ECON. 283 (2012).

William W. Bratton, *Berle and Means Reconsidered at the Century's Turn*, 26 J. CORP. L. 737 (2000).

Chad Bray & Reed Abelson, *Aetna Agrees to Acquire Humana for $37 Billion in Cash and Stock*, N.Y. TIMES: DEALBOOK (July 3, 2015), https://www.nytimes.com/2015/07/04/business/dealbook/aetna-agrees-to-acquire-humana-for-37-billion-in-cash-and-stock.html [https://perma.cc/FJH3-SFZY].

Bring Jobs Home Act, S. 3364, 112th Cong. (2012).

Joel Brockner et al., *Survivors' Reactions to Layoffs: We Get by with a Little Help for Our Friends*, 32 ADMIN. SCI. Q. 526 (1987).

David Brooks, Opinion, *What the Working Class Is Still Trying to Tell Us*, N.Y. TIMES (Nov. 8, 2018), https://www.nytimes.com/2018/11/08/opinion/midterms-working-class-labor.html [https://perma.cc/5YVF-AJ5V].

Brown Shoe Co. v. United States, 370 U.S.C. 294 (1962).

Barrett J. Brunsman, *P&G Sheds 2,700 Jobs as Buffett Deal Closes*, CINCINNATI BUS. J. (Mar. 1, 2016), https://www.bizjournals.com/cincinnati/news/2016/03/01/p-g-sheds-2-700-jobs-as-buffett-deal-closes.html [https://perma.cc/5TNV-36EN].

Building a New Boeing, ECONOMIST, Aug. 12. 2000, at 83.

BUS. ROUNDTABLE, *Statement on the Purpose of a Corporation* (Aug. 19, 2019), https://opportunity.businessroundtable.org/ourcommitment/ [https://perma.cc/NZM5-FFCA].

Pierre Cahuc et al., *Youth Unemployment in Old Europe: The Polar Cases of France and Germany*, 2:18 IZA J. EUR. LAB. STUD. 1 (2013).

Guido Calabresi, *The Pointlessness of Pareto: Carrying Coase Further*, 100 YALE L.J. 1211 (1990).

Ryan Calo, *Digital Market Manipulation*, 82 GEO. WASH. L. REV. 995 (2014).

Eric Cantor, *A Year of Living Dangerously*, in YOUNG GUNS: A NEW GENERATION OF CONSERVATIVE LEADERS 39 (Eric Cantor et al. eds., 2010).

David Card et al., *The Geography of Giving: The Effect of Corporate Headquarters on Local Charities*, 94 J. PUB. ECON. 222 (2010).

Oren Cass, *The Culture War on Work* (Dec. 12, 2018), https://medium.com/@orencass/the-culture-war-on-work-d1c6cae9db08 [https://perma.cc/MJT4-69P7].

OREN CASS, MANHATTAN INSTITUTE, THE WORKFORCE-TRAINING GRANT: A NEW BRIDGE FROM HIGH SCHOOL TO CAREER (July 2019), https://media4.manhattan-institute.org/sites/default/files/R-0719-OCass.pdf [https://perma.cc/U5TB-QBSN].

OREN CASS, THE ONCE AND FUTURE WORKER: A VISION FOR THE RENEWAL OF WORK IN AMERICA (2018).

CTR. FOR RESPONSIVE POL., *Lobbying*, https://www.opensecrets.org/federal-lobbying [https://perma.cc/WM9A-JQFC].

CTR. FOR RESPONSIVE POL., *Trends in Spending*, https://www.opensecrets.org/federal-lobbying/trends-in-spending [https://perma.cc/G9CY-K5XL].

CEO Pay: How Much Do CEOs Make Compared to Their Employees?, PAYSCALE, https://www.payscale.com/data-packages/ceo-pay [https://perma.cc/W2DV-KXEV].

Jim Chappelow, *Labor Force Participation Rate*, INVESTOPEDIA (Jan. 29, 2020), https://www.investopedia.com/terms/p/participationrate.asp [https://perma.cc/65JG-VBWN].

Charter of Fundamental Rights of the European Union, 2012 O.J. (C 326) 391.

Raj Chetty et al., *The Fading American Dream: Trends in Absolute Income Mobility since 1940*, 356 SCIENCE 398 (2017).

CHILD TRENDS DATABANK, *Key Facts About High School Dropout Rates* (2018), https://www.childtrends.org/indicators/high-school-dropout-rates [https://perma.cc/L3Y6-DRDF].

Clayton Act § 7, 15 U.S.C. § 18 (2018).

Ronald H. Coase, *How Should Economists Choose? G. Warren Nutter Lecture in Political Economy at the American Enterprise Institute for Public Policy Research (Nov. 18, 1981)*, in ESSAYS ON ECONOMICS AND ECONOMISTS 15 (1995).

Ronald H. Coase, *The Problem of Social Cost*, 3 J.L. & ECON. 1 (1960).

Patricia Cohen, *Bump in U.S. Incomes Doesn't Erase 50 Years of Pain*, N.Y. TIMES (Sept. 16, 2017), https://www.nytimes.com/2017/09/16/business/economy/bump-in-us-incomes-doesnt-erase-50-years-of-pain.html [https://perma.cc/FQL4-UC5X].

Patricia Cohen, *A Tax Cut That Lifts the Economy? Opinions Are Split*, N.Y. TIMES (Nov. 2, 2017), https://www.nytimes.com/2017/11/02/business/economy/corporate-tax-economists.html [https://perma.cc/V6FF-JQLKs].

Michael Collins, *Where Have All the Good Paying Jobs Gone?*, INDUSTRY WK. (Mar. 4, 2016), https://www.industryweek.com/the-economy/public-policy/article/22007276/where-have-all-the-good-paying-jobs-gone [https://perma.cc/Y6MN-LLEF].

Constitutzione [Cost.] (It.).

Brad Cooper, *Brownback Signs Big Tax Bill in Kansas*, KAN. CITY STAR (May 23, 2012), https://www.kansascity.com/latest-news/article303137/Brownback-signs-big-tax-cut-in-Kansas.html [https://perma.cc/Z9FN-59T2].

MARK COOPER, CONSUMER FED'N OF AM., THE SPECIAL PROBLEM OF SPECIAL ACCESS: CONSUMER OVERCHARGES AND TELEPHONE COMPANY EXCESS PROFITS (2016), https://consumerfed.org/wp-content/uploads/2016/04/4-16-The-Special-Problem-of-Special-Access.pdf [https://perma.cc/8HLN-BVYX].

ROBERT COOTER & THOMAS ULEN, LAW AND ECONOMICS (1988).

Dean Corbae & Pablo D'Erasmo, *A Quantitative Model of Banking Industry Dynamics* (Mar. 21, 2013), https://02e278dc-a-62cb3a1a-s-sites.googlegroups.com/site/deancorbae/research/bank032113.pdf [https://perma.cc/L8L8-4RUC].

WALTER CORSON ET AL., INTERNATIONAL TRADE AND WORKER DISLOCATION: EVALUATION OF THE TRADE ADJUSTMENT ASSISTANCE PROGRAM (1993).

ANTOINE COURNOT, RESEARCHES INTO THE MATHEMATICAL PRINCIPLES OF THE THEORY OF WEALTH (1897) (1838).

Bryce Covert, Opinion, *When Companies Supersize, Paychecks Shrink*, N.Y. TIMES (May 13, 2018), https://www.nytimes.com/2018/05/13/opinion/mergers-companies-supersize-workers-wages.html [https://perma.cc/R3VU-U5MN].

Cox v. Spirit Airlines, Inc., 786 F. App'x 283 (2d Cir. 2019).

Julie Creswell & Michael J. de la Merced, *Struggles at Procter & Gamble Draw Scrutiny of Nelson Peltz*, N.Y. TIMES (July 17, 2017), https://www.nytimes.com/2017/07/17/business/dealbook/procter-gamble-nelson-peltz-trian.html [https://perma.cc/J8HP-5JLT].

DONALD T. CRITCHLOW, THE CONSERVATIVE ASCENDANCY: HOW THE GOP RIGHT MADE POLITICAL HISTORY (2007).

Barry Z. Cynamon & Steven M. Fazzari, *Rising Inequality and Stagnation in the US Economy*, 12 EUR. J. ECON. & ECON. POLICIES: INTERVENTION 170 (2015).

RONALD D'AMICO & PETER Z. SCHOCHET, MATHEMATICA POL'Y RESEARCH, THE EVALUATION OF THE TRADE ADJUSTMENT ASSISTANCE PROGRAM: A SYNTHESIS OF MAJOR FINDINGS (2012), https://www.mathematica.org/our-publications-and-findings/publications/the-evaluation-of-the-trade-adjustment-assistance-program-a-synthesis-of-major-findings [https://perma.cc/G2KF-BSJB].

RALF DAHRENDORF, REFLECTIONS ON THE REVOLUTION IN EUROPE: IN A LETTER INTENDED TO HAVE BEEN SENT TO A GENTLEMAN IN WARSAW (1990).

Gerrit De Geest, *Any Normative Policy Analysis Not Based on Kaldor-Hicks Efficiency Violates Scholarly Transparency Norms, in* LAW AND ECONOMICS: PHILOSOPHICAL ISSUES AND FUNDAMENTAL QUESTIONS 183 (Aristides N. Hatzis & Nicholas Mercuro eds., 2015).

Michael J. de la Merced, *InBev to Buy Anheuser-Busch for $52 Billion,* N.Y. TIMES (July 14, 2008), https://www.nytimes.com/2008/07/14/business/worldbusiness/14iht-14beer.14460585.html [https://perma.cc/2Y7W-SQRM].

Michael J. de la Merced & Chad Bray, *Kraft Heinz Withdraws $143 Billion Offer to Merge with Unilever,* N.Y. TIMES: DEALBOOK (Feb. 19, 2017), https://www.nytimes.com/2017/02/19/business/dealbook/kraft-heinz-unilever-merger.html [https://perma.cc/C4XC-YPZF].

Laura Debter, *Dow Chemical to Cut 2,500 Jobs Ahead of DuPont Merger,* FORBES (June 28, 2016), https://www.forbes.com/sites/laurengensler/2016/06/28/dow-chemical-to-cut-2500-jobs-ahead-of-dupont-merger/ [https://perma.cc/8T5Y-ZPSH].

Delta Airlines, *Annual Report (Form 10-K)* (Feb. 23, 2018), https://www.sec.gov/Archives/edgar/data/27904/000002790418000006/dal1231201710k.htm [https://perma.cc/C9KY-C6KC].

Tuan Do, *The Real Production Costs of Smartphones,* TECHWALLS (Nov. 25, 2019), https://www.techwalls.com/production-costs-of-smartphones/ [https://perma.cc/2LRT-3X2D].

Craig Doidge, G. Andrew Karolyi, & René M. Stulz, *The U.S. Listing Gap* (Nat'l Bureau of Econ. Research, Working Paper No. 21181, May 2015), https://www.nber.org/papers/w21181 [https://perma.cc/748L-LWTR].

Domestic Market Share of Leading U.S. Airlines from February 2019 to January 2020, STATISTA, statista.com/statistics/250577/domestic-market-share-of-leading-us-airlines/ [https://perma.cc/5P7X-3VNX].

Dow Chemical Co., *Annual Report (Form 10-K)* (Feb. 9, 2017), https://www.sec.gov/Archives/edgar/data/29915/000002991517000011/dow201610k.htm [https://perma.cc/NM68-P3BR].

Dow Chemical Co., *Quarterly Report (Form 10-Q)* (July 27, 2017), https://www.sec.gov/Archives/edgar/data/29915/000002991517000035/dow-q2x6302017.htm [https://perma.cc/7AP9-8JRH].

Mario Draghi, President, Eur. Cent. Bank, Keynote Speech at Henry Grattan Lecture Series at Trinity College, Dublin: Youth Unemployment in the Euro Area (Sept. 22, 2017), https://www.ecb.europa.eu/press/key/date/2017/html/ecb.sp170922_1.en.html [https://perma.cc/VJB8-G4CM].

Erin Duffin, *U.S. Household Income Distribution from 1990 to 2018 (by Gini-Coefficient),* STATISTA (Sept. 24, 2019), https://www.statista.com/statistics/219643/gini-coefficient-for-us-individuals-families-and-households/ [https://perma.cc/MXJ5-2LK3].

ECON. POLICY INST., ECON. POLICY INST., MISSING WORKERS: THE MISSING PART OF THE UNEMPLOYMENT STORY (July 7, 2017), https://www.epi.org/publication/missing-workers/ [https://perma.cc/8GRQ-VHG6].

Thomas B. Edsall, Opinion, *Whose Party Is It Anyway?,* N.Y. TIMES (July 8, 2015), https://www.nytimes.com/2015/07/08/opinion/thomas-b-edsall-whose-party-is-it-anyway.html [https://perma.cc/4GNZ-25AX].

Gauti B. Eggertsson et al., *Kaldor and Piketty's Facts: The Rise of Monopoly Power in the United States* (Nat'l Bureau of Econ. Research, Working Paper No. 24,287, 2018), http://www.nber.org/papers/w24287 [https://perma.cc/D3VT-BZE9].

THRÁINN EGGERTSSON, IMPERFECT INSTITUTIONS: POSSIBILITIES AND LIMITS OF REFORM (2005).

Thráinn Eggertsson, *Knowledge and the Theory of Institutional Change*, 5 J. INSTITUTIONAL ECON. 137 (2009).

Thráinn Eggertsson, *Mapping Social Technologies in the Cultural Commons*, 95 CORNELL L. REV. 711 (2009).

THRÁINN EGGERTSSON, NORMS IN ECONOMICS: WITH SPECIAL REFERENCE TO ECONOMIC DEVELOPMENT (1999).

Thráinn Eggertsson, *The Old Theory of Economic Policy and the New Institutionalism*, 25 WORLD DEV. 1187 (1997).

Niv Elis, *Federal Deficit Jumps 20 Percent after Tax Cuts, Spending Bill*, HILL (Aug. 8, 2018), https://thehill.com/policy/finance/400876-federal-deficit-jumps-20-percent-after-tax-cuts-spending-bill [https://perma.cc/XA3W-8E6T].

Christopher Elliott, *Got a Complaint About the Travel Industry? It's Got One About You, Too*, WASH. POST (Sept. 27, 2017), https://www.washingtonpost.com/lifestyle/travel/got-a-complaint-about-the-travel-industry-its-got-a-complaint-about-you-too/2017/09/26/707c59ec-97d3-11e7-87fc-c3f7ee4035c9_story.html [https://perma.cc/KSA3-KV5W].

Christopher Elliott, *It's Time for Congress to Stand Up for Air Travelers*, WASH. POST (Feb. 18, 2016), https://www.washingtonpost.com/lifestyle/travel/its-time-for-congress-to-stand-up-for-air-travelers/2016/02/18/2a21b7aa-d4d7-11e5-b195-2e29a4e13425_story.html [https://perma.cc/T3QZ-JNH2].

Christopher Elliott, *Three Top Airlines Changed the Pricing of Multi-City Tickets. Here's How to Avoid Paying More.*, WASH. POST (Apr. 14, 2016), https://www.washingtonpost.com/lifestyle/travel/three-top-airlines-changed-the-pricing-of-multi-city-tickets-heres-how-to-avoid-paying-more/2016/04/14/59cf234e-00c8-11e6-b823-707c79ce3504_story.html [https://perma.cc/BK27-E72K].

Christopher Elliott, *The Wifi on Planes Makes a Convincing Argument for the In-flight Novel*, WASH. POST (Apr. 21, 2016), https://www.washingtonpost.com/lifestyle/travel/the-wifi-on-planes-makes-a-convincing-argument-for-the-in-flight-novel/2016/04/21/e130c592-df06-11e5-846c-10191d1fc4ec_story.html [https://perma.cc/HS7U-Q8QX].

EXEC. OFFICE OF THE PRESIDENT, COUNCIL ECON. ADVISERS, BENEFITS OF COMPETITION AND INDICATORS OF MARKET POWER (2016), https://obamawhitehouse.archives.gov/sites/default/files/page/files/20160414_cea_competition_issue_brief.pdf [https://perma.cc/CS72-XZL3].

FAKE NEWS: UNDERSTANDING MEDIA AND MISINFORMATION IN THE DIGITAL AGE (Melissa Zimdars & Kembrew McLeod eds., 2020).

Richard H. Fallon Jr., *Legitimacy and the Constitution*, 118 HARV. L. REV. 1787 (2004).

Mike Faulk, *Nonprofits Fishing for Dollars in a More Crowded Pond*, ST. LOUIS POST-DISPATCH (Sept. 19, 2016), https://www.stltoday.com/business/local/nonprofits-fishing-for-dollars-in-a-more-crowded-pond/article_70cff4cd-429f-5329-b65e-b1fd5d5d4dab.html [https://perma.cc/3JJY-25NC].

FED. BANK OF ST. LOUIS, U.S. DEP'T OF TREAS., *Federal Debt Held by the Public*, https://fred.stlouisfed.org/graph/?g=k977 [https://perma.cc/YYJ9-Z74M].

Brian S. Feldman, *How America's Coastal Cities Left the Heartland Behind*, ATLANTIC (Apr. 18, 2016), https://www.theatlantic.com/business/archive/2016/04/how-americas-coastal-cities-left-the-heartland-behind/478296/ [https://perma.cc/JWE9-D9J8].

Brian Feldt, *A Decade after Anheuser-Busch's Sale, Beer Still Pours from St. Louis Brewery but Much Has Changed*, ST. LOUIS POST-DISPATCH (July 13, 2018), https://www.stltoday.com/business/local/a-decade-after-anheuser-busch-s-sale-beer-still-pours/article_5a9faf1c-d7c9-5d46-99de-b11b1e22f703.html   [https://perma.cc/HW7K-FPLV].

Brian Feldt, *Scottrade Layoffs Climb to over 1,000*, ST. LOUIS POST-DISPATCH (Mar. 22, 2018), https://www.stltoday.com/business/local/scottrade-layoffs-climb-to-over/article_6dc4f951-b4ae-53b1-8066-63e4b9436222.html   [https://perma.cc/4C64-7CB9].

Gary M. Fink, *F. Ray Marshall: Secretary of Labor and Jimmy Carter's Ambassador to Organized Labor*, 37 LAB. HIST. 463 (1996).

Samuel Fleischacker, *Adam Smith's Moral and Political Philosophy*, STAN. ENCYCLOPEDIA OF PHIL. (Jan. 27, 2017), https://plato.stanford.edu/entries/smith-moral-political/ [https://perma.cc/T9US-LPE6].

John Bellamy Foster et al., *Monopoly and Competition in Twenty-First Century Capitalism*, MONTHLY REV., Apr. 2011, at 1.

Stuart Fox, *What Causes Corporate Greed?*, LIVESCIENCE (Apr. 30, 2010), https://www.livescience.com/6394-corporate-greed.html [https://perma.cc/G2TA-CUUT].

Theo Francis & Ryan Knutson, *Wave of Megadeals Tests Antitrust Limits in U.S.*, WALL ST. J. (Oct. 18, 2015), https://www.wsj.com/articles/wave-of-megadeals-tests-antitrust-limits-in-u-s-1445213306 [https://perma.cc/XH9A-2MMX].

MILTON FRIEDMAN, CAPITALISM AND FREEDOM (1962).

Milton Friedman, *Monopoly and the Social Responsibility of Business and Labor*, in MONOPOLY POWER AND ECONOMIC PERFORMANCE: THE PROBLEM OF INDUSTRIAL CONCENTRATION 105 (Edwin Mansfield ed., 1964).

F.T.C. v. Actavis, Inc., 570 U.S. 136 (2013).

F.T.C. v. Lundbeck, Inc., 650 F.3d 1236 (8th Cir. 2011).

GALLUP, *Trust in Government*, https://news.gallup.com/poll/5392/trust-government.aspx [https://perma.cc/CR2B-M4K4].

Antoine Gara, *More Job Cuts at Kraft Heinz under 3G Capital and Warren Buffett*, FORBES (Nov. 4, 2015), https://www.forbes.com/sites/antoinegara/2015/11/04/more-job-cuts-at-kraft-heinz-under-3g-capital-and-warren-buffett/ [https://perma.cc/J6SM-TAZ4].

Martin Gaynor et al., *The Industrial Organization of Health Care Markets* (Nat'l Bureau of Econ. Research, Working Paper No. 19800, 2014), https://www.nber.org/papers/w19800.pdf [https://perma.cc/8NUG-Q98G].

Kenneth M. Geisler II, Note, *Fissures in the Valley: Searching for a Remedy for US Tech Workers Indirectly Displaced by H-1b Visa Outsourcing Firms*, 95 WASH. U. L. REV. 465 (2017).

David Gelles, *Want to Make Money Like a C.E.O.? Work for 275 Years*, N.Y. TIMES (May 25, 2018), https://www.nytimes.com/2018/05/25/business/highest-paid-ceos-2017.html [https://perma.cc/2CM8-VAZE].

Howard Gleckman, *The Great Kansas Tax Cut Experiment Crashes and Burns*, FORBES (June 7, 2017), https://www.forbes.com/sites/beltway/2017/06/07/the-great-kansas-tax-cut-experiment-crashes-and-burns/#1e2e2aa45508   [https://perma.cc/9ATE-RCYB].

Elaine Glusac, *Fly Farther, for Cheaper. For Now.*, N.Y. TIMES (July 13, 2018), https://www.nytimes.com/2018/07/13/travel/summer-airline-fares.html [https://perma.cc/AYQ9-XB29].

John Godard, *The Exceptional Decline of the American Labor Movement*, 63 INDUS. & LAB. REL. REV. 82 (2009).

Vindu Goel, *IBM Now Has More Employees in India Than in the U.S.*, N.Y. TIMES (Sept. 28, 2017), https://www.nytimes.com/2017/09/28/technology/ibm-india.html [https://perma.cc/2UZV-N8TJ].

AMY GOLDSTEIN, JANESVILLE: AN AMERICAN STORY (2017).

KENT GREENFIELD, THE FAILURE OF CORPORATE LAW: FUNDAMENTAL FLAWS AND PROGRESSIVE POSSIBILITIES (2006).

Aaron Gregg, *Raytheon to Merge with United Technologies, Creating a Military-Industrial Behemoth*, WASH. POST (June 9, 2019), https://www.washingtonpost.com/business/2019/06/09/raytheon-merge-with-united-technologies-creating-military-industrial-behemoth/ [https://perma.cc/CF9G-VMZL].

William Greider, *The Education of David Stockman*, ATLANTIC (Dec., 1981), https://www.theatlantic.com/magazine/archive/1981/12/the-education-of-david-stockman/305760/ [https://perma.cc/CH9Y-CQQY].

Stephen Grocer, *A Record $2.5 Trillion in Mergers Were Announced in the First Half of 2018*, N.Y TIMES (July 3, 2018), https://www.nytimes.com/2018/07/03/business/dealbook/mergers-record-levels.html [https://perma.cc/G5KF-HX7Y].

Gustavo Grullon, Yelena Larkin, & Roni Michaely, *Are US Industries Becoming More Concentrated?*, 23 REV. FIN. 697 (2019).

GRUNDEGESETZ [GG] [Basic Law], art. 9(3) (Ger.), *translation at* https://www.gesetze-im-internet.de/englisch_gg/englisch_gg.html#p0054 [https://perma.cc/E6CR-6729].

JOANNE GUTH & JEAN LEE, U.S. INT'L TRADE COMM'N, EVALUATIONS OF THE TRADE ADJUSTMENT ASSISTANCE PROGRAM FOR WORKERS: A LITERATURE REVIEW (2017), https://www.usitc.gov/publications/332/executive_briefings/ebot_taaevaluationsguthlee.pdf [https://perma.cc/GL6V-S8DB].

GURUFOCUS, *American Airlines Group WACC %*, https://www.gurufocus.com/term/wacc/NAS:AAL/WACC-/American-Airlines-Group-Inc [https://perma.cc/2EJJ-8HS7].

GURUFOCUS, *Delta Air Lines WACC %*, https://www.gurufocus.com/term/wacc/NYSE:DAL/WACC-/Delta-Air-Lines-Inc [https://perma.cc/MQJ3-5LQS].

GURUFOCUS, *Southwest Airlines Co WACC %*, https://www.gurufocus.com/term/wacc/LUV/WACC-Percentage/Southwest%20Airlines%20Co [https://perma.cc/MK8S-FNZ4].

GURUFOCUS, *United Airlines Holdings WACC %*, https://www.gurufocus.com/term/wacc/UAL/WACC-Percentage/United%20Airlines%20Holdings [https://perma.cc/3FUZ-Z4JN].

JAMES D. GWARTNEY ET AL., MICROECONOMICS: PRIVATE AND PUBLIC CHOICE (9th ed. 2000).

JACOB S. HACKER & PAUL PIERSON, WINNER-TAKE-ALL POLITICS: HOW WASHINGTON MADE THE RICH RICHER—AND TURNED ITS BACK ON THE MIDDLE CLASS (2011).

James Hamblin, *The Money Spent Selling Sugar to Americans Is Staggering*, ATLANTIC (Sept. 27, 2015), https://www.theatlantic.com/health/archive/2015/09/the-money-spent-selling-sugar-to-americans-is-staggering/407350/ [https://perma.cc/Q6PM-PE6S].

Donald C. Hambrick & Albert A. Cannella Jr., *Relative Standing: A Framework for Understanding Departures of Acquired Executives*, 36 ACAD. MGMT. J. 733 (1993).

Oscar Handlin & Mary Flug Handlin, Commonwealth: A Study of the Role of Government in the American Economy: Massachusetts, 1774–1861 (1969).

Russell Hardin, *The Crippled Epistemology of Extremism, in* Political Extremism and Rationality 3 (Albert Breton et al. eds., 2002).

Hart-Scott-Rodino Act, 15 U.S.C. § 18a (2018).

Drew Harwell, *Heinz to Acquire Kraft Foods in Mega-Merger*, Wash. Post (Mar. 25, 2015), https://www.washingtonpost.com/business/economy/heinz-will-buy-kraft-foods-in-megamerger-for-american-food/2015/03/25/9ed45bd4-d316-11e4-8fce-3941fc548f1c_story.html [https://perma.cc/T82K-RWA3].

Richard L. Hasen, *Lobbying, Rent-Seeking, and the Constitution*, 64 Stan. L. Rev. 191 (2012).

Albert H. Hastorf & Hadley Cantril, *They Saw a Game; a Case Study*, 49 J. Abnormal & Soc. Psychol. 129 (1954).

Paul M. Hayashi et al., *An Analysis of Pricing and Production Efficiency of Electric Utilities by Mode of Ownership, in* Regulating Utilities in an Era of Deregulation 111 (Michael A. Crew ed., 1987).

Thomas Lee Hazen, *The Short-Term/Long-Term Dichotomy and Investment Theory: Implications for Securities Market Regulation and for Corporate Law*, 70 N.C. L. Rev. 137 (1991).

David R. Henderson, *Burying Good Ideas*, Reg., Spring. 2011, at 56 (book review).

Lauren Hirsch & Chris Prentice, *AB InBev, SABMiller Deal Wins U.S. Approval, Adds Craft Beer Protections*, Reuters (July 20, 2016), https://www.reuters.com/article/us-sabmiller-m-a-abinbev-idUSKCN1002HJ [https://perma.cc/PB4K-GYP6].

Ian Holloway, *The Constitutionalization of Employment Rights: A Comparative View*, 14 Berkeley J. Emp. & Lab. L. 113 (1993).

Scott Horsley, *From a Napkin to a White House Medal—The Path of a Controversial Economic Idea*, NPR: Morning Edition (June 19, 2019), https://www.npr.org/2019/06/19/733779337/from-a-napkin-to-a-white-house-medal-the-path-of-a-controversial-economic-idea [https://perma.cc/5QG4-Q7ZT].

Scott Horsley, *Ronald Reagan's Legacy Clouds Tax Record*, NPR: Morning Edition (Feb. 4, 2011), https://www.npr.org/2011/02/04/133489113/Reagan-Legacy-Clouds-Tax-Record [https://perma.cc/PJ9R-V7DP].

Herbert J. Hovenkamp, *Appraising Merger Efficiencies*, 24 Geo. Mason L. Rev. 703 (2017).

How to Germany, *Termination of an Employment Contract in Germany*, https://www.howtogermany.com/pages/termination-employment-contract.html [https://perma.cc/77DZ-PNGQ].

Benjamin G. Hyman, *Can Displaced Labor Be Retrained? Evidence from Quasi-Random Assignment to Trade Adjustment Assistance* (Nov. 5, 2018), https://papers.ssrn.com/sol3/papers.cfm?abstract_id=3155386 [https://perma.cc/48RY-XLP6].

David Ihrke, *United States Mover Rate at a New Record Low*, Census Blogs (Jan. 23, 2017), https://www.census.gov/newsroom/blogs/random-samplings/2017/01/mover-rate.html [https://perma.cc/C5NN-4JGS].

Christopher Ingraham, *Household Net Worth Falls by Largest Amount since the Great Recession, New Fed Data Shows*, Wash. Post (Mar. 7, 2019), https://www.washingtonpost.com/us-policy/2019/03/07/household-net-worth-falls-by-largest-amount-since-great-recession-new-fed-data-show/ [https://perma.cc/Y874-L2XA].

Inst. Chartered Sec'y & Adm'rs & Inv. Ass'n, The Stakeholder Voice in Board Decision Making: Strengthening the Business, Promoting Long-Term

Success (Sept. 2017), https://www.icsa.org.uk/assets/files/free-guidance-notes/the-stakeholder-voice-in-Board-Decision-Making-09-2017.pdf [https://perma.cc/LWD5-7BY8].

Interview by Julie Pace with President Donald Trump, in Washington, D.C. (Apr. 23, 2017), https://apnews.com/c810d7de280a47e88848b0ac74690c83/Transcript-of-AP-interview-with-Trump [https://perma.cc/M2FY-9Z3Q].

WALTER ISAACSON, STEVE JOBS (2011).

Chris Isidore, *P&G to Buy Gillette for $57b*, CNN MONEY (Jan. 28, 2005), https://money.cnn.com/2005/01/28/news/fortune500/pg_gillette/ [https://perma.cc/8X6C-E9RU].

Michael C. Jensen, *Value Maximization, Stakeholder Theory, and the Corporate Objective Function*, J. APPLIED CORP. FIN., Fall 2001, at 8.

Michael C. Jensen & Kevin J. Murphy, *CEO Incentives—It's Not How Much You Pay, but How*, J. APPLIED CORP. FIN., Winter 2010, at 64.

Alfred E. Kahn, *Surprises of Airline Deregulation*, 78 AM. ECON. REV. 316 (1988).

Michael S. Kang, *Democratizing Direct Democracy: Restoring Voter Competence through Heuristic Cues and "Disclosure Plus,"* 50 UCLA L. REV. 1141 (2002).

Louis Kaplow, *Why (Ever) Define Markets?*, 124 HARV. L. REV. 437 (2010).

Sudip Kar-Gupta, *France Wants FCA-Renault Job Guarantees and Nissan on Board*, REUTERS (May 28, 2019), https://www.reuters.com/article/us-renault-m-a-fiat-chrysler/france-wants-fca-renault-job-guarantees-and-nissan-on-board-idUSKCN1SY0FR [https://perma.cc/547N-Y8KJ].

John F. Kennedy, *Attack on the Steel Price Increase (Apr. 11, 1962)*, *in* MONOPOLY POWER AND ECONOMIC PERFORMANCE: THE PROBLEM OF INDUSTRIAL CONCENTRATION 87 (Edwin Mansfield ed., 1964).

John F. Kennedy, *Press Conference, 11 April 1962*, JOHN F. KENNEDY PRESIDENTIAL LIBRARY & MUSEUM, https://www.jfklibrary.org/asset-viewer/archives/JFKWHA/1962/JFKWHA-086/JFKWHA-086 [https://perma.cc/U3YS-4AS3].

JOHN MAYNARD KEYNES, THE GENERAL THEORY OF EMPLOYMENT, INTEREST, AND MONEY (1964).

Neil Kokemuller, *Why Do People Buy Brand Names?*, HOUS. CHRONICLE (Jan. 28, 2019), https://smallbusiness.chron.com/people-buy-brand-names-69654.html [https://perma.cc/7PKK-3KCQ].

Julia Kollewe, *Renault-Fiat Chrysler Merger Collapses*, GUARDIAN (June 6, 2019), https://www.theguardian.com/business/2019/jun/06/renault-fiat-chrysler-merger-collapses [https://perma.cc/43A3-4R2A].

Rita D. Kosnik & Debra L. Shapiro, *Agency Conflicts between Investment Banks and Corporate Clients in Merger and Acquisition Transactions: Causes and Remedies*, ACAD. MGMT. PERSP., Feb. 1997, at 7.

Kraft Heinz Co., *Annual Report (Form 10-K)* (Feb. 23, 2017), https://www.sec.gov/Archives/edgar/data/1637459/000163745917000007/0001637459-17-000007-index.htm [https://perma.cc/MQH6-R5TK].

Kraft Heinz Co., *Quarterly Report (Form 10-Q)* (Aug. 4, 2017), https://www.sec.gov/Archives/edgar/data/1637459/000163745917000101/form10-qq22017.htm [https://perma.cc/7FK6-PWH7].

Steve Kraske, *Gov. Sam Brownback Suffers a Political Brownout*, KAN. CITY STAR (May 2, 2014), https://www.kansascity.com/sports/spt-columns-blogs/article348571/Gov.-Sam-Brownback-suffers-a-political-brownout.html [https://perma.cc/S8KN-HV3T].

Nicholas Kristof, Opinion, *Trump Finds a Brawler for His War on Workers*, N.Y. TIMES (Aug. 10, 2019), https://www.nytimes.com/2019/08/10/opinion/sunday/labor-unions. html [https://perma.cc/CSE6-TQ9U].

Alan B. Krueger, *Where Have All the Workers Gone? An Inquiry into the Decline of the US Labor Force Participation Rate*, 2017 Brookings Papers on Econ. Activity 1 (2017).

Paul Krugman, Opinion, *Apple and the Fruits of Tax Cuts*, N.Y. TIMES (May 3, 2018), https://www.nytimes.com/2018/05/03/opinion/apple-tax-cuts.html [https://perma. cc/V62P-SBLL].

Paul Krugman, Opinion, *Manufacturing Ain't Great Again. Why?*, N.Y. TIMES (Oct. 31, 2019), https://www.nytimes.com/2019/10/31/opinion/manufacturing-trump.html [https://perma.cc/XQY2-E2ZH].

Paul Krugman, Opinion, *Profits without Production*, N.Y. TIMES (June 20, 2013), https://www.nytimes.com/2013/06/21/opinion/krugman-profits-without-production.html [https://perma.cc/P5HU-FF3T].

John E. Kwoka Jr., *Does Merger Control Work: A Retrospective on US Enforcement Actions and Merger Outcomes*, 78 ANTITRUST L.J. 619 (2013).

William M. Lafferty, *Work as a Source of Political Learning among Wage-Laborers and Lower-Level Employees*, in POLITICAL LEARNING IN ADULTHOOD: A SOURCEBOOK OF THEORY AND RESEARCH 89 (Roberta S. Sigel ed., 1989).

Edmund Lee & Cecilia Kang, *U.S. Loses Appeal Seeking to Block AT&T–Time Warner Merger*, N.Y. TIMES (Feb. 26, 2019), https://www.nytimes.com/2019/02/26/business/media/att-time-warner-appeal.html [https://perma.cc/2U7H-S89D].

Legge 23 Luglio 1991, N. 223, G.U. July 27, 1991, N.175 (It.).

Pierre Lemieux, *France: The End of the Road, Again*, REG., Fall 2016, at 34.

David Leonhardt, Opinion, *The Charts That Show How Big Business Is Winning*, N.Y. TIMES (June 17, 2018), https://www.nytimes.com/2018/06/17/opinion/big-business-mergers.html [https://perma.cc/JPG7-S4ZA].

David Leonhardt, Opinion, *The Monopolization of America*, N.Y. TIMES (Nov. 25, 2018), https://www.nytimes.com/2018/11/25/opinion/monopolies-in-the-us.html [https://perma.cc/5LJ6-H97G].

David Leonhardt, Opinion, *We're Measuring the Economy All Wrong*, N.Y. TIMES (Sept. 14, 2018), https://www.nytimes.com/2018/09/14/opinion/columnists/great-recession-economy-gdp.html [https://perma.cc/2S2M-XJBY].

Sydney Levin, *China's Spring Airlines Lobbies for Vertical Seats*, AOL (Feb. 4, 2015), https://www.aol.com/article/2015/02/04/china-s-spring-airlines-lobbies-for-vertical-seats/21139087/ [https://perma.cc/MH6T-S55N].

Ben Lewis, *The Social Responsibility of Big Business*, in MONOPOLY POWER AND ECONOMIC PERFORMANCE; THE PROBLEM OF INDUSTRIAL CONCENTRATION 95 (Edwin Mansfield ed., 1964).

WALTER LIPPMAN, THE PHANTOM PUBLIC: A SEQUEL TO PUBLIC OPINION (1927).

Eric Lipton, *G.O.P. Hurries to Slash Oil and Gas Rules, Ending Industries' 8-Year Wait*, N.Y. TIMES (Feb. 4, 2017), https://www.nytimes.com/2017/02/04/us/politics/republicans-oil-gas-regulations.html [https://perma.cc/7MVP-2HHG].

Arthur Lupia, *Dumber Than Chimps? An Assessment of Direct Democracy Voters*, in DANGEROUS DEMOCRACY?: THE BATTLE OVER BALLOT INITIATIVES IN AMERICA 66 (Larry Sabato et al. eds., 2001).

N. Gregory Mankiw, *Why Aren't More Men Working?*, N.Y. TIMES (June 15, 2018), https://www.nytimes.com/2018/06/15/business/men-unemployment-jobs.html [https://perma.cc/9HTU-EMJC].

N. Gregory Mankiw & Mark P. Taylor, Economics (1st ed. 2006).

Henry G. Manne, *The "Higher Criticism" of the Modern Corporation*, 62 Colum. L. Rev. 399 (1962).

Leah E. Marcal, *Does Trade Adjustment Assistance Help Trade-Displaced Workers?*, 19 Contemp. Econ. Pol'y 59 (2001).

Ioana Elena Marinescu & Eric A. Posner, *Why Has Antitrust Law Failed Workers?* (Mar. 7, 2019), https://papers.ssrn.com/sol3/papers.cfm?abstract_id=3335174 [https://perma.cc/32N7-5P8G].

Donald N. McCloskey, *The Rhetoric of Economics*, 21 J. Econ. Lit. 481 (1983).

Duff McDonald, The Golden Passport: Harvard Business School, the Limits of Capitalism, and the Moral Failure of the MBA Elite (2017).

Tim McLaughlin, *Off the Radar: U.S. CEOs' Jet Perks Add Millions to Corporate Tax Bills*, Reuters (Dec. 2, 2019), https://www.reuters.com/article/us-usa-taxes-jets-insight/off-the-radar-u-s-ceos-jet-perks-add-millions-to-corporate-tax-bills-idUSKBN1Y6131 [https://perma.cc/ZV4C-A9NK].

Richard M. Merelman, *The Development of Political Ideology: A Framework for the Analysis of Political Socialization*, 63 Am. Pol. Sci. Rev. 750 (1969).

Robert A. Meyer, *Publicly Owned Versus Privately Owned Utilities: A Policy Choice*, 57 Rev. Econ. & Stat. 391 (1975).

Microsoft Corp., *Annual Report (Form 10-K)* (July 31, 2014), https://www.sec.gov/Archives/edgar/data/789019/000119312514289961/0001193125-14-289961-index.htm [https://perma.cc/7QT7-PCZ4].

Microsoft Corp., *Annual Report (Form 10-K)* (July 31, 2015), https://www.sec.gov/Archives/edgar/data/789019/000119312515272806/d918813d10k.htm [https://perma.cc/FLC8-6MFC].

Microsoft Corp., *Annual Report (Form 10-K)* (July 28, 2016), https://www.sec.gov/Archives/edgar/data/789019/000119312516662209/d187868d10k.htm [https://perma.cc/2QVD-ZU65].

Mitbestimmungsgesetz [Mitbestg] [Codetermination Act], May 4, 1976, BGBl I at 1153, § 9 (Ger.), https://www.gesetze-im-internet.de/mitbestg/BJNR011530976.html.

Walter F. Murphy & Joseph Tanenhaus, *Publicity, Public Opinion, and the Court*, 84 Nw. U. L. Rev. 985 (1989).

Peter Noel Murray, *The Myth of the Rational Consumer*, Psychol. Today (Mar. 8, 2016), https://www.psychologytoday.com/us/blog/inside-the-consumer-mind/201603/the-myth-the-rational-consumer [https://perma.cc/8438-5K6D].

Nat'l Center for Educ. Statistics, *Fast Facts: Graduation Rates* (2019), https://nces.ed.gov/fastfacts/display.asp?id=40 [https://perma.cc/2QXE-UCTQ].

Stephen Nellis, *Apple's iPhone X Has Higher Margin Than iPhone 8: Analysis*, Reuters (Nov. 6, 2017), https://www.reuters.com/article/us-apple-iphone/apples-iphone-x-has-higher-margin-than-iphone-8-analysis-idUSKBN1D62RZ [https://perma.cc/K8JD-SWCP].

David Nicklaus, *A Decade Later, the Recession Has Caused Big Changes in St. Louis*, St. Louis Post-Dispatch (Dec. 24, 2017), https://www.stltoday.com/business/columns/david-nicklaus/a-decade-later-the-recession-has-caused-big-changes-in/article_c6be3164-49a1-50fd-b24b-23b8607b3962.html [https://perma.cc/PG2T-543X].

David Nicklaus, *Merger Boom Is a Sign of Confidence, or Maybe Overconfidence*, St. Louis Post-Dispatch (Sept. 22, 2015), https://www.stltoday.com/business/

columns/david-nicklaus/nicklaus-merger-boom-is-a-sign-of-confidence-or-maybe/article_f41e7d73-e47d-521f-802b-3202cc3a2c76.html   [https://perma.cc/8WYY-UZ47].

Richard G. Niemi & Barbara I. Sobieszek, *Political Socialization*, 3 ANN. REV. SOC. 209 (1977).

Tony Nitti, *What Will the Trump Tax Cuts Mean for Your Wallet?*, FORBES (July 13, 2017), https://www.forbes.com/sites/anthonynitti/2017/07/13/what-will-the-trump-tax-cuts-mean-for-your-wallet/ [https://perma.cc/7MY4-S8CY].

DOUGLASS C. NORTH, UNDERSTANDING THE PROCESS OF ECONOMIC CHANGE (2005).

Douglass C. North, *Cognitive Science and the Study of the "Rules of the Game" in a World of Uncertainty, in* NORMS AND THE LAW 48 (John N. Drobak ed., 2006).

DOUGLASS C. NORTH, INSTITUTIONS, INSTITUTIONAL CHANGE AND ECONOMIC PERFORMANCE (1990).

DOUGLASS C. NORTH, UNDERSTANDING THE PROCESS OF ECONOMIC CHANGE (2005).

N. Sec. Co. v. United States, 193 U.S. 197 (1904).

ORG. ECON. COOPERATION & DEV., *Wage Levels (Indicator)* (2020), https://data.oecd.org/earnwage/wage-levels.htm [https://perma.cc/WDU4-4YHX].

Alan L. Otten, *Call for Volunteers: Nixon Plans to Foster Private-Group Attacks on Big Social Problems*, WALL ST. J., Jan. 21 1969, at 1.

Outsourcing: Where's Uncle Sam?, BUSINESSWEEK: THE DEBATE ROOM (2007), https://web.archive.org/web/20070305113458/http://www.businessweek.com/debateroom/archives/2007/02/outsourcing_whe.html [https://perma.cc/2BEX-J3S6].

John Paintcrown, *Why Do People Pay More Just for a Brand Name or Logo?*, QUORA (Mar. 31, 2018), https://www.quora.com/Why-do-people-pay-more-just-for-a-brand-name-or-logo [https://perma.cc/7PFS-YLQB].

Donn R. Pescatrice & John M. Trapani III, *The Performance and Objectives of Public and Private Utilities Operating in the United States*, 13 J. PUB. ECON. 259 (1980).

Melody Petersen, *Drug Prices Surge Even When Rivals Join Market*, ST. LOUIS POST-DISPATCH (Sept. 3, 2016), https://www.stltoday.com/business/local/drug-prices-surge-even-when-rivals-join-market/article_303648e5-9c27-583f-9bec-37abe05340e1.html [https://perma.cc/8YDQ-4NPV].

Hayley Peterson, *Whole Foods Is Cutting Medical Benefits for Hundreds of Part-Time Workers*, BUS. INSIDER (Sept. 12, 2019), https://www.businessinsider.com/whole-foods-cuts-medical-benefits-for-part-time-workers-2019-9 [https://perma.cc/PY2D-WQZD].

Matt Phillips, *Trump's Tax Cuts in Hand, Companies Spend More on Themselves Than on Wages*, N.Y. TIMES (Feb. 26, 2018), https://www.nytimes.com/2018/02/26/business/tax-cuts-share-buybacks-corporate.html [https://perma.cc/64JS-FA6S].

THOMAS PIKETTY, CAPITAL IN THE TWENTY-FIRST CENTURY (Arthur Goldhammer trans., 2014).

H. Plecher, *Youth Unemployment Rate in Europe August 2019*, STATISTA (Oct. 15, 2019), https://www.statista.com/statistics/266228/youth-unemployment-rate-in-eu-countries/ [https://perma.cc/Y7LD-K4B7].

Brad Plumer, *The Outsized Returns from Lobbying*, WASH. POST (Oct. 10, 2011), https://www.washingtonpost.com/blogs/ezra-klein/post/the-outsized-returns-from-lobbying/2011/10/10/gIQADSNEaL_blog.html [https://perma.cc/8W7W-RB2R].

MICHAEL G. POLLITT, OWNERSHIP AND PERFORMANCE IN ELECTRIC UTILITIES: THE INTERNATIONAL EVIDENCE ON PRIVATIZATION AND EFFICIENCY (1995).

Eduardo Porter, *Reviving the Working Class without Building Walls*, N.Y. Times (Mar. 8, 2016), https://www.nytimes.com/2016/03/09/business/economy/a-few-solutions-to-the-working-class-revolt.html [https://perma.cc/K33N-Q39R].

Richard A. Posner, *The Deprofessionalization of Legal Teaching and Scholarship*, 91 Mich. L. Rev. 1921 (1993).

Ned Potter, *Senate Kills Anti-Outsourcing Bill; Democrats Point to Romney*, ABC News (July 19, 2012), https://abcnews.go.com/blogs/politics/2012/07/senate-kills-anti-outsourcing-bill-democrats-point-to-romney [https://perma.cc/BT6T-46FZ].

Procter & Gamble Co., *Annual Report (Form 10-K)* (Aug. 29, 2005), https://www.sec.gov/Archives/edgar/data/80424/000095015205007351/l15436ae10vk.htm [https://perma.cc/CP42-CBHJ].

Ralf Ptak, *Neoliberalism in Germany: Revisiting the Ordoliberal Foundations of the Social Market Economy*, *in* The Road from Mont Pelerin: The Making of the Neoliberal Thought Collective 98 (Philip Mirowski & Dieter Plehwe eds., 2009).

John Quiggin, Zombie Economics: How Dead Ideas Still Walk Among Us (2012).

James A. Reichley, Conservatives in an Age of Change: The Nixon and Ford Administrations (1981).

Return of the Big Deal, Economist (May 1, 2014), https://www.economist.com/business/2014/05/01/return-of-the-big-deal [https://perma.cc/X79S-BQDM].

Kara M. Reynolds & John S. Palatucci, *Does Trade Adjustment Assistance Make a Difference?*, 30 Contemp. Econ. Pol'y 43 (2012).

Samuli Rikama et al., *International Sourcing of Business Functions*, Eurostat (June 2013), https://ec.europa.eu/eurostat/statistics-explained/index.php/Archive:International_sourcing_of_business_functions [https://perma.cc/TT7H-V5A5].

Lionel Robbins, An Essay on the Nature and Significance of Economic Science (1932).

Joan Robinson, The Economics of Imperfect Competition (2d ed. 1969).

Carol M. Rose, *Privatization-the Road to Democracy?*, 50 St. Louis L.J. 691 (2005).

Stephanie Rosenbloom, *Hotels Rake in Record Fees, and Travelers Foot the Bill*, N.Y. Times (Sept. 29, 2017), https://www.nytimes.com/2017/09/29/travel/hotels-rake-in-record-fees-and-travelers-foot-the-bill.html [https://perma.cc/P837-9PNV].

Elisabeth Rosenthal, Sunday Review, *Ask Your Doctor If This Ad Is Right for You*, N.Y. Times (Feb. 27, 2016), https://www.nytimes.com/2016/02/28/sunday-review/ask-your-doctor-if-this-ad-is-right-for-you.html [https://perma.cc/C9QU-4DVX].

Elisabeth Rosenthal, Opinion, *The Lesson of Epipens: Why Drug Prices Spike, Again and Again*, N.Y. Times (Sept. 2, 2016), https://www.nytimes.com/2016/09/04/opinion/sunday/the-lesson-of-epipens-why-drug-prices-spike-again-and-again.html [https://perma.cc/YP2Q-VUC9].

Allen Rostron, *The Dickey Amendment for Federal Funding for Research on Gun Violence*, 108 Am. J. Pub. Health 865 (2018).

Jonathan Rothwell, *Myths of the 1 Percent: What Puts People at the Top*, N.Y. Times: Upshot (Nov. 20, 2017), https://www.nytimes.com/2017/11/17/upshot/income-inequality-united-states.html [https://perma.cc/NM9H-GV3N].

Nouriel Roubini, *Supply Side Economics: Do Tax Rate Cuts Increase Growth and Revenues and Reduce Budget Deficits? Or Is It Voodoo Economics All over Again?*, Stern Sch. of Bus. (1997), http://people.stern.nyu.edu/nroubini/SUPPLY.HTM [https://perma.cc/EHG4-DEJ8].

Greg Roumeliotis & Ludwig Burger, *Bayer Clinches Monsanto with Improved $66 Billion Bid*, REUTERS (Sept. 14, 2016), https://www.reuters.com/article/us-monsanto-m-a-bayer-deal-idUSKCN11K128 [https://perma.cc/XK2A-S8EJ].

Seth B. Sacher & John M. Yun, *Twelve Fallacies of the "Neo-Antitrust" Movement*, 26 GEO. MASON L. REV. 1491, 1495–96 (2019), https://papers.ssrn.com/sol3/papers.cfm?abstract_id=3369013 [https://perma.cc/R9GZ-TFU7].

Rachel E. Sachs, *Mylan Announces Generic Epipen; Baffles Health Policy Wonks Everywhere*, BILL OF HEALTH (Aug. 30, 2016), https://blog.petrieflom.law.harvard.edu/2016/08/30/mylan-announces-generic-epipen-baffles-health-policy-wonks-everywhere/ [https://perma.cc/9KC4-KHMZ].

Rachel E. Sachs, *The Uneasy Case for Patent Law*, 117 MICH. L. REV. 499 (2018).

Emmanuel Saez et al., *The Elasticity of Taxable Income with Respect to Marginal Tax Rates: A Critical Review*, 50 J. ECON. LITERATURE 3 (2012).

Josh Sager, *The Effects of Corporate Lobbying, Pt. 1*, SARCASTIC LIBERAL (May 29, 2012), http://sarcasticliberal.blogspot.com/2012/05/wolf-pac-effects-of-corporate-lobbying.html [https://perma.cc/N54R-Z2BW].

Paul A. Samuelson, *Where Ricardo and Mill Rebut and Confirm Arguments of Mainstream Economists Supporting Globalization*, 18 J. ECON. PERSP. 135 (2004).

Rachel Sandler, *How the iPhone Changed the Telecommunications Industry*, USA TODAY (July 4, 2017), https://www.usatoday.com/story/tech/news/2017/07/04/how-iphone-changed-telecommunications-industry/103154146/ [https://perma.cc/3CE3-8EPE].

Bill Saporito, Opinion, *C.E.O. Pay, America's Economic "Miracle,"* N.Y. TIMES (May 17, 2019), https://www.nytimes.com/2019/05/17/opinion/ceo-pay-raises.html [https://perma.cc/TBJ7-NUYN].

Thomas R. Saving, *Concentration Ratios and the Degree of Monopoly*, 11 INT'L ECON. REV. 139 (1970).

Frederic M. Scherer, *Some Principles for Post-Chicago Antitrust Analysis*, 52 CASE W. RES. L. REV. 5 (2001).

Mary Schlangenstein, *Southwest's $49 Fares Signal Summer Bargains Despite Pricier Oil*, BLOOMBERG (May 21, 2018), https://www.bloomberg.com/news/articles/2018-05-21/southwest-s-49-fares-signal-summer-bargains-despite-pricier-oil [https://perma.cc/L53C-VANS].

Michael Schudson, *America's Ignorant Voters*, WILSON Q., Spring 2000, at 16.

Michael Schuldt, Comment, *A Statutory Proposal for the Regulation of Fairness Opinions in Corporate Control Transactions*, 56 MO. L. REV. 103 (1991).

Michael Schuman, *Does Germany Know the Secret to Creating Jobs?*, TIME (Feb. 25, 2011), https://business.time.com/2011/02/25/does-germany-know-the-secret-to-creating-jobs/ [https://perma.cc/N2AA-AGLR].

Norbert Schwarz et al., *Metacognitive Experiences and the Intricacies of Setting People Straight: Implications for Debiasing and Public Information Campaigns*, 39 ADVANCES EXPERIMENTAL SOC. PSYCHOL. 127 (2007).

ROBERT E. SCOTT, ECON. POL'Y INST., HEADING SOUTH: U.S.-MEXICO TRADE AND JOB DISPLACEMENT AFTER NAFTA (May 3, 2011), https://www.epi.org/files/page/-/BriefingPaper308.pdf [https://perma.cc/VSW9-U7ER].

ROBERT E. SCOTT & WILL KIMBALL, ECON. POL'Y INST., CHINA TRADE, OUTSOURCING AND JOBS (Dec. 11, 2014), https://www.epi.org/files/2014/bp385-china-trade-deficit.pdf [https://perma.cc/3ASC-KURD].

Second Amended Class Action Complaint & Demand for Jury Trial, Cox v. Spirit Airlines, Inc., 340 F. Supp.3d 154 (E.D.N.Y. May 10, 2018).

Seventeenth Mobile Wireless Competition Report, 29 FCC Rcd. 15311 (19), 17 (2014), https://www.fcc.gov/document/17th-annual-competition-report [https://perma.cc/9YCD-CM5B].

SGL GROUP, *Fundamentals of German Corporate Governance*, https://web.archive.org/web/20190201194846/http://www.sglgroup.com/cms/international/investor-relations/corporate-governance/principles-of-german-corporate-governance/index.html?__locale=en [https://perma.cc/4J9B-K66C].

SIDNEY A. SHAPIRO & JOSEPH P. TOMAIN, REGULATORY LAW AND POLICY (1993).

Jeremy N. Sheff, *The Myth of the Level Playing Field: Knowledge, Affect, and Repetition in Public Debate*, 75 MO. L. REV. 143 (2010).

DENNIS A. SHIELDS, CONG. RESEARCH SERV., CONSOLIDATION AND CONCENTRATION IN THE U.S. DAIRY INDUSTRY, RL41224 (2010).

Jonathan Shorman, *Kansas Legislature Approves Budget Deal after Lawmakers Deliver Blistering Critiques of State's Finances*, TOPEKA CAP.-J. (May 2, 2016), https://www.cjonline.com/news/2016-05-02/kansas-legislature-approves-budget-deal-after-lawmakers-deliver-blistering-critiques?page=2 [https://perma.cc/P3V2-F99D].

Donald S. Siegel & Kenneth L. Simons, *Assessing the Effects of Mergers and Acquisitions on Firm Performance, Plant Productivity, and Workers: New Evidence from Matched Employer-Employee Data*, 31 STRATEGIC MGMT. J. 903 (2010).

Roberta S. Sigel, *Conclusion: Adult Political Learning—A Lifelong Process*, in POLITICAL LEARNING IN ADULTHOOD: A SOURCEBOOK OF THEORY AND RESEARCH 458 (Roberta S. Sigel ed., 1988).

Nirvkar Singh & Xavier Vives, *Price and Quantity Competition in a Differentiated Duopoly*, 15 RAND J. 546 (1984).

Aaron Smith & Jackie Wattles, *Aetna-Humana & Anthem-Cigna: Two Mergers Die in One Day*, CNN MONEY (Feb. 14, 2017), https://money.cnn.com/2017/02/14/investing/aetna-humana/index.html [https://perma.cc/6VCR-NCXB].

ADAM SMITH, AN INQUIRY INTO THE NATURE AND CAUSES OF THE WEALTH OF NATIONS (R.H. Campbell & A.S. Skinner eds., Liberty Fund 1981) (1776).

ADAM SMITH, THE WEALTH OF NATIONS (Edwin Cannan ed., Modern Library 1994) (1776).

Noah Smith, Opinion, *Trump's Tax Cuts Failed to Deliver*, BLOOMBERG (June 7, 2019), https://www.bloomberg.com/opinion/articles/2019-06-07/trump-s-tax-cuts-failed-to-deliver-the-promised-boom [https://perma.cc/YT7K-X4GQ].

Jeff Sommer, *Apple's Watch Is Smarter, but My Casio Keeps Getting the Job Done*, N.Y. TIMES (Aug. 23, 2019), https://www.nytimes.com/2019/08/23/business/apple-watch-iphone-casio.html [https://perma.cc/R9RK-D4Y7].

Tobie Stanger, *Get More Wedding for Your Money*, CONSUMER REPS. (Apr. 26, 2016), https://www.consumerreports.org/weddings/get-more-wedding-for-your-money/ [https://perma.cc/9BLD-LK54].

Jonathan Stempel, *Spirit Airlines Must Face Lawsuit over "Gotcha" Carry-on Bag Fees: Court*, REUTERS (Sept. 10, 2019), https://www.reuters.com/article/us-spirit-airlines-lawsuit-bag-fees/spirit-airlines-must-face-lawsuit-over-gotcha-carry-on-bag-fees-court-idUSKCN1VV212 [https://perma.cc/C8LL-QCXH].

Steps to Increase Competition and Better Inform Consumers and Workers to Support Continued Growth of the American Economy, Exec. Order No. 13,725, 3 C.F.R., 2016 Comp., at 452 (2017).

GEORGE J. STIGLER, ESSAYS IN THE HISTORY OF ECONOMICS (1965).

Joseph E. Stiglitz, *America Has a Monopoly Problem—And It's Huge*, THE NATION (Oct. 23, 2017), https://www.thenation.com/article/archive/america-has-a-monopoly-problem-and-its-huge/ [https://perma.cc/3ZCN-BQTY].

George W. Stocking & Willard F. Mueller, *The Cellophane Case and the New Competition*, 45 AM. ECON. REV. 29 (1955).

Lynn A. Stout, *The Dumbest Business Idea Ever. The Myth of Maximizing Shareholder Value: The Dominant Business Philosophy Debunked*, EVONOMICS, https://evonomics.com/maximizing-shareholder-value-dumbest-idea/ [https://perma.cc/RT2X-PVBB].

LYNN A. STOUT, THE SHAREHOLDER VALUE MYTH: HOW PUTTING SHAREHOLDERS FIRST HARMS INVESTORS, CORPORATIONS, AND THE PUBLIC (2012).

Lynn A. Stout, *Social Norms and Other-Regarding Preferences*, *in* NORMS AND THE LAW 13 (John N. Drobak ed., 2006).

Lynn A. Stout, *The Toxic Side Effects of Shareholder Primacy*, 161 U. PA. L. REV. 2003 (2013).

Leo E. Strine Jr., *Human Freedom and Two Friedmen: Musings on the Implications of Globalization for the Effective Regulation of Corporate Behaviour*, 58 U. TORONTO L.J. 241 (2008).

Stephanie Strom, *Shareholders Demand More Drastic Shifts at Nestlé*, N.Y. TIMES (June 26, 2017), https://www.nytimes.com/2017/06/26/business/nestle-activist-investor.html [https://perma.cc/LE8X-VUDN].

RANDY M. STUTZ, AM. ANTITRUST INST., THE EVOLVING ANTITRUST TREATMENT OF LABOR-MARKET RESTRAINTS: FROM THEORY TO PRACTICE (2018).

CASS R. SUNSTEIN, REPUBLIC.COM 2.0 (2007).

T1INTERNATIONAL, *8 Reasons Why Insulin Is So Outrageously Expensive* (Jan. 20, 2019), https://www.t1international.com/blog/2019/01/20/why-insulin-so-expensive/ [https://perma.cc/W65Z-QLMQ].

Philip Taft & Philip Ross, *American Labor Violence: Its Causes, Character, and Outcome*, *in* VIOLENCE IN AMERICA: HISTORICAL AND COMPARATIVE PERSPECTIVES: A REPORT TO THE NATIONAL COMMISSION ON THE CAUSES AND PREVENTION OF VIOLENCE 221 (Hugh Davis Graham & Ted Robert Gurr eds., 1969).

Sabrina Tavernise, *Frozen in Place: Americans Are Moving at the Lowest Rate on Record*, N.Y. TIMES (Nov. 20, 2019), https://www.nytimes.com/2019/11/20/us/american-workers-moving-states-.html [https://perma.cc/M9ZB-YX6W].

Chad Terhune, *Health Insurer Cigna Rejects Anthem's $54-Billion Takeover Bid*, L.A. TIMES (June 21, 2015), https://www.latimes.com/business/la-fi-anthem-cigna-talks-20150621-story.html [https://perma.cc/6ECA-W4RK].

In re Text Messaging Antitrust Litig., 782 F.3d 867 (7th Cir. 2015).

LEO TOLSTOY, WAR AND PEACE (E. Zaydenshnur trans., 2009).

Mathias Trabandt & Harald Uhlig, *The Laffer Curve Revisited*, 58 J. MONETARY ECON. 305 (2011).

Trade Expansion Act of 1962, tit. III, Pub. L. 87-794, 76 Stat. 872, 883.

Dalia Tsuk, *From Pluralism to Individualism: Berle and Means and 20th-Century American Legal Thought*, 30 L. & SOC. INQUIRY 179 (2005).

21 CONG. REC. (1890) (statement of Sen. Sherman).

United States v. Aetna, Inc., 240 F. Supp. 3d 1 (D.D.C. 2017).

United States v. AT&T Inc., 310 F. Supp. 3d 161 (D.D.C. 2018).

United States v. Phila. Nat'l Bank, 374 U.S. 321 (1963).

U.S. Bureau of Labor Statistics, *BLS 2013 Sequestration Information* (Mar. 4, 2013), https://www.bls.gov/bls/sequester_info.htm [https://perma.cc/89FN-JT7E].

U.S. Bureau of Labor Statistics, *Labor Force Statistics from the Current Population Survey*, https://data.bls.gov/timeseries/LNS11300000 [https://perma.cc/5TLF-2LBW].

U.S. Bureau of Labor Statistics, *Labor Force Statistics from the Current Population Survey* (Feb. 21, 2020), https://www.bls.gov/web/empsit/cpseea01.htm [https://perma.cc/SV2K-G47A].

U.S. Bureau of Labor Statistics, *Mass Layoff Statistics*, https://www.bls.gov/mls/home.htm [https://perma.cc/JF74-NLGK].

U.S. Bureau of Labor Statistics, *MLS Databases*, https://www.bls.gov/mls/data.htm [https://perma.cc/PC6U-CU29].

U.S. Dep't of Justice, Competition and Monopoly: Single-Firm Conduct under Section 2 of the Sherman Act (2008), https://www.justice.gov/sites/default/files/atr/legacy/2009/05/11/236681.pdf [https://perma.cc/Z8RK-AVDU].

U.S. Dep't of Justice & Fed. Trade Comm'n, Horizontal Merger Guidelines (2010), https://www.justice.gov/atr/file/810276/download [https://perma.cc/672Q-5RSB].

US Unemployment Rate by Year, Multpl, https://www.multpl.com/unemployment/table/by-year [https://perma.cc/R7KY-BUWP].

U.S. Fed. Trade Comm'n & Dep't of Justice, Hart-Scott-Rodino Annual Report: Fiscal Year 2018, https://www.ftc.gov/system/files/documents/reports/federal-trade-commission-bureau-competition-department-justice-antitrust-division-hart-scott-rodino/fy18hsrreport.pdf [https://perma.cc/MF2C-TBF5].

Hal R. Varian, *Recent Trends in Concentration, Competition, and Entry*, 82 Antitrust L.J. 807 (2019).

Vill. Johnson City, N.Y., *The History of Johnson City, NY*, http://www.villageofjc.com/history.html [https://perma.cc/8GWU-LJE9].

W. Kip Viscusi et al., Economics of Regulation and Antitrust (2005).

David Vogel, Fluctuating Fortunes: The Political Power of Business in America (2003).

David Vogel, Kindred Strangers: The Uneasy Relationship between Politics and Business in America (2016).

James P. Walsh, *Top Management Turnover Following Mergers and Acquisitions*, 9 Strategic Mgmt. J. 173 (1988).

Julie Weed, *In the Race for Cheap Airfare, It's You vs. the Machine*, N.Y. Times (Jan. 27, 2020), https://www.nytimes.com/2020/01/27/business/cheap-airfare.html [https://perma.cc/R7ZT-K3C2].

Murray Weidenbaum, *Conversion and the Future Direction of Defence Contractors*, in Economic Issues of Disarmament: Contributions from Peace Economics and Peace Science 97 (Jurgen Brauer & Manas Chatterji eds., 1993).

Murray Weidenbaum, *Conversion and the Future of Defense Contractors*, in One-Armed Economist: On the Intersection of Business and Government 187 (2004).

Charles W. Wessner, *How Does Germany Do It?*, Mechanical Engineering (Nov. 13, 2013), https://www.asme.org/topics-resources/content/how-does-germany-do-it [https://perma.cc/4VEH-8R79].

Alex Williams, *Why Don't Rich People Just Stop Working?*, N.Y. Times (Oct. 17, 2019), https://www.nytimes.com/2019/10/17/style/rich-people-things.html [https://perma.cc/VPQ8-KFUZ].

Joan C. Williams, White Working Class: Overcoming Class Cluelessness in America (2017).

Oliver E. Williamson, *Economies as an Antitrust Defense: The Welfare Tradeoffs*, Am. Econ. Rev., Mar. 1968, at 18.

Johan Willner, *Ownership, Efficiency, and Political Interference*, 17 Eur. J. Pol. Econ. 723 (2001).

Nick Wingfield, *Cutting Jobs, Microsoft Turns Page on Nokia Deal*, N.Y. Times (July 8, 2015), https://www.nytimes.com/2015/07/09/technology/microsoft-layoffs.html [https://perma.cc/VR7J-GR7E].

Morgan Winsor & David Caplan, *Clinton's "Deplorables" Comment Show Disdain for Working People, Trump Camp Says*, ABC News (Sept. 10, 2016), https://abcnews.go.com/Politics/hillary-clinton-half-donald-trumps-supporters-basket-deplorables/story?id=41993204 [https://perma.cc/3VE4-CNLS].

Justin Wolfers, *How to Think About Corporate Tax Cuts*, N.Y. Times (Mar. 30, 2018), https://www.nytimes.com/2018/03/30/business/how-to-think-about-corporate-tax-cuts.html [https://perma.cc/PXQ7-AW9Z].

Christopher T. Wonnell, *Efficiency and Conservatism*, 80 Neb. L. Rev. 643 (2001).

World Population Rev., *Gini Coefficient by Country 2020* (Feb. 17, 2020), http://worldpopulationreview.com/countries/gini-coefficient-by-country/ [https://perma.cc/7D5U-NA97].

Tim Worstall, Opinion, *The Epi's Terribly Strange Calculation About Trade and the Effect on Jobs*, Forbes (Mar. 13, 2016), https://www.forbes.com/sites/timworstall/2016/03/13/the-epis-terribly-strange-calculation-about-trade-and-the-effect-on-jobs/ [https://perma.cc/A5ZW-NNU9].

Tim Wu, *Blind Spot: The Attention Economy and the Law*, 82 Antitrust L.J. 771 (2017).

Tim Wu, The Curse of Bigness: Antitrust in the New Gilded Age (2018).

Gerald Zahavi, *Negotiated Loyalty: Welfare Capitalism and the Shoeworkers of Endicott Johnson, 1920–1940*, 70 J. Am. Hist. 602 (1983).

Gerald Zahavi, Workers, Managers, and Welfare Capitalism: The Shoeworkers and Tanners of Endicott Johnson, 1890–1950 (1988).

Owen Zidar, *Tax Cuts for Whom? Heterogeneous Effects of Income Tax Changes on Growth and Employment*, 127 J. Pol. Econ. 1437 (2019).

Luigi Zingales, *Preventing Economists' Capture*, in Preventing Regulatory Capture: Special Interest Influence and How to Limit It 124 (Daniel Carpenter & David A. Moss eds., 2014).

Index

For the benefit of digital users, indexed terms that span two pages (e.g., 52–53) may, on occasion, appear on only one of those pages.